THE FLYING CARPET *of* SMALL MIRACLES

A WOMAN'S FIGHT TO SAVE TWO ORPHANS

HALA JABER

"Jaber maps the ancient roads of the human heart. . . .
Family, finally, is those who love us, and those we choose to love."
—Melissa Fay Greene, author of *Praying for Sheetrock*

PRAISE FOR

The Flying Carpet of Small Miracles

"The author of this fascinating memoir is—by her own admission—hot-tempered, prone to depressions and tantrums, extremely prone to tears. . . . None of that interferes with her award-winning journalistic work, however, as she reports on an out-of-control war that must have seemed to someone like a good idea, at the time."

—*The Washington Post*

"Blessed with courage, humanity, a Lebanese background, and the support of a British newspaper, Hala Jaber had the credentials to spell out the true ugliness of 'collateral damage' in the Iraqi war. . . . Devastating."

—*The Economist*

"If there is one book that stands as evidence of the simple human cost of the Iraq war, it is Hala Jaber's *Flying Carpet of Small Miracles*. Jaber is a brave war correspondent, a canny British journalist, but also a profoundly motherly woman. Her personal journey and genuine grief are told sparingly and unflinchingly, without sentimentality or self-pity and with a rare degree of feeling for the orphans and the dispossessed of Iraq. This book will stand when others are forgotten."

—Radio 4

"By any measure, Hala Jaber is a courageous woman. . . . Hers is an often harrowing tale, but its conclusion offers an unexpected measure of redemption. . . . Jaber skillfully weaves together the different strands of her story. She does not attempt to equate the devastation of war with her own woes. But she does allow a reader to feel the way that one fueled the other in her own experience. This is a story that brings readers face to face with the horror of war and the suffering of the Iraqis. Sometimes it feels almost unbearable. Fortunately, however, Jaber also writes of the familial love that sustained her and the occasional heroes who inspired her."

—*The Christian Science Monitor*

"A painful reminder of the toll taken by the Iraq war, offering details that rarely made it into the headlines. . . . Jaber's memoir is a compelling read that tracks the trajectory of a woman who finally comes to understand the rewards of maternal love." —*More*

"Maternal instincts fuel Hala Jaber's *The Flying Carpet of Small Miracles*, which follows the Lebanese journalist to war-torn Baghdad, where she finds her own fate intertwined with that of two young girls, their family's lone survivors of a bombing. Kinship, it seems, can be discovered in the most unexpected places." —*Vogue*

"It is essential that we learn from other cultures. Recounting the traumas of war and sacrificed innocence . . . Hala Jaber brings us into this other world in a way that enlightens our understanding of ourselves. A moving and sober book, to be read and considered thoughtfully." —Yasmina Khadra, author of *The Swallows of Kabul*

"The beauty, courage, and drama of this book absolutely floored me. Jaber finds compassion in war, love in grief, and a way to mother despite childlessness. *The Flying Carpet of Small Miracles* offers vital perspective on contemporary women's choices and reminds us there are myriad paths to a creative, meaningful, generative life." —Peggy Orenstein, author of *Waiting for Daisy*

"A powerful, unforgettable memoir, Jaber paints heartbreaking portraits of children who have lost everything during the Iraq war, but also of the fearless, selfless journalists, doctors, and volunteers who work at great risk to themselves to help these devastated people."

—Nahid Rachlin, author of *Persian Girls*

"Jaber maps the ancient roads of the human heart, where a childless woman longs for a baby of her own and embraces Baghdad's smallest victims instead. The result is a unique and haunting tale. Family, finally, is those who love us, and those we choose to love."

—Melissa Fay Greene,
author of *Praying for Sheetrock* and *There Is No Me Without You*

The Flying Carpet of Small Miracles

A WOMAN'S FIGHT
TO SAVE TWO ORPHANS

HALA JABER

RIVERHEAD BOOKS

New York

RIVERHEAD BOOKS
Published by the Penguin Group
Penguin Group (USA) Inc.
375 Hudson Street, New York, New York 10014, USA
Penguin Group (Canada), 90 Eglinton Avenue East, Suite 700, Toronto, Ontario M4P 2Y3, Canada
(a division of Pearson Penguin Canada Inc.)
Penguin Books Ltd., 80 Strand, London WC2R 0RL, England
Penguin Group Ireland, 25 St. Stephen's Green, Dublin 2, Ireland (a division of Penguin Books Ltd.)
Penguin Group (Australia), 250 Camberwell Road, Camberwell, Victoria 3124, Australia
(a division of Pearson Australia Group Pty. Ltd.)
Penguin Books India Pvt. Ltd., 11 Community Centre, Panchsheel Park, New Delhi—110 017, India
Penguin Group (NZ), 67 Apollo Drive, Rosedale, North Shore 0632, New Zealand
(a division of Pearson New Zealand Ltd.)
Penguin Books (South Africa) (Pty.) Ltd., 24 Sturdee Avenue, Rosebank, Johannesburg 2196,
South Africa

Penguin Books Ltd., Registered Offices: 80 Strand, London WC2R 0RL, England

Book design by Nicole LaRoche

First Riverhead hardcover edition: May 2009
First Riverhead trade paperback edition: July 2010
Riverhead trade paperback ISBN: 978-1-59448-466-7

The Library of Congress has catalogued the Riverhead hardcover edition as follows:

Jaber, Hala.
The flying carpet of small miracles : a woman's fight to save two orphans / Hala Jaber.
p. cm.
ISBN 978-1-59448-867-2
1. Iraq War, 2003—Personal narratives, British. 2. Iraq War, 2003—Children. 3. Jaber, Hala.
4. Journalists—Great Britain—Biography. I. Title.
DS 79,76.J312 2009 2009009665
956.7044'3092—dc22

PRINTED IN THE UNITED STATES OF AMERICA

10 9 8 7 6 5 4 3 2 1

To Zahra, Marla, Lara, and Hawra

Prologue

APRIL 4, 2003, BAGHDAD

It was not until the windows exploded that Ali and Rasmiyeh Kathem realized they had to get out. For hours, they had clutched their seven children to them as the firestorm approached. The brighter the flashes of hot, white light outside, the more coldly their sweat ran as they shielded the eyes of the little ones. The louder the booms that reverberated around their single-story concrete house, the more softly they whispered reassurance in the ears of their terrified girls. Perhaps the most petrified was three-year-old Zahra, for a child of that age is old enough to know when something is terribly wrong and too young to control her fear. At least Hawra, the baby, could be rocked back to sleep in her mother's arms if she was woken by a shaking of the ground.

Ali kept up a brave face for his sons, but inside he was tormented by alternating visions of hell. Stay holed up at home and his family could be blown to smithereens by a stray bomb intended for the barracks nearby. Race away in the taxi he drove for a living and they could be consumed by an inferno on the open road. When the glass blew in over some mattresses the older children had pushed together on the living room floor, their screams made up his mind.

He barked orders and bundled paperwork into a folder. Rasmiyeh parceled up clothes in a large piece of cloth and tipped her few gold trinkets into a handbag. Then, as quickly as they could, they assembled their priceless cargo in Ali's vehicle on the road outside: Muntather, their eighteen-year-old son, took charge of his three younger brothers and one sister on the backseat, while Rasmiyeh squeezed her youngest daughters together on her lap in the front and began to pray.

As he slid behind the wheel and switched on the engine, Ali, too, was reciting the opening verse of the Koran. He understood that mayhem had descended on this district because it was full of military facilities and families. To get his children to safety, all he had to do was drive to his mother's house across town, as he had done hundreds of times before. It was difficult to concentrate on the road when so much was happening in the air, however. He craned his neck out the window to see what was making all the noise. Helicopters were swooping across the dawn sky like big black birds of prey. What if they were to start firing missiles on the highway? Ali pressed his foot down hard on the accelerator.

Ahead, two trucks were rolling up the road in convoy. Ali saw their high sides and thought they could protect his car from the force of any blast. He overtook the second truck and swerved in behind the first.

If it had occurred to him for one moment that these trucks might be the helicopters' targets, he would never have been driving between them, looking at his five eldest children in the rearview mirror and glancing down at the youngest, Zahra and Hawra, in the arms of his wife in the front passenger seat. Nobody in that car suspected that the firestorm they had fled was sweeping back toward them at unstoppable speed. It struck in a split second with a white-hot bolt from the blue. By the time the thunderous roar of the erupting missile had faded away, Ali and Rasmiyeh Kathem were dead and all but two of their seven treasures were dying.

One

FINDING ZAHRA

If it had not been for a strange request from my office, I would never have followed the trail that led me through a teeming, terrified city at war to the hospital where I found Zahra.

"We need an orphan," my boss said. "Not just any orphan. A special one."

His instructions were as meticulous as they were startling. I should not settle for the first injured orphan I came across, he told me firmly. I should scan all the hospitals with pediatric wards for the special one.

A baby would be no good because it would not have an expressive enough face. The orphan we needed would be slightly older but still young enough to look defenseless. A girl would be better because she would seem more vulnerable than a boy. Ideally, she would be badly injured but still beautiful: she had to make a great picture.

So, to summarize, I was looking for a wounded girl, between one and five years old, whose parents had died and whose pretty face was more or less unscathed.

"Okay," I said.

I repeated the details to my husband, Steve, who was also the photographer on my assignment, and alerted our driver to be ready to leave in five minutes. For a moment, I wondered whether anyone at the office in London understood what it meant to drive through Baghdad, with all its shooting and looting, on a mission to select and reject injured children with inconsolable families for a slot on the inside pages of our newspaper.

Yet I did not mind the cynicism of my brief. I knew it was for a good cause. The paper was planning a fund-raising campaign for the children worst affected by the war. My task was to find the face of that campaign and write the story that would launch it. The face and the story had to move readers, otherwise they would not give money. Since I had begged my boss to set up this appeal in the first place, I was in no position to complain. On the contrary, I had seen so many children hurt by the bombardment that I would have done anything to help.

I MADE A LIST of hospitals for the driver. Searching them for our "ideal orphan" would be tougher now than at the start of the fighting three weeks earlier. Barricades were going up to fortify all medical facilities against attack. Armed guards were being hired by the hundred to repel rampaging gangs. Doors had been barred to prevent any looters who pushed past the guards from plundering the sick and frail. I had heard that even doctors sworn to preserve life were carrying guns in case they had to kill in self-defense. Not only were hospital staff overwhelmed by the influx of civilians wounded in the American bombing, but a fear of the violence suddenly being inflicted by their fellow citizens had turned them into vigilantes on their own wards. If ever there was a warning sign that the fall of the country's security apparatus would lead to the rise of a peculiarly ruthless anarchy, this was it.

Setting off from our downtown hotel in a hired Mercedes, we wound slowly past ministries once renowned for crude aggression, which had been left with no defense against the Americans' smart bombs. Their roofs had been wrecked and their interiors razed, leaving little more than the crumbling facades of their former glory. The Ministry of Information, the propaganda mouthpiece of the fallen dictator, Saddam Hussein, had collapsed in a cloud of dust. Smoke was still billowing from the rubble of one of the dictator's palaces.

On we drove toward our first hospital, past row upon charred row of burned-out buses, cars, and vans, each one representing an undisclosed story of personal loss for owners immobilized in a city that everyone but the looters seemed intent on fleeing. Hundreds of honking motorists lined up for fuel at the few garages still operating since thieves had started commandeering the tankers.

From one of the main highways, I saw the entrances to residential roads sealed off with barriers made from tires, planks, scrap metal—anything that came to hand—to keep out militias that were forming fast and staking claims to clusters of streets they intended to control now that the dictator's army and police had been smashed. Some of the militias had already begun to fight over their territory.

"It reminds me of Beirut just before the civil war," I said as Steve peered through one of his lenses. "Still, no need to worry. As long as we can dodge the missiles, the hijackers, and the gun battles, we'll be fine."

He gave me a broad grin and went back to checking his camera.

AT OUR FIRST DESTINATION, a teaching hospital we had visited every day at the start of the war, we found the operating rooms empty and an evacuation under way. A doctor we had befriended greeted us with a warning to leave.

"There are a lot of armed men around," he said. "Nobody knows who anybody is anymore. I can't even protect my patients here. Please go away."

In any case, he told us bitterly, there were no injured children in this hospital. Only children's bodies were left.

Our route to the second hospital took us into a slum of 2 million Shi'ites that had been known as Saddam City until the dictator was ousted. The old name was being blacked out on road signs and the new one—Sadr City—painted over it. Shi'ite militiamen were driving out loyalists of the Sunni-dominated Ba'ath Party that Saddam had led. The thud of rocket-propelled grenades and the crackle of machine-gun fire reverberated around the narrow streets, and our driver retreated into alleyways to avoid them.

When we reached the children's ward of the local hospital, we found a girl crying because she had lost her leg when a missile hit her house. But she was eleven years old and I knew the office would not want to know about her.

We moved on to Saddam Children's Hospital, where a small boy was screaming as nurses held him down so that doctors could clean a gaping wound in his left leg. The calf muscle had been torn away by shrapnel from another missile strike. But although his father had been killed, his mother had not. Our hunt for an orphan continued.

The fourth hospital, a modern, single-story building with a beautiful garden full of fragrant flowers and birdsong, seemed useless at first sight. Once we had persuaded the security controller to open the gate, we found white-coated doctors making their rounds of the wards with AK-47 assault rifles slung over their shoulders, just as we had heard. They were not guarding any children, however. This was a hospital for adults only.

I was beginning to despair, when one of the exhausted doctors invited us to sit down with him for a cup of tea. We explained what we were looking for. He paused for a moment, searching his memory, then told us about a young man of eighteen who had been admitted to this hospital as the battle for Baghdad was reaching its peak. The youth had been burned from head to foot and never stood much of a chance. He had died in agony after four days, but not before telling a story that had so touched the doctor that he wanted me to hear it.

"It's about a little girl," he said. "She lost seven members of her family, including her parents and her brothers. She was severely burned."

I gazed at the doctor intently, thinking the end of my search was coming into view.

"How do you know the story's true?" Such was the general hysteria at that time that many of the tales being told to journalists turned out to be wildly exaggerated.

"I know it's true, because my patient was one of the little girl's brothers," he replied. "She could die if her burns are anything like his."

"Where is she?"

"I really don't know," he said. "But there are many like her."

At that moment, I did not care about the "many like her." Perhaps because I was tired or perhaps because this girl had lost so many people she loved all at once, I found myself unexpectedly moved and mesmerized by her story. The cool professional detachment that had got me through the day was gone. I was captivated by this child and consumed by an urge to find her. All I wanted were the names of other hospitals where I might look.

My agitation must have been obvious to the doctor as I demanded them. I was on my feet as soon as he had finished his list. How rude he must have thought me when I dashed out of his office. Steve gave me that wide-eyed look he reserves for moments when he thinks I am getting carried away.

The late-afternoon sun was setting as we emerged from the hospital. I knew the curfew was looming and I did not want to wait another day to find this girl. It was already Wednesday and I would have to write on Friday for that weekend's paper. I headed for the main gates, where the driver was waiting.

"Madam, stop!" a voice cried.

I looked over my shoulder to see an old nurse running toward me. I thought I knew what she wanted. Journalists from the Western media were in great demand for their satellite phones. Landlines were down and there were no mobile phones, so wherever we went, there was always somebody pleading to call loved ones abroad, even for a minute or two, with the news that they were safe. Usually, I found it impossible to turn my back on these people; if the office got mad at me for running up an astronomical bill, I would deal with that later. But with time running out fast for me to find my little girl that afternoon, I did not want to hang around while this nurse chattered to her grandchildren. I hurried on.

"Madam," she called again. "Wait, I know where the little girl is." Her words stopped me in my tracks. She had overheard my conversation with the doctor.

"Don't waste your time looking all over the place," the nurse said. "Go straight to the Karameh hospital. She's there."

I thanked, hugged, and kissed her and rushed off.

In the car, Steve and I went through what the doctor had told us. Steve was looking at it from a purely professional point of view. An injured toddler who had lost seven members of her family was a hell of a good story, he reasoned, especially if she was the sole survivor. I agreed. Yet something more was drawing me toward this girl, an enigmatic force that I preferred to keep to myself for the moment. So when our driver grumbled that it was late, the hospital was far away, and we should leave the journey until morning, I snapped at him.

"No, we're going now. Please, I don't care how, just take us there—right now."

EVENING WAS ALMOST UPON US by the time we arrived. Not only that, but we could not find the burn unit at first. Our time for this assignment was being squeezed and I was feeling the pressure.

Eventually, we were met by a rather strict doctor at the entrance to the unit.

"Please take off your shoes and jackets, and leave your bags outside," he said. "Wear these gowns. Wear these masks over your mouth and come barefooted." He apologized for having no slippers to offer us.

As we padded down a disinfected corridor, waves of apprehension swelled in my stomach and rippled out to my racing heart. It was not just that I was worried about getting back to the hotel before curfew; I was bracing myself for the shock that awaited me in the ward. My whole body tensed as we followed the doctor through a door at the end of the corridor.

I saw her immediately: a tiny figure in that huge room, swathed in bandages like a miniature mummy and sleeping on her side beneath a blanket that was draped over a tunnel-shaped lattice to keep it from touching her skin.

She was oblivious to the pain of the burned women in the beds beyond hers, but something was disturbing the child. As she slept, her pale eyelids twitched as toddlers' do when they are having a nightmare. She moaned softly, as if too exhausted by her suffering to cry out. By her bed stood her grandmother, who was fanning her with a piece of cardboard. Tears were running down the old woman's face. She looked as if she had been weeping around the clock for days.

I hardly dared breathe as I approached, for fear of exhaling microbes that might harm so delicate a child. When I reached the bedside, I saw that her arms were shaking uncontrollably and although she appeared to be unconscious, I could make out some words.

"Cold . . . cold," she whimpered. I glanced at the doctor, thinking he might move forward to make her warm somehow, but he stared impassively. I presumed it was normal for someone who has been burned to feel cold.

"Cover me up, Mama," the little girl said. "Baba [Daddy], where are you? I'm cold." The same words were repeated over and over again. Whether she was conscious or not, she had never needed her mother more desperately and yet she was an orphan.

The doctor was clinical. This three-year-old patient had sustained deep second- and third-degree burns to her face, back, arms, and legs, he said, and contusions to the right arm and both legs. There were already signs of septicemia, he added coolly. If she could not be transferred from his nonsterile ward into a more appropriate environment within a few days, she would die. It was as simple as that, the doctor said. He did not have the facilities she needed and he could not provide the care that was required for her condition. His words were devoid of emotion, but by the time he had finished speaking, I was in tears.

Steve placed a hand on my shoulder and I met his eyes. Only he really understood why I was making such an exhibition of myself. He knew that I was prone to extremes of emotion when I was run down and that, like a lot of foreign correspondents, I always struggled to cope with the sight of a child hurt by war. He also realized instinctively that this encounter was especially poignant for me. The little girl was calling for a mother who would never come. And I had longed for a daughter like her who would never appear. I had been unprepared for how strongly I would respond as a childless woman to this motherless child. The ferocity of my reaction made me shudder. It would have been selfish to pity myself at such a moment and I did not do so. But I had no defenses left against all these feelings that assailed me. I was overwhelmed.

Something about my reaction stirred the girl's grandmother, however. She motioned me into the corridor outside, and there she recounted the family tragedy. The child's name was Zahra—it means "flower" in Arabic—and she was three and a half. She did not yet know the terrible truth: that her mother, father, four brothers, and a sister she adored had all been killed by a missile from an American warplane that had hit their car on the morning of April 4. Only Zahra and her three-month-old baby sister, Hawra, had survived.

"Zahra's too young to understand what it must have been like for her mother in that blazing car with her children dying around her," the grandmother said. "But perhaps one day, when she has children of her own, she'll know how difficult it must have been for her mother to choose which of them to save." She had hurled Hawra through a broken window of the vehicle, and the baby had survived virtually uninjured. But by the time she threw Zahra out a few seconds later, the flames had taken hold. That was why Zahra had been so badly burned.

One of the boys had got out after that, but his clothes had been on fire and nobody had thought he would last more than a few days. Their father, Ali, their mother, Rasmiyeh, and the other children had perished in seconds where they sat, or soon afterward in the hospital.

I could not speak.

"Please help my little girl, Zahra," the grandmother said, clutching my hand. She had watched me crying on the ward, had seen my concern for the child, and imagined that I could make everything all right.

"Please don't let her die, please take her away, please make her better for me," she begged. "You mustn't let her die. She's lost everyone. You owe it to her to help her live. I'm appealing to you to help her."

With that, my tears flowed again.

I hate big promises. Yet I could not deny this old woman. I wanted to help. So I looked her straight in the eye and gave her my word.

"Your granddaughter will live," I told her solemnly. "I'll make sure she receives the treatment she needs, whatever the cost."

The old woman wept once more, drained by the effort of pleading with me and buoyed by relief at my response. She squeezed my hand more tightly than before and brought her face up close to mine.

"Zahra is yours now," she said sweetly.

It was a figure of speech, or so I assumed. What she meant, surely, was that it was my job to make sure Zahra got the care that could save her. In that sense, Zahra had become my responsibility.

She would have life, I vowed. She would have hope. She would have a future. No one could be more determined than I to see to that.

LATER, IN THE DEAD OF NIGHT, I thought of nothing but saving Zahra. I was not indifferent toward the other children: I would have liked to help them all. My instructions, however, had been to find one child, a marketable orphan for a newspaper campaign. I had tried my hardest to remain aloof like a good journalist, because I would never have accomplished my search otherwise. Yet the discovery of a girl who encapsulated the anguish of all the rest had made me see these wounded innocents in a different light. Their suffering meant more than a powerful news story showing the sadness of war. It was far removed from the selling of newspapers. Some of the traumatized children in those hospitals would not survive, and the others had been changed for life. I could not merely report this. I resolved that I would use my paper's appeal to rescue Zahra, as well as raise money for the others. God knows Zahra needed help more than any of them.

For as long as I can remember, I have lain in bed and imagined a magic carpet transporting me from the anxieties of the present to an exotic, far-flung future where all my wishes come effortlessly true. When I was a little girl, the carpet would rise serenely above my bombed-out hometown of Beirut while I slept. It would fly me away from the war to a towering fairy castle where adoring crowds waited to hail the return of the enchanted Princess Hala. As a teenager, I glided away from my banal British boarding school to glamorous fashion shows in New York, Paris, and Milan. When I became a reporter in my twenties, the carpet showed me a blissful marriage; clever, handsome sons; and bright, beautiful daughters. This seemed more tangible than my other dreams at the time, though eventually it would prove just as difficult to grasp.

But on the first night I dreamed of Zahra, my ambitions were not for myself. The carpet took her away, leaving me behind to pray that she would reach a modern hospital, a sterile ward, and skilled specialists.

I knew from the start that saving Zahra would require a little magic and a lot of medical expertise. I made up my mind to get her flown to the finest doctors. It was her one chance of staying alive and my only hope of keeping my promise to her family.

Why, you may wonder, was I obsessed with the fate of one orphan of war among so many? What madness drove me to fight for her, when countless such battles were being lost across the beleaguered city? Why in God's name did I, a crazy journalist, believe I could achieve more than Zahra's surgeon, so much so that I promised her life when he predicted her death? To explain, I need to take you back to another time in a different war zone, where I fell in love and first conceived the fierce desire for a child whose destiny I could shape with my devotion.

Two

"THIS WOMAN WILL NEVER BEAR A CHILD"

I married Steve Bent twice: at a register office in London, with his family and friends, and then a few weeks later in Beirut, with mine. Most years, I ignore the anniversary of the chilly October ceremony in which we were formally married and my new mother-in-law was so overjoyed that she sobbed throughout. I celebrate on December 1, when it was my dear father's turn to shed tears as he walked me down the stairs of a gaily decorated Lebanese restaurant to a groom protected by guns and guards.

This was a wedding to remember. It took place in 1988, when Lebanon's civil war was raging and Beirut was particularly perilous for Westerners. The Church of England envoy, Terry Waite, had come to free three Western hostages, Terry Anderson, Brian Keenan, and John McCarthy, only to be kidnapped himself. The threat of abduction hung over every British visitor until he checked in for the flight out. Steve could not ask relatives to hop on a plane and watch him get hitched in a war zone. But he did bring his closest friends from Britain, all battle-worn photographers and reporters who knew the risks that were waiting for them in Lebanon and still did not want to miss the party.

As a reporter with the Reuters news agency, I received a tip-off on the day of their arrival that kidnap gangs were watching the airport road. The gangs apparently hoped to seize fresh victims in retaliation for some political statement in the West that had riled them. To make matters worse, fighting had broken out on the route we were planning to take through a Shi'ite southern suburb to the relative safety of Christian east Beirut, where Steve and his six "best men" would be staying.

All were briefed to avoid attracting attention after their flight touched down. They were not permitted to utter a single word of English when I greeted them, when their travel documents were being stamped, or when they were collecting their baggage. But there was no getting away from the fact that they looked Western, and the militant groups had spies at the airport. So no sooner had the last of Steve's friends climbed into our convoy of vehicles lined up outside than the drivers took off on the wrong side of the road, bodyguards hanging out of the front passenger-seat windows, waving their pistols wildly and firing into the air to clear the way. Our guards wanted everyone to think they were protecting Lebanese politicians rather than British partygoers.

There was no letup in speed or gunfire until the convoy reached the Green Line that marked our entry point into the Christian sector. After a swift change of vehicles to fool any persistent pursuers, we arrived in east Beirut, dazed but exhilarated.

"Now that's what I call driving," said one of Steve's photographer friends. "Can you get me through the London traffic like that?"

Our marriage took two days. First came a religious ceremony, then a full wedding celebration the following night. On security advice, the initial ceremony was performed at my parents' apartment. It was considered safer than a mosque, where we might have attracted attention from the militants. Steve converted to Islam and the presiding sheikh treated our British visitors to an hour-long lecture on the importance of allowing me to preserve my Muslim faith. He concluded by looking them greedily up and down.

"Seven Englishmen, one million dollars a head—I could retire," he said.

It was meant as a joke, but it did nothing to relieve my poor parents' tension. Nor did a power cut that trapped me in an elevator between two floors as I went to freshen my makeup at a nearby beauty salon. Our friends made light of it by forcing open the doors and taking endless photographs from the landing below me.

"Look down, darling, turn to this side—yes, great that way," they shouted until I screamed at them to get me out of there.

When the sheikh left, we dispensed with the traditional pink and white sugarcoated almonds and lemonade. The wine flowed and the table was laid for a sumptuous dinner of stuffed vine leaves, lamb, chicken, and *fatoush*, a favorite salad of mine with radishes and sweet peppers tossed in pomegranate syrup.

I escorted our guests back to their accommodations for the night and left them with the strict instruction: "You are not to leave the premises of this hotel under any circumstances."

I HAD MET STEVE when I was writing about the Lebanese civil war and he was photographing it. Shortly after I broke the story of Terry Waite's kidnapping, Steve turned up in Beirut with a reporter to investigate. One of my colleagues asked me to have a drink with them, but I had been trapped in my office for seventy-two hours by fighting outside and was not in the best of humor. When I saw how Steve's long fair hair and drooping mustache spoiled a handsome face, I was distinctly unimpressed.

"Who do you work for?" I asked.

"The Mail on Sunday," he said. I had never read it, though I knew it was a tabloid.

"Oh, that shitty paper," I said, hoping to deter him from bothering me again.

The next morning, however, he came into the office where I sat with my friends Diana and Samia. The three of us were young, green reporters, but we knew the story in Beirut so much better than the visiting veterans of the international press that we did not always treat them with the respect they were accustomed to from the agencies that served their newspapers.

The reporter with Steve asked the best way for them to find out where Terry Waite had gone on the day he disappeared.

"Let me save you the trouble," I said irritably. "Turn left out of the office, cross the bridge, and you'll find him in the second office block on the right."

For some reason, Steve was amused by my insolence. Later, we bumped into each other in The Back Street, a Beirut bar whose manager was renowned for keeping correspondents in a relaxed, free-spending frame of mind by turning up the music loud enough to cover the din of any shelling nearby. Before I knew it, Steve was smitten. One night after I turned up late for dinner with some of the "war corrs," Steve drew hearts and arrows in my Filofax and we drank port and brandy until four a.m. On the day he left, he dropped into the office with bouquets for Diana, Samia, and me, but his phone call from the airport left no doubt about which of us was on his mind. After that, he flew out for weekends, defying his newspaper's ban on travel to Beirut. He stayed with my parents and did his best to charm them with his fascination for me.

"Are you sure you know what you're doing, Hala?" my father would ask tenderly, his brow furrowing. "You come from different cultures and I've seen friends who went into mixed marriages end up divorced. Isn't it better to marry somebody from one's own culture?"

As I became more and more open to the idea of marrying Steve, it fell to my father to think of all the cons. "What happens when his Western political views clash with your Arab beliefs about the regional issues that matter a lot to you?" was one question on which I was urged to reflect.

Another was: "What happens when you listen to an Arabic song and you translate the words and Steve is unable to get the exact essence that moves you?"

Then, when there was talk of my moving to London, he asked: "What will you do when you start missing your own language and you want to express things in your own words and ways?"

In the end, I gently told my father that it was thanks to him I could not be the traditional Arab Muslim woman he had presumed I would become. I could not settle for this, because he had spent too much on my education, devoted too much time to developing my mind, put too much effort into encouraging me to seek something more in life. While he had been running a coffee factory in Sierra Leone, I had attended boarding schools in Lebanon until war came, then in England, where I had gone on to study business.

"There is a part of me that is very Arab, but then again another side of me belongs in the West where you sent me to be educated," I told him. "You meant well, but at times I feel like an outcast—I belong neither here nor there. I will have to reinvent myself and put to use my two worlds."

My softly spoken father, who had never once raised his voice to me, accepted what I had said. As I thought it all through for the final time before my wedding, his acceptance reassured me.

THE WEDDING HERALDED two new dreams. Not only would I be the wife of a Westerner, but there was also the prospect of becoming a mother. I knew I would want this and was certain I would have it. It was in the back of my mind on the day my smartly booted and suited father walked me through that restaurant, half choking with emotion as he handed his daughter over to the Englishman.

Rana, my petite sister, led the way, belly dancing a vibrant *zafet al-arrouss* (giving away the bride) to wild applause from our one hundred guests. Steve's best men, who had met them at the door with bows for the gentlemen and kisses for the ladies, were so inspired that they belly danced the night away. My sister was three years younger than I and had already had her first baby, a daughter, Lara, who was bounced from one relative to another all evening. If anyone had told me then that motherhood would not be part of my future, I would have laughed in his face.

IT IS ACCEPTED in the Middle East that after the first month of marriage, family and friends will begin to ask whether you are expecting a baby. To preempt this, I had told my parents that I did not want to conceive immediately. I explained that because I was marrying someone from a different culture and moving to Britain, I would need time to adjust to my new life and surroundings, and to get to know my husband better before starting a family.

For the first couple of years, we worked, partied, and enjoyed the occasional carefree holiday in the sun. Our apartment in Maida Vale became known among journalists in that part of West London for open-house Sundays. Anyone who was on his own was welcome to come to a lunch of roast lamb with all the trimmings. Nobody needed an invitation. The food was plentiful in Hala's kitchen and the drinks flowed from Steve's bar.

I was deeply in love with this blond, blue-eyed husband of mine, who had become not only my lover and best friend but my agent, directing me toward opportunities for work on his newspaper and others. There was also an impishness in Steve that I soon longed to see replicated in our sons. At the supermarket checkout one day, I found some tins of dog food at the bottom of the cart. As we did not have a dog, I removed them and apologized to the cashier.

"But they're for Goggy," Steve said. Then he told the cashier that I was a mean woman who would not feed our dog. Goggy had been a prop in Steve's stunts since childhood, his mother told me. He had once put worms in her bed and insisted that his imaginary dog was the culprit.

"I want boys so I can teach them all the naughty things and drive you crazy, Hala," he would tell me. Our boys probably would drive me mad, I thought, but there would be little girls with his golden curls to compensate.

Even so, we were determined to wait awhile. On visits to Beirut, I began to loathe people, including total strangers, who would ask, *"Mish m'khabayitilna shee?"*—Are you not hiding something from us, dear? In other words, are you pregnant? My mother and I would explain that I was taking my time.

"Well, don't take too long," they would all tell me. "It's not good." I would smile back at them, thinking, "What do you know?"

It was in 1990, when I was thirty years old, that I told Steve it was time we made our first baby. We had been married two full years. We had survived the initial ups and downs of getting used to each other's ways and our relationship was strong.

"I can't wait to see half of you and half of me joined together, Haloul," Steve said, using his pet name for me. "A child with my blond hair and your olive skin. We'll be seeing our kids off to school before we know it."

SEX EDUCATION HAD NO PART in a conservative Arab upbringing. Girls were forbidden to go out with boys and expected to remain virgins until they married. If a couple did not conceive, it was taken as a sign of incompleteness or imperfection. The possibility that there could be problems conceiving wasn't something I was even aware of. There was no talk of fertility or infertility.

So when we started trying, I became more and more mystified with each cycle of blood. My instincts began to tell me that something was wrong, and I went to see my gynecologist at his clinic in Harley Street.

He asked all the obvious questions: How long had we been trying, how often did we have sex, how often were we apart? When he heard how much Steve was traveling for *The Mail on Sunday*, he laughed and said I was worrying too much, too soon.

I asked him to humor me. I explained that I was troubled by an incident from the past. Some friends had told me about a marvelous fortune-teller who did readings from a cup of Turkish coffee grounds.

"Bring her around," I said. But although the fortune-teller read my friends' cups, she refused to look at mine. She made every excuse you could possibly imagine and just left. I thought she must be busy.

The following day one of my friends said she had refused because the minute she saw me, she had felt something.

"This woman will never bear a child," she had told my friend. She had not been able to bring herself to tell me.

At the time, I had been flabbergasted. I had talked to a doctor friend who had rebuked me for taking any notice of such nonsense. Yet here I was, telling my crazy story again to a specialist.

"Please," I begged him. "Could we start some preliminary tests, just in case?"

I expected to be dismissed out of hand. But the specialist saw how emotional I was and agreed to a test. He probably thought that if he could reassure me, I would calm down and stand more of a chance of getting pregnant.

"Go home, Hala," he said. "Make love with Steve first thing in the morning and come back to me shortly afterward."

THE NEXT DAY, I waited nervously as the specialist stared through his microscope. This is it, I thought. The sample he had collected would show that there was nothing to fret about. He would lecture me on the virtues of patience. These things take time, he would say. Getting stressed about it would not help. I expected to leave the clinic with a smile of self-deprecation on my lips, chiding myself for being so superstitious and stupid. Perhaps I would indulge myself by looking at some baby clothes on the way home. I would picture tiny toes fitting snugly into little white socks, crinkled fingers in woolen mittens, bright eyes that would make my heart leap every time I performed the routine chore of dressing and undressing my child.

My reverie was interrupted by an intake of breath from the doctor.

"Good God," he said, without looking up from the microscope. "I've never seen anything quite like this."

My mouth suddenly felt dry. I wanted him to explain immediately but dreaded what he might say. The wait while he checked his findings was agonizing.

"We seem to have a slight problem, Hala," he said finally.

As he explained, I could barely take it in.

"This is a small obstacle," he insisted gently. If Steve and I could not overcome it, medicine had so much to offer these days. There was artificial insemination and, failing that, in vitro fertilization. If he thought I would take heart from the prospect of clinical procedures, he was sadly mistaken. The visions they conjured of syringes, test tubes, and endless examinations compounded my distress. I left feeling battered and bruised.

I do not remember much about that afternoon except that I walked in the cold for hours, thinking to myself, "I am a murderer. I kill every sperm, every possibility of life."

I felt violated, as if something inside me had been removed without my consent. I did not understand what it was at first. Then I realized: I had been stripped of my confidence in the future, robbed of my certainty that I would become a mother. In my mind—and here my Arab culture plays a large role—I was a woman if I could make babies. But at nearly thirty, an age when most of my Lebanese contemporaries already had several children, I had just been told by this doctor that I was not like most women.

Now I started to hit the panic buttons, one after the other. How could I tell my parents that I might not be able to give them grandchildren? Far worse, what was I going to say to Steve, who longed to teach our son photography and play soccer with him on the common?

I was sobbing by the time I reached Steve's office, so I called him from outside and asked him to meet me for a coffee. My poor husband. I ranted, cursed, and cried. I even screamed at him for being normal.

"Why does it have to be me who has the problem? Why couldn't it be you?" I let the emotions pour out of me in torrents and nothing my husband said to reassure me could staunch the flow.

"I'm a Hitler," I remember shrieking at the height of it. "I just butcher everything."

"Look at me, Hala," he said, shaking me gently. "I love you . . . I promise you I'll make sure you have that bundle of joy in your arms."

TOGETHER, we tried everything we could. I strained every sinew and swallowed every prescription. After three months, I went back to the gynecologist, hoping that his pills would have cured the problem. They had not.

Traveling between London and Beirut, where I was doing assignments for British papers, I listened to various doctors, friends, and the inevitable old wives.

"Drink this herbal concoction, Hala . . . Take these new pills . . . Try this position," said some. Others counseled: "Don't even think about it . . . Just take a holiday . . . Relax."

Nothing worked. No test or scan signaled any way forward. I noticed that Steve would watch me intently when a child was introduced to us. He saw an increasingly desperate desire in me to say, "This is my son," or "That's my daughter."

Gradually, we accepted that we were never going to achieve this naturally. So be it, we thought. We would try every unnatural method known to medicine. I underwent a laparoscopy to check the state of my uterus and, as if my misery were not abject enough, suffered a punctured bowel for my pains. I surrendered my dignity to doctors practicing artificial insemination, heedless of my embarrassment as I lay on my back with my feet in stirrups and legs akimbo. But I returned home with fresh hope in my heart every time.

"This will be the month," I would tell myself.

"Don't carry heavy shopping bags," my mother would say on the phone from Beirut. "Stay home, don't go up and down stairs, rest, eat well."

That did not work, either.

We moved out of our apartment and into a beautiful Victorian home in south London with several floors of spacious rooms that I longed to fill up with our children. There was a basement kitchen where I would make my own baby food; a dining room overlooking the lush green garden where I would chase my toddlers around the swings and slide; the quiet back bedroom with its own bathroom where I would wrap them in warm towels and sprinkle them with talcum powder before tucking them in with teddy bears and goodnight stories.

A different specialist advised us to try IVF, so I learned how to inject myself with fertility drugs to stimulate my ovaries. This was hard for a person who freaks out at the sight of needles. I could not push them into my stomach, as the doctor advised, but forced myself to shoot up into my thigh, saying out loud: "Come on, Hala, you can do it. Think of the babies." Then I would take satisfaction from the scans that showed my eggs had multiplied, ready to be removed and fertilized.

"I need you to be at the hospital on such and such a day at such and such a time," I would tell Steve. He turned up when he had to, but I was angry with him for not coming with me unless his presence was strictly necessary. I knew he had to work, but I felt the burden of making our babies was falling mainly on me. I sought solace in Internet chat rooms with women who had the same problems, finding encouragement in their successes and doing my best to encourage those who failed to keep trying.

As the months became years, I worried more and more about the expense. I racked up bills for thousands and thousands of pounds' worth of IVF, with nothing to show for the investment of our life savings.

My father sent a check for £3,500, the cost of one cycle of treatment at that time, with a note saying: "Perhaps this will be the one, Hala." His generosity made me cry because I knew he was not a rich man. I returned the check, saying this was something we could fund ourselves.

"Promise me you will ask if you need, Hala," he said, choking up on the phone.

EVENTUALLY, I began to tire of the sterile rooms, the harsh fluorescent lights, the relentless merry-go-round of smiling doctors who boosted my hopes, only to watch them die each month in a trickle of blood.

It was too exhausting to keep challenging God's will. My mother had always told me that this would happen if it was meant to be, though her fatalism did not deter her from supplying the names of one doctor after another with a reputation for working miracles on women who had been trying for longer than I.

In Beirut, she forced me to see an obstetrician who worked partly in America and partly in the Middle East. It took a long time to get an appointment, but I used up most of it by venting my frustrations.

"I've tried it all. Why should you be any different?" I said. Then I lost it. "I hate you all," I told this eminent specialist. I walked out in tears, screaming at my mother that she should never have put me through this. Later, I cried and cried. I begged Mama's forgiveness, thanked her for all she had done but told her I did not know how much more I could take of these hospital endurance tests.

Not only was my faith in medical miracles fading fast, but with it was vanishing the passion for work that had driven me through militias' roadblocks as a journalist in Beirut. The focus on having a child pushed everything else into oblivion. My ideas for assignments were drying up and so were the offers from newspapers.

I was not a mother. I was barely a journalist anymore. I was nothing but a total failure.

Never was this more acutely felt than at Christmas. Our first Christmas in London, a few years earlier, with my newly divorced sister, Rana, and her then two-year-old daughter, Lara, had been such a delight.

"Rana," I had told her when her marriage fell apart and she ran short of money, "whatever happens, we'll make sure between us that Lara has the best things in life. This I promise you."

"But Hala," she had replied, "Lara isn't mine alone. She's your daughter, too, so be prepared. You'll be involved in every decision. This is a responsibility you won't get out of easily."

I bought Lara so many presents that the parcels spread out from my heavily decorated tree to cover much of the living room floor. My sister joked about how the child would grow up confused as to which of us was really her mother. Steve played the role of substitute father to perfection. I watched him talk to Lara, bathe her, and put her to bed. I thought how gentle he would be with our own children.

When our own children did not arrive, I came to hate Christmas. I refused to put up a tree because I did not want one without children to play around it. I was reminded over and over again of a friend of my father's who had asked why we did not have children and who had received an equivocal reply.

"But Hala, my dear child," he had said as my mother and I looked at each other in horror, willing him to stop but unable to interrupt. "Listen to this old man's wisdom and trust it. A house without a child is a house without a soul."

He could not have known that each word was a jab to my heart. Even though I believed he was right, I hated him for saying it. Each Christmas, when I looked back on another year of failure, his words returned to haunt me, like the ghosts of the babies I had imagined but had failed to deliver to this world.

AS ANY WOMAN who has failed to get pregnant will know, it is hard to put up with the glad tidings of a friend who has succeeded. For the most part, I managed to put on a happy face, clink glasses, and toast the expectant mother. I abhorred the self-pity that made me curl up in bed and sob for hours on end when I reached home. But I loathed myself more for being the barren, miserable one in a social circle of fun-loving young mothers who took fecundity to absurd extremes. Some of these women even got pregnant when they did not want to.

When Diana told me that she was expecting a baby she wanted very much, I stayed with her in Dubai for a few weeks to finish writing a book. I was ecstatic for her but envious, too. As I watched her belly grow, I could not help but wonder how I would look if I should be so lucky. In the end I held her tiny son in my arms but cried like a lunatic in a children's clothes shop when I went to buy him a present.

Steve was named godfather, and we found ourselves looking after the child while his parents went away for a few days. It made me long for my own baby more than ever.

Only Lara could soothe the pain. She was growing into a beautiful, sensitive girl with a wisdom beyond her years, who seemed to sense the need in me long before I articulated it to her. Ever since she was small, she has sent me a card on Mother's Day, signed, "Your daughter, Lara."

Rana longed for me to become a mother almost as much as I did. When the fourth course of IVF, with all its attendant expectancy, resulted in nothing more than my usual period, I fled the dear London friends whose sympathy was more than I could bear for the sanctuary of Rana's house in Cairo.

One night, she came into my room with a bottle of wine and two glasses, and locked the door behind her.

"Hala," she said in a very serious tone. "Please listen to me and don't cut me off until I'm finished."

She poured our glasses. "I know you're older and I always turn to you for help, but for once there's something I can do for you." I had no idea what she was talking about.

"Hala, if it's fine with you, I'll be happy to act as a surrogate mother for you and Steve. It will still be your baby, from your IVF, but instead of being planted in you, I'll carry him for you."

"Oh God, Rana," was all I managed to say. As she went on, I could only think that as much as I had always cherished my sister, I had never loved her more than I did at that moment. Not until she had finished her piece did I begin to explain why I could not let her do this. For one thing, I pointed out softly, it was prohibited in Islam for a woman to become pregnant with the sperm of any man other than her husband's.

"But Hala, not even Allah would find this sinful. I'm sure He would bless it," said my sister, who has never been a great one for religious constraint.

I gave her a huge hug and said I was still hopeful that another way would be found for me to have a baby. After all, most doctors had described my infertility as "unexplained," and none had said it was impossible for me to conceive. In the meantime, I would praise the first words and tottering steps of other women's children but would quickly block them out of my mind and try to think of something else.

What, though? Adoption? I could not face it. I craved a child, but I wanted one that had grown inside me, one that had heard my heartbeat for nine months. I wanted one that had Steve's blood running through its veins. You could be sure of your own child, but there were no guarantees with someone else's. I feared the unknown. What if the stranger's baby had bad genes? What if I could not love him enough? Would British social workers not think me too old to adopt a baby? If we tried to adopt in Lebanon, would Steve not be barred as a foreigner? I worried about it all and changed the subject whenever adoption was broached by friends.

WE WERE COMING to the end of the 1990s. We had been trying for nearly ten years and I was almost forty. The dawn of the millennium was hailed by many as a time of renewed hope for the future. I took a different view. For Steve and me, it would mark the end of hope. There would be no more tests, no more drugs, no more prodding and poking. I had endured too much humiliation and too many devastating disappointments. I could not go on weeping for babies I had dreamed of so vividly that I could almost feel them in my arms. The pressure on Steve was becoming unbearable, too. If the IVF cycles of hope and despair continued, they would force us apart.

When my mother said that perhaps this was not meant to be after all, I agreed.

"Never hate anything that happens," she said. "It may turn out to be best for you." I could not think of any way my infertility could be a good thing. But I knew it was time to change.

"Let go of the dream, Hala," I told myself solemnly. "Make do with what you have. Reinvent yourself. So you were not supposed to be a mother—you can do other things instead."

IT WAS NOT UNTIL I saw United Airlines Flight 175 slice through the South Tower of the World Trade Center on September 11, 2001, that I knew precisely what I had to do. Like everyone else who saw the TV images of this second plane striking its target in New York, I was filled with awe at the scale of the attack, and pity for its victims. But the collapse of the Twin Towers sparked something inside me that I thought had long been extinguished. An enormous news story was breaking in front of my eyes and I realized I wanted to be one of the thousands of reporters covering it.

It was a shock to feel the journalistic passion stirring again after so long, warming the blood and firing up the brain. Okay, so I was not meant to be a mother, but by God I was a good reporter. What was to stop my becoming one of the best? Nothing—nothing would stand in my way, because I could give myself to assignments with a devotion other women reserved for their families. Not only that, I could work with Steve. We would reinvigorate our marriage.

I started with some assignments for Steve's latest newspaper, *The Sunday Telegraph*, including a couple of trips to Iraq as war began to loom there. Unbeknownst to me, the foreign editor of the rival *Sunday Times*, Sean Ryan, was reading my dispatches. He was struggling to get his journalists into Baghdad because the authorities would not issue visas to the British and Americans. As a Lebanese, I could get a visa in a day. Sean rang me.

No sooner had we shaken hands in his office than we clicked. A tall, blond man in his late thirties, he greeted me with a courteous smile and some rather formal questions. But when I mentioned a couple of ideas, his reserve melted and his eyes shone. He was seized by the potential of this Arab reporter who could gain access to people no Westerner could reach, whether in Baghdad or elsewhere in the Middle East. He saw how my ideas could be built up into big pieces with bold projection. His excitement thrilled me.

I said I had contacts in Hamas, one of the groups behind a wave of suicide bombings in Israel. No one else had penetrated Hamas and found out who the bombers were.

"Great idea," Sean said. "Could you interview one? We have no sense of why these people volunteer, how they're prepared, whether they think about the women and children they kill. What drives them, Hala? Let's find out."

Over lunch a week later, I said I thought it would take six weeks to earn the trust of Hamas. If I did, they might give me access to bombers undergoing training. I could rent a tiny flat in Gaza for a couple of months for next to no money and see if I could win them over.

"Let's do it," Sean said.

I left in London all thoughts of motherhood, traveled to Gaza, and eventually interviewed three educated young men whose families had lost their land to Israel and who were preparing to take revenge in the belief that their "martyrdom" would secure them a place in paradise. *The Sunday Times* ran three thousand words, starting on page one and turning to a two-page spread inside.

My career had been relaunched. I had found a paper I could work with and a boss who believed in me. Other front-page stories followed, interspersed with discreet trips to Baghdad to cultivate contacts, grease palms, and organize accommodations, transport, and visas in the buildup to a conflict that had seemed inevitable from the moment the Bush administration alleged—erroneously, as it turned out—a link between that city and the 9/11 attacks.

Would I consider basing myself there when the blitz came? I was asked.

"Absolutely," I heard myself telling the boss in a strangely confident tone. It was not courage that made me say this. I had already made my choice. This was one of the biggest news stories of the new century. I did not want to miss it.

As a Lebanese and a Muslim, I knew the Arab perspective. As the wife of an Englishman and the employee of a London paper, I understood the Western way of thinking. I was in the privileged position of being able to straddle two worlds and explain one to the other.

So it was no surprise to be asked a few months later if I would report on the anticipated invasion of Iraq. It was only to be expected that I would be speeding across the desert toward thronging Baghdad, several weeks before the bombardment was likely to start. What no one—least of all myself—could have predicted was that however hard I tried to bury myself in the new role of action-girl foreign correspondent, something within me would resurface in Baghdad—my maternal instincts disarmingly intact.

Three

SHOCK AND AWE

Nobody could accuse us of being ill prepared: by the time we reached the Iraqi border, our four-wheel drive was packed to bursting point. We had bags stuffed with laptops and cameras, cables and clothes. There were flak jackets and first-aid kits, batteries and something called an M4 that would give us Internet access in the field. We also brought enough food and drink to see us through a siege. Military analysts were predicting that Baghdad would be encircled by invading forces, so supplies were vital. We carried boxes of mineral water, jars of coffee, and cartons of fruit juice, staples such as rice and sugar, and chocolate treats we knew we would earn.

The adventure before us was the most daunting of our professional lives but also the most exciting: it would keep the adrenaline pumping for months. If it was terrifying, we would be brave. If it was heartbreaking, we would be tough enough to get the job done and save our tears for later. I knew Steve and I would be strong together because we had endured so much without falling apart. The effort of trying to get pregnant and the hollowness it had left inside me were being replaced with a sense of purpose and the promise of another kind of fulfillment. We had made our wills and asked our families to pray for us. We were fired up and ready for anything.

OUR BRITISH PHONES could still pick up a signal at this point, but once we drove over the border, we would be cut off from colleagues and contacts, family and friends, during the ten-hour desert drive to the city. Satellite telephones were prohibited by the Iraqi authorities, although we were smuggling one in for emergencies.

My phone beeped with a text message: "Hala, before you cross over, call me urgently. Sean x."

I shouted at our driver to stop before we lost our signal.

"Thank God I got you in time," said the boss when I dialed his number. "Listen carefully. We can't discuss this once you've crossed, so I'd better fill you in on the latest decisions here. We need you to start preparing for the day the regime falls."

The senior editors had just held a council of war. They knew that Saddam Hussein's regime, like the Nazis, documented everything meticulously. In which case, they reasoned, the documents would contain all his secrets, ranging from weapons programs to covert contacts with Western politicians, from links with international terrorists to the executions of dissidents in hellhole prisons. This could mean one front-page scoop after another.

What Hala should do, they decided, was remove the files from key buildings when the dictator fled. A former special-forces officer was being hired to help me.

"Could you arrange vehicles and drivers so that the documents can be put in safe houses before the Americans come looking for them?" I was asked.

I felt like saying, "Are you guys serious?" but instead heard myself saying, "Okay." I knew that they were not really crazy in the office, that every newspaper was probably thinking along the same lines and making similar plans. We would see what happened.

"Everything okay?" Steve asked as I switched off my phone.

"Yes." I smiled back. "All's well."

MY MOTHER ALWAYS TOLD ME not to question Allah's will. "It's not personal, Hala," she said when I realized that I was not going to have a baby. "He doesn't work that way. Do not blaspheme. Just accept Him and thank Him for what you already have."

I could not do so for a long, long time. I was in mourning. Mine was an irrational grief for someone who had never existed. I was crying for all the hopes that had died—hope for life, for the future, for the person my child might have been and the person I might have become.

For the most part, I have learned to hold this pain inside me, but the desire for children is a demon that cannot be locked away. Every now and then it creeps out and catches me unaware, bringing back all the emotions in a surge of realization.

"Perhaps this is why it was never meant to be," I thought as our vehicle powered on to the six-lane highway that stretched for 650 miles ahead of us. "Where I'm going, I'll be glad I don't have children left behind in London."

THE PECULIAR THING ABOUT DRIVING into Baghdad was that we noticed nothing out of the ordinary. The war fever that had gripped everyone in London was nowhere to be seen in the city of 6 million people where the fighting was actually going to take place. Women still trudged to market for fish, spices, and fruit. Men with clipped mustaches and oiled hair smoked gloomily in their cars to relieve the frustration of being caught in gridlocked traffic on their way to the office. Small boys chased a soccer ball around some wasteland and dreamed of bending it like Beckham, just like small boys everywhere.

A newly arrived visitor from Baghdad might have been viewed with some suspicion in Britain, so strong was the association in people's minds between that city and its tyrant with his supposed weapons of mass destruction. Britons arriving here were greeted with warm smiles.

"Engleezee, ahlan, ahlan"—Welcome, welcome—we heard everywhere. Western sanctions had impoverished the ordinary inhabitants of this place for years, yet the hospitality they offered us was generous and kind. It seemed strangely at odds with the preparations our country was making to attack with missiles, bombs, and crack troops. Did these people know what we were about to do to them? I wondered.

One had only to stroll down the street to see that if they did know, the inhabitants of Baghdad preferred not to think about it. Rich and poor families alike crowded into restaurants to feast on roast chicken and freshly grilled lamb kebabs. In the coffee shops, old men played drafts and smoked their hubble-bubbles in clouds of apple-scented smoke. Many of the younger ones busied themselves with building work. Cranes swung to and fro over monumental office blocks, and the fancy private villas going up nearby seemed to reflect faith in the future rather than fear of imminent destruction.

There were two signs of trouble. Men, women, and children alike spoke of an undying love for the dictator whose poster loomed over the main roads, yet their voices were devoid of passion. In a country where Internet access was all but a dream and satellite television was banned for fear that people would demand the freedoms enjoyed elsewhere, everyone understood that any failure to show loyalty to Saddam could lead to punishment and perhaps to death. So when I asked passersby if they were afraid of war, they merely uttered the ruling party mantra that they would fight if necessary, then hurried on with their daily lives.

More than anything else, however, it was the joyous frequency of wedding celebrations around me that showed that Baghdadis sensed sorrow might not be far away. On one night alone I must have seen eighty young women in shimmering white gowns clutching their husbands' arms on the grounds of my hotel. It was a mass wedding arranged by the regime. Each bride was so beautifully made up that any anxiety about the fate of her groom was masked. Exultant family and friends ululated and honked horns around them as they departed. But what I saw in some of the couples' eyes was a determination to seize their chance of pleasure before it disintegrated in the painful weeks that stretched ahead.

STEVE AND I were always being teased about being together as husband and wife while our colleagues were remote from their loved ones. What they refused to believe was that when we were away on assignment, we ceased to live as a married couple and operated as a purely professional duo. We brainstormed and watched each other's back. But if Steve did not have the right picture for my story, I blamed him. If my piece was not strong enough to get his picture a good placement, he blamed me. In that sense, we were the same as any other reporter and photographer.

The dread we all shared was of being arrested, carted off into the desert, and tied up at some remote installation on the American target list to deter the bombers. So it was strange to come across British people in hotel lobbies who had actually volunteered to become "human shields" in this way. They truly believed that they could make Bush think again about the wisdom of going to war.

"I do think if we have a large number of people in the sites, it will be very difficult for them to bomb," said an Old Etonian and Cambridge graduate who had retired to his country house after a long career in the Foreign Office. "I really do think so."

However naive they might have seemed, they earned our respect. Joe Letts, a bus driver from Dorset, had delivered fifty human shields to Iraq.

"I'm not keen on dying," he said in his understated English way. "But if I die, I want everybody to know I was here and why I was here."

I wished I could have been half as brave.

The most pressing issue for journalists, however, was what to do if we were ordered out of the country. No reporter wanted to endure all that waiting, only to miss the war. So we debated whether safe houses could be arranged where we could hide from the prying eyes of the regime if visas were revoked. These refuges could be lifesavers later on if the bombardment provoked anti-Western mobs to attack our hotels or try to take us hostage. But could we trust the drivers we had befriended not to betray our whereabouts?

I wanted to try something different. I had entered Iraq with a visa in my British passport. But I had a second passport from Lebanon. If I could get a visa in that one, too, it would give me more options than my competitors. If I was thrown out on one passport, for instance, I could still reenter the country anytime I liked.

There was only one problem. They were used to seeing me at the ministry every day and I stood out in their eyes, partly because I had made it my business to flirt shamelessly with them and partly because I liked to smoke a pipe. I had become known everywhere as "the pipe woman" and I was sure my absence would be noted if I took off to Beirut for a few days.

It was decided in the end that I would sneak away on a Friday evening and drive to the Syrian border. If I traveled all night, I could cross from Syria into Lebanon and reach Beirut on Saturday morning. The aim was to return to Baghdad via the same route on Sunday so that I would be out of the ministry officials' sight for only a day or two. Given the quality of our diet, my absence could easily be explained away as an episode of food poisoning. Steve would stay in our room and say that he was also suffering with his stomach. I was briefed to switch on my radio before crossing over into Syria. President George W. Bush was due to address his nation.

"Listen carefully, Hala—there are bound to be some clues about the timing of the war," my boss said. If it sounded as if Bush was about to order the attack, I would return immediately to Baghdad rather than risk being out of the country when the bombing started. If he presented one last option for averting war, I would continue on my way.

My driver was instructed to stop just before we reached the crossing, and we tuned in to BBC World Service. Bush's voice crackled across the airwaves but his message was clear. The dictator was being given an ultimatum to leave—a few more days to save his country and his people from the inevitable. That meant a few more days for me to get myself organized.

"Hit the accelerator," I told the driver.

I WAS AWAY FROM BAGHDAD for just forty-eight hours, but by the time I returned, the atmosphere had been transformed. Bush's ultimatum had destroyed any remnant of doubt that bombing was imminent. The men were not driving to their offices anymore with cigarettes clamped to their lips. They were at home, moving chairs and beds away from windows, which they had taped with cardboard to prevent shards of shattering glass from lacerating their children.

"How do people protect themselves from bombing?" the dictator asked provincial governors at a televised meeting. "Tell them to dig trenches in their gardens."

Some families followed this decree; others went further and dug wells. The streets were empty, save for women hurrying to stock up on food and water, anxious to make sure that husbands and children would not go hungry under bombardment. As for the small boys I had been watching with their soccer balls, they were kept indoors on pain of death.

I found myself drawn to the maternity department of one of the city's great hospitals, the Alwiya. Whether I was seeking a striking angle for an article or satisfying my curiosity, I do not know. But the sight of mothers with swollen bellies walking through the entrance, their toddlers in tow, made something stir inside me. I believed I had learned to control my emotions in the face of pregnant women, but what would I say if one of these mothers asked whether I had children? Would I be able to interview them without betraying my old longings for the euphoria of a positive pregnancy test, the wonder of seeing my child curling and uncurling minute fingers on a scan, and the joy, pride, and relief of holding him in my arms for the first time?

Determined though I was to avoid embarrassing myself with tears, I was shaken by my reaction to the first newborn I saw in the waiting area. Envy of his mother convulsed me and I trembled with the shame of it. I took a deep breath, steadied myself, and tried to concentrate on the reporting I had come to do.

Whatever my motive in entering the hospital, a poignant drama was unfolding that excited me professionally and moved me personally. Here were dozens of women struggling to bring new life into the world before it could be asphyxiated by war. They were asking doctors to induce labor now rather than risk giving birth while trapped in their homes a few days later.

"There is a sense of hysteria among pregnant women," said one of the busy obstetricians. "They are coming seven and eight months pregnant and saying, 'I want my baby now.' These mothers tell me they are afraid in case they cannot make it to the hospital on their due date, in case they have no fuel in their cars, or bridges are blown up or air raids are going on. We do what we can for them."

Several cesarean sections were performed by this doctor on the day of my visit—purple-skinned babies pulled from their sleeping places and rudely awoken by latex-covered fingers clearing their throats of fluid. They were placed unceremoniously on scales before being passed to mothers whose joy was surely tempered by the grave responsibility of protecting them from the fighting that would begin in the first days of their infancy.

Other births were induced, even though everyone knew that there would be no drugs to relieve the pain of these longer labors. The hospital was saving its anesthetic for the legion of wounded who would be stretchered in before the week was out. The shrieks that resounded through the corridors seemed to impart not only the agony of the women giving birth but their anguish at the loss of life that would soon be all around them.

Some mothers whose babies had been born prematurely insisted on taking them home despite doctors' warnings that the infants should be left in their incubators.

"Whatever happens, at least we'll be together," said a twenty-eight-year-old woman who already had three children and had started to bleed a month before her fourth was due. The doctors had been compelled to perform a cesarean and then, when she did not stop bleeding, a hysterectomy. One of them was soothing her and gazing anxiously at the skinny son she insisted on removing from his incubator.

"I can't leave him behind, not knowing if I'll even be able to visit him," she cried.

Away from the hospital, I found another group of young mothers who had tried to make their newborns safe by taking them out of the country, only to be turned back by stony-faced soldiers at the border. One woman cradling a two-week-old baby boy in a shawl told me that when she had pleaded to be allowed through, the soldiers had told her she had the wrong kind of passport. A new, smaller passport was required now. That was the law.

"I'm frightened," this woman told me, "not for me, but for my baby. He's sick. I am worried he might die without proper medicine."

While these people were trapped in the city, our media friends were getting out. Gone was the late-night, beer-fueled bravado of reporters bragging about their determination to remain regardless of the risks. The Ministry of Information was in chaos as they lined up to pay their bills and leave. The rumor mill had gone into overdrive. One journalist assured me that a mass kidnapping of Westerners was imminent. Another who had been ordered to leave claimed that female reporters held as human shields would also be raped.

The panic was spreading to editors back home, many of whom decided to withdraw their staff. The correspondents of our sister paper, *The Times*, were among those told to go, on the grounds that the risks were "unprecedented and unacceptable." My office telephoned to relay the thinking at *The Sunday Times* just as Steve and I were deciding what we would do.

"You should leave if it's too dangerous to stay," Sean said. "No one will think any the less of you if you get out now."

"No," I replied calmly. "We've talked about this and come to the conclusion that we'll be safe."

It was no use explaining that I did not believe Saddam had weapons of mass destruction, because Sean would have accused me of going native. Instead, I told him I did not think it was in the military's interests to use such weapons in the city, because the scale of civilian casualties would wreck any chance of sustaining sympathy in the Arab world.

"We'll be safe in the city," I repeated. "The Americans know which hotels the Western media are in. There's no way they'll blow up CNN. The regime isn't going to take us hostage. On the contrary—it will probably help us with reporting and pictures. It will want pictures of wounded people to go round the world."

"Come off it, Hala, they've used human shields before," Sean said, though I could tell from his tone that I was winning the argument.

"No," I told him, my own voice rising in alarm at the thought that months of preparation might come to nothing if we were pulled back to London. "We came in here knowing the risks and we came for this moment. It's where I want to be. Please ask the editor not to order us out of here. Please tell him to trust our judgment on the ground and allow us the freedom to make this decision ourselves. If we feel it necessary to leave, we'll say so and nothing will stop us from getting out of here."

It worked. We were told we could stay even though the other British media were pulling out, bar *The Guardian*, *The Independent*, Sky, and the BBC.

IT WAS 5:34 A.M. when we were woken by the wailing of sirens. Steve and I glimpsed a moment's panic in each other's eyes and scrambled out of bed. Within seconds, muezzins were chanting from nearby minarets. Their call to prayer almost drowned out the clattering anti-aircraft fire at first, but the thump of cruise missiles finding their targets was unmistakable. It was enough to put the fear of God into anyone.

As we huddled together in the corridor outside our room, a pause in the cacophony of war was filled by the screeching of a solitary motorist's tires, the shrill barking of terrified dogs, and another, less familiar sound. It took me a few seconds to realize that it was a donkey braying. For days afterward, he would bray just before the attacks began. He became my imaginary friend, my early-warning call. I made a note in my head to find him when it was all over and present him with a feast of carrots.

The "shock and awe" that had been promised by Donald Rumsfeld, the man in charge of the Pentagon, had finally begun. It was no surprise after the weeks of waiting, yet shock and awe were precisely what we felt. The city center where we were holed up was now the bull's-eye target of some of the most lethal weaponry ever devised, and it was coming closer.

As we ventured on to our hotel balcony to start documenting the bombardment, the emergency equipment stacked in one corner of the room caught my eye: flak jackets, helmets, first-aid kits, and the "NBC" suits that were supposed to protect us against a nuclear, biological, or chemical onslaught.

"Ya Rab yasser wall tu'aaseer," I prayed over and over again. "God, please help. Do not put obstacles in our way."

I switched on the radio for any news of the attack or counter-attack, but all that was being broadcast at first was a mixture of traditional patriotic songs and some modern ones dedicated to "the great leader." Later, they were interspersed with poems expressing "the people's love of the leader." Then the leader's son came on.

"This is the day we have been waiting for," he said. "Bush and

Blair have proved they are the bastard sons of whores. Rise, celebrate, resist, and be steadfast against this foreign aggression."

As news began to circulate that both father and son had narrowly escaped one of the cruise missile strikes, the leader himself appeared on television in military fatigues and a black beret, urging his countrymen to "draw your sword and be not afraid."

THEY WERE, OF COURSE, deeply afraid, as I saw that morning when the bombs stopped falling and I went to visit a family whose diary of war I was compiling for the paper.

I had chosen this family partly because the man of the house, Farouq Mohammed Ali, had spent seven years studying civil engineering in Britain, and partly because his wife, Iman, was four months pregnant. I felt an instinctive connection with her. Although she had a girl of thirteen and boys of twelve and eleven, it had taken ten years to conceive the child she was now carrying.

They lived with Iman's divorced sister, Anthra, and her two daughters in one of the oldest houses in Baghdad. It stooped and creaked, and although its fine wooden doors, ten feet high, looked out onto an attractive courtyard, the roof and plaster had seen better days in the early part of the last century. The first time I met them, they had reminisced about the days when the Iraqi dinar was worth three American dollars, when they had traveled together on holiday in Europe and bought good clothes. Now one American dollar was worth three thousand Iraqi dinars.

By the time I arrived on the first day of the bombardment, Farouq had gone to work in the video rental shop he now managed. This would be a particularly busy week for him, Iman explained. The one thing the people of the city could do while the electricity lasted was to stay at home and let their favorite films transport them to another, more familiar world other than the Hades outside their own front doors.

"It was an awful night and the children cried as I held them in my arms, whispering soothing words to them," Iman said. She shuddered as she explained how, as the sky rumbled overhead, the house had shaken. Some of the plaster had tumbled down the walls, the glass windows had shattered, and Iman had been convinced the fragile roof would cave in.

"I had to get the children out of their rooms so that we could take cover by the entrance to the house," she explained. "I couldn't walk—my feet wouldn't carry me—so I crawled on all fours. I know I'm pregnant but I had no choice. I don't know if I'll lose this baby out of sudden panic from those loud explosions."

I pretended to sound knowledgeable in the hope that I could reassure her.

"Babies are tougher than you think," I said.

She took my hand and guided it toward her. I knew what she was going to do next and I had to stop myself from recoiling. If there was one thing guaranteed to melt the glacial sangfroid with which I had come to view my own infertility, it was a pregnant woman placing my hand on the warm, taut skin of her bloated belly.

"I don't know whether the heart is beating," Iman was saying, as if I should be able to feel it. For a moment, I could not answer.

"My nightmare is that my fear will affect my pregnancy and I'll give birth to an abnormal child," she went on. "I know one thing: if anything happens to this child, it will be America's and Britain's fault."

I felt for the baby as best I could.

"All seems well," I said, trying to hide my hopeless ignorance of such matters. "You'll be fine, Iman, as will your baby. I am sure your child is kicking."

To my astonishment, her face brightened. She believed me.

I felt myself sway slightly and allowed my hand to drop away from her. The bulge of her fetus had reminded me of my desolate emptiness, and I realized that my demon had returned, or more likely had never gone away.

"Snap out of it, Hala," I thought as I left Iman's house.

I went back to Steve and did not say a word about it.

Four

"WILL I GET MY ARMS BACK?"

A few hours later I heard a knock at my door, and who should be standing there but my hero. Jon Swain, a *Sunday Times* correspondent who has covered every war from Vietnam in the 1970s to Afghanistan in the 2000s, had driven across the desert overnight to replace a colleague who had left. He had careered into the city under bombardment, in defiance of a specific instruction from the editor not to take that risk, and he already had a story in his notebook about the first civilian casualty of the war.

"Salut, habibi!" he cried, greeting me with his habitual mixture of French and Arabic, and a hug.

Swain was a legendary reporter. As a teenager, he had rejected college in favor of a stint in the French Foreign Legion. When other journalists were fleeing Cambodia, he had flown into Phnom Penh on the last plane before the fall of that city to the Khmer Rouge in 1975. He would have been summarily executed but for the intervention of the *New York Times* interpreter Dith Pran—a story told in the film *The Killing Fields*. He had survived a kidnapping by Ethiopian rebels who held him hostage for three months and an attack on his car by Indonesian soldiers who had murdered his interpreter. There had been one marriage but many love affairs. Swain's colorful past and gentle charm ensured that he was surrounded by women at every party. But to work with, he was a perfect gentleman. I could not have been more delighted to see him.

Steve and I settled him down with a glass of wine to toast his arrival and hear the extraordinary story of his journey. The bombing had begun as he entered the country, but officials at the border post continued to process his papers. They said they could not understand why the Americans had just destroyed a nearby car pound, even though it contained only vehicles confiscated by customs.

Swain's taxi and a bus carrying twenty-five human shields from South Africa were the only signs of life on the road when he had arrived at a rest station with a public telephone office that had been the target of an equally mysterious air strike. A lone American bomber flying high above it in the darkness had dropped a guided one-thousand-pound bomb through the roof. According to witnesses, the ground had erupted and the building had leaped into the air before settling back into rubble.

The sole victim was Ahmad Walid, a thirty-six-year-old driver who had been phoning ahead to his boss in Baghdad to check that it was safe to proceed with his two passengers. Most of his body was buried, but his brown corduroy jacket and blood-streaked head were just visible beneath the huge slab of concrete that had crushed him. He had died at one a.m., several hours before Bush appeared on television to announce that the war had begun, and Swain could find nothing in the debris that could conceivably have linked it to military communications. He concluded that by no stretch of the imagination could the office have represented one of the "selected targets of military importance" the Americans said they had been hitting that night.

SWAIN AND I TEAMED UP to report on some of the most fearsome nights of the war, when the bombing intensified to a magnitude that no city in the modern world had seen before. First would come the braying of the donkey, more agitated each time; then sirens would blare as the sky sparkled with tracer fire. Antiaircraft guns opened up with a deafening roar, and suddenly buildings around our hotel were evaporating in orange fireballs. The city shook from one shock wave after another.

One evening there was a commotion in the hotel lobby as Ministry of Information officials arrived to escort any journalists reckless enough to venture out into the conflagration.

"Quick, Hala, get your driver," shouted one of them. "Hurry, there's no time to waste."

Steve ran downstairs with our driver, Rafed, who sped his little car into position in a convoy of media and minders. A balding man with a broad smile, Rafed had earned our affection with his ability to produce coffee or water for his passengers just when they needed it most. He was also brave enough to take us anywhere. But as we hurtled through the darkness with boiling infernos to either side and bombs plunging to earth ahead, my heart was pounding so hard that I thought it would explode. In my terror, I kept thinking that if I got hit by shrapnel, my boss would be mad at me for having left my flak jacket behind.

We were being taken to a hospital. They wanted us to see the casualties, just as I had predicted. But I could not have known how profoundly I would be affected by what we were about to witness.

Walking into the Shifaa hospital in al-Shuula, an impoverished Shi'ite suburb, was like entering a charnel house. Blood ran along corridors that resounded with the wailing of women and the sobbing of men. Doctors were shouting frantic instructions to nurses who could not hear them above the shrieks of the wounded they were trying to save.

One of them, Dr. Osama Fadel, detached himself from the mayhem to brief us. Twice that day, once in the morning and once in the afternoon, missiles had struck markets where families were buying fruit and vegetables, he said. In the second attack, just before nightfall, fifty-five people had been killed and forty-nine injured.

"Is this enough? Is this enough for America and Britain?" he asked, his voice cracking under the force of his anger. He saw Steve's European face beside mine and turned on me.

"So you are from the countries of these crimes?" he said, accusingly.

Dr. Fadel apologized when he saw a tear rolling down my face. Then he showed me one of the reasons for his rage: a gurney where a six-year-old girl was lying with her eyes half open as if she were falling asleep. Her orange sweatshirt was dotted with some of the 101 dalmatians from the book loved by children the world over. Blood oozed from her sleeve. She had been hit in the back of the head by a piece of shrapnel in her home after the morning explosion. Her name was Sara.

On the same gurney, partly hidden beneath Sara, was her seven-year-old brother, Karar. Part of his face had been torn off and there was a gaping wound in his chest. Little pieces of his toes were missing.

Neither child had survived the injuries. We were in the morgue.

I stepped back to speak to the doctor, who was now crying openly, so that Steve could take pictures. As I scribbled notes, I bowed my head, unable to control the flow of my own tears.

"Tony Blair should come and have a look at his day's deeds here in this poor neighborhood," said the doctor, who seemed to be in shock. "Too many civilians have been killed. Please tell him. I have a baby of my own and I cry today for all the babies I've seen."

Steve and I walked solemnly through corridors where mothers, aunts, friends, and neighbors of the wounded stood weeping in black chadors. We searched wards where fear in the eyes of children with bloody bandages around their heads was reflected in the despair of adults who had been injured with them. Eventually we found the mother of the girl and boy we had seen on the gurney.

Her name was Shafaa Awaid, and she was tending her two other children, Sujud, two, and Sajad, three. Both had been badly hurt. Both required surgery for wounds to their tummies.

"My tears are strangled in my eyes," said Shafaa, her pale face framed by a black veil. "They will not gush. They are burning my soul. They will stay inside me as an everlasting reminder of my anger with the Americans and British who did this to my babies."

She described what had happened. It was nine-thirty and she had just finished giving breakfast to her own children and her brother's in the house where they all lived together. One minute she could hear the children singing, laughing, and playing as she washed the breakfast dishes in the kitchen. The next minute came the explosion. She did not know what had caused it.

"All I could see was blood spattered against the walls," she said, as her daughter Sujud moaned beside us.

She rushed out of the kitchen, calling the children's names and peering desperately through the smoke. As soon as she saw Sara and Karar, she knew they were dead. Their younger brother and sister were lying in a pool of blood with a fourteen-year-old cousin, who had also been injured.

"Tell Bush and Blair that their end is near," she concluded with a coolness that chilled me. "Tell them that the scalding tears of Iraq's mothers will burn them and send them to hell."

We drove back in silence, save for my sobbing. I did not feel like a journalist. I was no longer responding in a professional way: my objectivity had deserted me. All I had wanted to do was to wrap in my arms the children we had seen and carry them to safety. Any one of them could have been my own. I did not understand why they had to suffer. I was helpless to protect them. I was hopeless in the knowledge that others would die in the days ahead.

The city was as black as my mood: the missiles had hit home and the electricity had finally been cut off. With no elevators at the hotel, we walked up seventeen floors and reached our room physically and emotionally drained. I wanted to curl up in bed, but Saturday was dawning. While Steve slept, I wrote. I did so in anger and sorrow, pouring my heart into every word to describe what I had seen. I found myself crying again—for the dead, of course, but also for the living.

The intensity with which Iman had pressed my hand into her belly as I felt for her baby's feet, the clamor of the maternity ward women straining to give birth, and now the sight of these beautiful, china-faced children in the morgue had stirred a mass of conflicting emotions that I could barely contain inside me. I wept for the children of all the despairing mothers I had met, but there was something deeper.

I longed to do more than merely report the frenzy of these families in a Western newspaper that supported the war: I wanted to relieve their misery somehow. Okay, so I was writing about the human cost of a bombardment that was being executed with a good deal less precision than the spin doctors in London and Washington were leading people to think. The so-called smart bombs had turned out not to be so smart after all, and that needed to be said. But I longed to do something practical, too: I wanted to help the victims of this war.

However crazy it would seem if I said it out loud, I wanted to save the children.

IT WAS ON THE FOLLOWING SATURDAY that I received the call that would set me on a new path.

"Go to the Kindi hospital and ask for the young boy, Ali," said my contact, a Lebanese photographer friend with one of the international agencies who knew of my craving for stories about children. He also knew we were near deadline, and having seen the boy himself, he wanted to ensure that Ali's story was further publicized. "Go now before someone finds out."

With deadlines for the Sunday paper only hours away, there was no time to negotiate with the Ministry of Information for permission. Rafed, our driver, went to his car. I followed a few minutes later, and finally, after a pause to avoid arousing suspicion from anyone watching the comings and goings in the lobby, we were joined by Steve. We slumped low in our seats so that none of the ministry's spies would see us as Rafed pulled out of the hotel parking lot and headed for the Kindi, a large general hospital in a southern suburb of the city. I soon found the right doctor, but I had trouble persuading him to let me see his patient.

"Where's your escort from the ministry?" he demanded to know. I told him nobody had been available.

"You haven't come without permission, have you?" he asked. I swore that we would never dream of doing such a thing.

Perhaps the doctor thought we would take up less of his valuable time if he relented; or perhaps he understood that publicity might somehow help the boy. Whatever the reason, he beckoned us to follow him along a scruffy, poorly lit corridor, explaining as we went that he could allow us only a few minutes.

"Ali shouldn't have visitors," the doctor cautioned. "He must not be caught seeing anyone without official permission. It could mean trouble for both of us."

He opened a door and directed us inside, saying he would wait in the corridor to make sure nobody discovered us. No sooner had I stepped into the room than I heard the voice of a young boy asking a question that I shall never forget.

"Have you come to give me my arms back?"

For a moment I stood stock-still, trying to make sense of the question, struggling to take in the sight before me. I was looking at the foot of a standard single bed, but there was something unusual about it. A rickety metal contraption had been erected above the middle section, with a tattered old blanket draped over part of it. I guessed that the struts were there to keep the blanket from touching the child beneath it. His skin must be burned, I thought. Poor boy. I moved forward to see his face, expecting it to be irrevocably scarred, but instead saw a handsome child with hazel eyes. It was then that I noticed his shoulders were wrapped in thick bandages. Below the shoulders were two heavily bandaged stumps where his arms should have been.

"Will I get my arms back?" he asked tearfully. "What about my hands?"

I felt myself choking, unable to utter a word. He was evidently in shock. He could not as yet comprehend his injury. How could I tell him I did not have the power to grant his wish to be whole again? I had to say something, I realized: I could not let him see my own shock. I calmly asked him his name, and he told me he was Ali Abbas Ismail, twelve years old. If Steve and I had had a son when we started trying for our baby, he would have been the same age.

I watched Steve move silently around the bed as he took his pictures. There was a tautness around his mouth that told me he was angry, although to anyone walking in on us he would have appeared the consummate cool professional. Instinctively, I knew what he was doing. He was focusing on Ali's handsome face. It was a face that newspaper readers would relate to when they looked at it. A face in which they would be able to see their own children. Even a cursory glance would bring home the scale of Ali's injury, suffering, and loss. Steve's skill would see to that.

"What happened?" I said.

The brief sentences that followed were punctuated by sobs. Ali had been asleep a few nights before when a missile had crashed into his house. He had woken up in the middle of a fierce fire, soaked in his own blood.

"I couldn't find my arms," he said. His father and mother had both been killed. His mother had been expecting a baby in the summer. His brother had also died in the explosion. So had his uncle, aunt, and their four children; and three other relatives' homes on the same row as Ali's family were also destroyed.

"What will happen to my arms?" he asked. "A missile cut them off, you know. Will I get my arms back, please?"

Steve was talking to him gently as he took his photographs, telling him he was going to be okay. Ali seemed to take comfort from this, even though he could not understand what my husband was saying.

The doctor came in to say our time was up.

"Don't worry, Ali. I'll be back," I reassured him in Arabic. "We'll make sure you're okay."

WE DROVE BACK TO THE HOTEL as fast as possible, but it was a long way and deadlines were looming. The main pieces for the next day's paper had already been edited, and I knew it would be a struggle to get Ali's story in at such a late stage. We had been breaking up our longest features with little boxes of quotations from a variety of people caught up in the war to show its impact on them. I thought the least we could do was to get Ali's story into a quote box. I sent the boss an urgent e-mail to that effect and attached what little Ali had said. A reply came back right away.

"Christ, pls file quotes immediately as we're very close to deadline," Sean wrote. "Hala, I want to get this in but to make it work I need more quotes. . . . Do you have any?"

I sent what I could, but I had not had enough time with Ali to do a full story, and besides, my editors were preoccupied with updating Swain's accounts of the first American soldiers entering Baghdad.

THE AMERICANS WERE COMING. They had stormed the airport just outside Baghdad, and now they were mounting quick, darting raids in and out of the city to test the level of resistance. We could even hear some of the fighting from the balcony of our hotel in the center of town. There was only one man left in Baghdad who refused to accept that things were going badly for the regime, and that was its information minister. He wore a military uniform and beret, and his name was Mohammed Saeed al-Sahhaf.

The tyrant and his brother, a general known as Chemical Ali because he had used chemical weapons to put down an uprising some years earlier, were about to be deposed, yet the information minister was having none of it. He insisted that the regime was winning the war. His briefings for the media were becoming hysterical. We nicknamed him Comical Ali.

"There are no American infidels in Baghdad," he said as U.S.

Marines occupied the airport. The "bloodsucking bastards" and "wild donkeys," as he called the coalition forces, were "nowhere near the airport." "They are lost in the desert. . . . They cannot read a compass. . . . They are retarded."

When film of Marines on the airport runway was broadcast on satellite channels, there was only one way for Comical Ali to save face.

"We have retaken the airport," he announced. "There are no Americans there. I will take you and show you in one hour. . . . We kicked them out. We pulverized them, defeated them, surrounded them. . . ."

Bush found the minister so entertaining that he broke up meetings to watch the latest outbursts. Someone in Alaska set up a website, WeLoveTheIraqiInformationMinister.com, which attracted up to four thousand hits per second and sold T-shirts and mugs emblazoned with the funniest quotes. The greater the defeats for the regime's army, the more triumphal the minister's statements became. To listen to him, anyone would have thought the U.S. Army was facing its most ignominious rout.

"These rascals are now committing suicide on the gates of Baghdad. I would encourage them to increase their rate of committing suicide," he declared. "God is grilling their bellies in hell. I think we will finish them soon."

Comical Ali's performances gave Swain, Steve, and me a bit of light relief at a critical time when civilian casualties were mounting and we were growing apprehensive about our own prospects. What would happen when the fighting reached us? we wondered. Would the regime's army grab Western journalists? And if they did, would it deter the Americans for one second from bringing their onslaught to a bloody climax in the heart of the city? We doubted it. As the American forces advanced, we hunkered down in our hotel.

The regime was disintegrating, and as long as its remnants left us alone, we believed we would be safe in our own rooms.

How wrong we were. On the day we first saw hostilities in the distance from our hotel, I was getting worried about the way Steve was filming and photographing everything from our balcony. He could just pick out a column of tanks approaching from the far side of the river we overlooked. There was fighting around the tanks, and although it was a long way off, helicopters were already strafing buildings nearby, perhaps to take out any snipers preparing to fire on the column as it trundled toward us.

Steve had just stepped into our room to change the film on his video camera when a huge explosion beneath us shook the entire building. It was so loud, so powerful, and so close that I fell off my chair, screaming.

"Flak jackets," Steve cried, picking himself up off the floor and half running, half crouching to the corner where we kept the equipment that had been supplied for moments such as this.

My legs were so wobbly that it was all I could do to crawl over to him, grabbing my boots as I went. But my hands were shaking violently. Helpless as a child, I could not even tie my laces. Steve sorted out my boots and the straps on my flak jacket, then dashed back to the balcony to unhook the dish we used for Internet access while I shut down the laptop.

Our training told us to evacuate any building as soon as it was hit in case of further attacks. We opened our door to the sound of pandemonium as other journalists rushed from their rooms and bumped along the darkened corridor with their flashlights. We barged down the stairs from the seventeenth story, buffeted by panic-stricken people who were joining the stampede on every new floor we reached.

Outside, a group of men were shrieking incomprehensibly as they carried a young woman in a bloodied bedsheet toward their car. The terror rose in me again. I recognized this woman. Not only did she have the balcony room on the fifteenth floor—just two below ours—but we had worked together at Reuters in Beirut. It was Samia, who had been at my side when Steve had first walked into my office. Slender, stylish Samia, who had always looked like a million dollars with her insistence on covering the war in matching outfits and shoes. She and I had competed for stories and comforted each other during the years of conflict that had torn our beloved hometown apart. But now that she had been wounded in a strange foreign place where she had few friends, she was beyond my help. It was obvious from the bloodstains that she had been hit in the head by shrapnel. Her rescuers were saying that two cameramen with her had died instantly.

The sight of television cameras around us reminded me that I needed to act fast. Whatever had caused the explosion, news of it would be reaching my office and my family within minutes. I set up our dish, hooked it up to the laptop, and went straight to e-mail. There were already two messages from Sean asking me to call him immediately.

"It's me," I told him a few seconds later. "We're all well. Steve, Jon, and I are all downstairs. We are sitting outside, a bit shaky but safe."

"Thank God for that," he said.

"My friend Samia has taken a hit, Sean, I have to go look for her." First, though, I had to phone my mother. I had hoped to reach her before she panicked, but it was too late. She had seen the footage of Samia, whom she knew well from our days together. She was reciting verses from the Koran and praying that I was unhurt. She was remembering the terror she had felt one night when my sister, Rana, had been hit by a sniper's bullet that sliced through her neck as she drove through Beirut.

"We can't go through this anymore," Mama said when I finally got through. "This could have been you. It is too much. Enough, *habibi*. Please leave."

"We'll be fine, *inshallah*"—God willing—I told her, trying to sound braver than I felt. "The end of the war is near. We couldn't leave now even if we wanted to. It's more dangerous to drive out now. We're safer if we stay put." I did my best not to choke up as I told her how much I loved her and missed her.

"Just keep on praying, Mama."

WE THOUGHT THE REGIME must have turned against us, fired on us, tried to kill us on its own dying day. In fact, an American M1A1 Abrams tank striking out for the center of Baghdad had fired the round that had smashed into the hotel fifteen feet from where I had been sitting. Samia was seriously injured but would survive.

The mood in the blasted building remained somber as joyful American soldiers rolled into the center of the city, smiling incredulously at the speed of their conquest and the alacrity with which the dictator's opponents tore down his statue and battered it with their shoes, a classic insult in the Muslim world.

It was obvious in the first few days after the American victory that the collapse of the ousted regime's security forces had not brought peace. For one thing, looters were on the rampage. For another, soldiers from an army that no longer officially existed were banding together to attack communities that had opposed the tyrant. This in turn triggered the formation of militias to fend them off. It was the start of what would become a long, bitter, and almost unimaginably bloody sectarian conflict.

The effects of all this on Ali became clear when Steve and I went to the Kindi hospital to check up on him. By now, one of Steve's pictures of the boy had made the front page of the *Daily Mirror*. It had prompted a huge outpouring of sympathy. There was talk of fund-raising with the aim of flying him to London and fitting him with far more sophisticated prosthetic arms than he would ever receive in his own country. But as we arrived at the hospital, the first thing I noticed was that the military guards were missing from their usual posts. Then I saw that at the entrance to the emergency unit, ambulances were being turned away.

I went in search of the doctor who had briefed us before and found that he was one of the few medical staff remaining.

"People are looting," he said as soon as he saw us. "Please go back your hotel—immediately!"

The doctor had already decided that a hospital where the heartless were helping themselves to everything from prescription medicines to patients' beds was no place for a child. Ali had been moved to another hospital, the Shawader, in an area where a ransacking was thought to be less likely. He said he had taken his family out of the hospital and left them at the home of some of his friends. Other patients had been evacuated and new casualties were being turned away. The majority of the hospital's staff had not shown up that day, and those who were at the hospital and had been there throughout the duration of the war, nurses and doctors alike, had finally abandoned it out of fear.

"I cannot even protect my patients here. Please go away," he said. "The only reason I remain behind is because of the medical vow I took and which I cannot break," he said, adding that even the director of the hospital had walked out that morning without telling him of his intentions.

He spoke as he turned away ambulances with casualties, explaining to the desperate people and drivers that he could not treat them for lack of staff, giving them directions to other hospitals in the area that he said would be of better service to them.

So we drove to the Shawader hospital, where we found a battle was raging between the tyrant's men and a local militia. Inside, we became trapped. For half an hour, I crouched against a wall, covering my head with my arms, while Saddam's special forces pumped machine-gun bullets through the windows for reasons I could not begin to comprehend.

Ali was distraught when we reached him. He had been made to leave his things behind at the other hospital when he was moved out in a rush. There were no toys or sweets for him here, not even a pillowcase. Beneath the plastic sheet on which he lay all day, the thinnest of mattresses provided scant protection from the bedsprings pressing against his back. Not only was he terrified of the shooting, but he was quivering with pain.

"When will you take me away from here?" Ali said, the moment I walked into his room. "I can't bear this anymore." He jumped at each new crack of gunfire. I asked him whether he was feeling any better.

"My arms hurt," he said. "A missile cut them off, you know. I don't have a house anymore. What will I do? Where will I go?"

An aunt sat at his bedside. Since he could not flick flies away from his wounds, she did this for him as she tried to soothe him with prayers. She explained that his parents had gone to heaven, but Ali had heard this before. He fixed his hazel eyes on me and I saw that there was a very determined look in them. I had promised to help, he recalled.

"When will you take me? Can you take me? Will you help me?" The questions came in a rush.

I explained that many people far away in England were concerned about him and some wanted him to be treated there.

"Really?" he said, his eyes widening. "Where's the new hospital? When will you move me? Is it near you? Where do you live?"

In the corridor, a nurse explained gently that with burns covering sixty percent of his body, he would succumb to septicemia unless he could be moved to a hospital with advanced intensive care.

I left Ali with chocolate, music tapes, and, it seemed, a little more hope than he had woken up with that morning, whatever the doctors' doubts about his prospects for recovery. But had I raised his hopes too high? Somehow, he had gained the impression that I was responsible for his welfare. In the absence of his own mother, he seemed to be looking to me to reassure him, to relieve his suffering, and to organize his rehabilitation far from Baghdad. I had to stop myself from telling him that I was no one's mother; that I had no experience as a mother; that he should not put his faith in me.

I had promised to help him, yet I could not even get my own paper to print an article publicizing his needs. As far as the office was concerned, we had covered Ali's story the previous week, albeit in a small way, and some of the daily newspapers had followed it up. That made Ali old news.

Sean was sympathetic. He liked the idea of launching an appeal for the injured children. But he wanted fresh cases.

"Let's find another Ali," he said.

Five

SAVING ZAHRA

The relentless years of repression, surveillance, and deprivation ended faster than anyone had expected. The citizens of Baghdad were suddenly informed that they had been liberated, and they wasted no time in exercising their newfound freedom to help themselves to anything they fancied, safe in the knowledge that there was no one left to report, arrest, or punish them.

Their own police force had vanished overnight. The American soldiers had no orders to maintain law and order, therefore they did not do so. Even when they saw the National Museum of Iraq being robbed of priceless artifacts that constituted thousands of years of heritage, they sat quietly in their armored vehicles rather than intervene.

On some streets in the city center, I saw emancipated people dancing. Around them, other emancipated people were emerging from official buildings with all manner of loot and not even looking furtive about it. On the contrary, they were unashamedly jubilant.

The most extraordinary items were catching the eye of the casual looter. I watched a woman dressed from head to toe in a black abaya coming out of one ministry building, weighed down with boxes of sneakers. Out of the same building came another woman with a litter bin and a man with a whole window. Stranger still was the sight of a small car stuttering down the street at a snail's pace, dragging a generator that looked as if it might have come from one of the state-owned factories and must have weighed a ton. The owner smiled delightedly as he passed me. He did not care that the generator was almost certainly too big for his house, nor that he probably would not be able to afford the fuel to run it. He had got it and he was proud of it. That was all that mattered.

A sanitation worker interrupted his pillaging of another ministry to tell me he had worked from dawn to dusk for ten years under the old regime to scrape together enough money for a one-bedroom house. He and his wife shared the bedroom with four children.

"This is not stealing," he said. "This is just getting what we're owed."

The rampage was unexpectedly orderly at first. The looters made their choices and staked their claims by sitting on an object if it was big, like a sofa, or simply by taking it away if it was small, like a cushion. I witnessed no arguing, let alone a scuffle. Women went for tables, chairs, and lamp shades to brighten the home. Men concentrated on computers and cars. It was finders keepers, and that was that.

The buildings that had held the greatest fear for Baghdadis were the most greedily stripped. I gasped when I realized what they were doing to the headquarters of the Iraqi National Olympic Committee, where the dictator's son Uday was said to have had his enemies tortured. Men, women, and children were swarming out of the compound with everything from ropes to running gear.

The fancy private homes of ousted government officials were also joyously plundered. Outside the mansion of Tariq Aziz, the deputy prime minister who had been the regime's international envoy, I saw a large freezer awaiting collection and peeped inside. It was lined with neatly packed bags of hand-cut vegetables. Baby carrots and French beans were arranged alongside chopped cauliflower and peeled garlic. Had the lady of the house slaved over these? I wondered. No, it was far more likely that she had had servants to do her work. How they must have envied her well-fed family in a place where millions went hungry.

Aziz had been meticulously prepared when I interviewed him in his office before the war. Now, in his house, I found a ledger in which his family's possessions had been scrupulously listed, right down to the last teaspoon and mop. The figurehead of a regime renowned for documenting every detail of its activities had evidently imposed the same discipline on his household. I sat on the floor, reading the paperwork as young men hauled their burdens around me. Beds and dressing tables, carpets and rugs, vases and ornaments, were disappearing fast. Even the light fittings were being removed.

With typical Iraqi entrepreneurship, some of the looters were quick to hawk their wares. "These carpets come from the house," said one as I strolled outside. "They're very good Persian rugs. I'll make you a good deal and give you a good price." He was asking $500 apiece, equivalent to a year's wages for some workers. Yet although he wanted to negotiate in U.S. dollars, he made it clear that he would also take familiar Iraqi dinars from anyone who was interested. Steve and I were not.

Another hawker brandished an item we did find intriguing. Having identified Steve as a Western photographer, he tried to sell us Aziz's family photograph album. We asked him to show us the pictures. There were dozens of them, portraying the deputy prime minister as a young man, on his wedding day, with his children and grandchildren, and with Saddam.

Steve returned them with a polite "No, thank you," but I could not bear the thought that these cherished family photos, which were of little value to anyone except those who appeared in them, might be discarded and destroyed. I thought of how I thumbed through my own family albums on rainy days in London to lighten my mood with thoughts of loved ones in sunny places. I had found that the older I grew, the more importance I attached to the moments captured by my parents as they chronicled my life from childhood to adulthood.

I told the thief that his pictures were not worth any money, but that if he would let us have some for free, we would be happy to use them for an article about Aziz's role in a regime that had oppressed people like him for years. He agreed and let us take our pick, even though we had no intention of publishing them. It would be two years before we located Aziz's family in exile and returned the pictures to their rightful owners.

In the home of the official who had lived next door to the deputy prime minister, I flipped through another pile of papers in the hope of uncovering some scandalous insight into the regime's relationships with the West. All I found was a notebook belonging to a student of biology and chemistry. He was the son of the homeowner and he was in love. On some pages, he had drawn hearts. On others, he had written poems to his sweetheart. That she returned his affections was clear from a dried red rose pasted in the middle of his lecture notes.

I wondered what would happen to the couple now that the man of the house had been driven from power. Would he have taken his family with him on the run? Had his romantically inclined son been forced to flee the country and separate from his girlfriend forever? In a theater of war with thousands on the move, many such dramas would be unfolding.

IT WAS TWO DAYS LATER that I received my instructions from the office to search Baghdad's pediatric wards for the little girl whose story would launch our Iraq appeal. The task filled me with revulsion.

As a journalist, I understood that the most heartrending orphan's story would raise the largest amount of money. The more harrowing her loss, the greater the sympathy. But as a woman longing for her own baby, I knew that the sight of distraught children with no mothers to wipe their tears would test me to the limits of emotional endurance.

It was not only the psychological ordeal ahead that troubled me. I knew that the injured child I chose would receive special treatment, while the innocents I rejected would be left to their fate in hospitals that clearly could not cope. Who would have relished that responsibility? Having taken it upon myself to "save the children," I was reduced to rescuing just one.

I had to remind myself that whatever my personal feelings, I had a job to do. And besides, it was better to save one child than none. I took a deep drag on my cigarette and tried to picture her. I would hold this image at the forefront of my mind as I went about my business. I would cling to the idea that I could help this child survive, and try not to think too hard about the others until I had got through the day.

In the car, I briefed Rafed just as I had been briefed by the office.

"We need a child who's a victim of war," I told him. "Not just any victim. This one has to be special." Dear God, I was beginning to sound like my boss. "She has to be a little girl, not a boy, and not a baby—preferably a toddler. Her injuries must be grave, her story must be heartbreaking, and she must have lost her parents like Ali."

Rafed looked at me as if I had gone mad.

"But Madam Hala, there are many injured from the bombings," he said reasonably.

"Yes, Rafed, and the best way to help them is to start a fund that will benefit as many as possible. To do that, we must focus on one child who will capture people's imagination. The sadder the case, the more money we'll get and the more children we'll help." As I said it, I could not stop myself from thinking of the many we would not help at all.

"As you wish, Madam Hala."

My driver was still resisting me and I could not afford a battle of wills. "Rafed," I said, flashing him the most dazzling smile I could muster as I launched a little charm offensive. "Help me find a child. Think of your own children, Rafed. This little girl we're looking for could have been yours. We don't have much time. Let's find her."

With that, he surrendered.

As we wove our way through the city, taking care to avoid routes blocked by bomb debris, Steve and I saw how sharply the mood had changed in forty-eight hours as Baghdadis began to fight one another for the dwindling supply of loot. Shops burned. Streets smoldered. The atmosphere had become so heated that at the Kindi hospital, where Ali's arms had been amputated, we found volunteers in camouflage trousers and plastic slippers pointing AK-47s at anyone who approached. I was bemused to see that they were wearing blue medical gowns over their T-shirts, presumably to denote their semiofficial status as guardians of the doctors inside.

The medical staff were moving patients out to hospitals in safer districts and turning away ambulances bringing fresh casualties from even more dangerous ones. We picked our way through the wheelchairs and the walking wounded in the hope of finding a doctor who could tell us what was going on, but everyone looked too busy to talk to us. The only comment I got that seemed of any importance was that there were more dead patients than live ones at the Kindi.

Eventually, an electrician with nothing better to do insisted on showing us to the morgue. I was not at all sure I wanted to see it and as soon as we entered I longed to be somewhere else. There were so many bodies that they had been piled on top of one another. Most were those of civilians. I saw men who looked too old to have run away from the onslaught; a woman whose charred fist was raised as if she had died fighting; and a child of about three, covered by a blanket except for some chubby fingers that stuck out. I looked away and felt the anger rising in me.

Why had this been allowed to happen? I wanted to know. I found myself questioning God's wisdom even though I knew it was blasphemous to do so. Why give a child life, only to end it so soon in this way? It made no sense.

I barely managed to glance at a dozen men, women, and children in a huge refrigerator whose double doors our guide swung open.

"In life they suffered and now in death they cannot rest," the electrician said, lamenting the fact that nobody had claimed them.

No less harrowing were our encounters with the injured at our next stop, the Saddam Children's Hospital. Already light-headed after the morgue, I felt a heaviness in my feet as Steve marched through the entrance ahead of me, camera at the ready. Ahead of us were scores of young patients on soiled gurneys. Some shrieked at the sight of their wounds, others begged for pills to relieve the pain. They had been wheeled into the foyer because this was the only part of the hospital with power. A doctor glanced down at a floor smeared with stale blood and explained that there was not enough water to clean it. In fact, he said, he could not even wash his hands as he moved from one patient to the next.

One little boy who had just been admitted was screaming louder than all the others, so I went over to see what the matter was. Two doctors were swabbing a leg that had been mangled by a missile slamming into his family's pickup truck. His name was Seif Karim. He was a scrawny seven-year-old with the frailty of a man ten times his age. I spoke to him softly and stroked his head as he described what had happened.

He swung his arm to show how a plane had swooped down. There had been a big boom, he said. "My baba died, my brother died, and I was hurt."

The bones in his lower leg were fractured, the muscle wasted, and the wound infected, a doctor explained. He needed surgery, skin grafts, special care. He stood little chance of receiving them.

The father of another boy approached. He begged us to help his son, who had been injured when a bomb landed in their back garden. Shrapnel had severed his spinal cord. The boy was paralyzed at fifteen.

"I have money," the father told me. "Please help. Please arrange for his evacuation."

I was shaking as I noted the details in my notebook. Much as I would have liked to help, I was just a journalist and what use was that? I primly expressed my regret and explained that there was nothing I could do.

"Your country is responsible," he retorted angrily. "You must do something." I turned away, unable to face his fury.

My country? Yes, I thought as I darted outside for some fresh air, I had always been an Arab, but Britain was my country now. I felt doubly ashamed for belonging to a country that had contributed to this chaos and for being unable to help my fellow Arabs.

In the hospital's dusty, unkempt grounds, more than one hundred children, women, and men had been tipped into shallow graves for want of any family to give them a proper burial. Each mound of sunbaked earth was marked by a bottle into which a handwritten note had been stuffed with a description of the victim for anyone who might come looking for a clue to the fate of a loved one.

One of the notes read: "Infant, two to three years old, wearing a T-shirt with blue and red squares and white cotton trousers." The child had been dead on arrival at the hospital ten days earlier.

The note did not say if it had been a boy or a girl, but from the clothing I guessed this must have been some unfortunate couple's cherished daughter. I thought how much worse it must be to have a child and lose her than to be denied a baby in the first place. For a while, I sat by her grave and said the Fatiha, the opening verse of the Koran, which should always be read for the soul of someone who has died. As I prayed, I wondered how she had perished, why her parents had not come for her, and whether they had been killed, too. I stared at Steve as he photographed the makeshift graveyard.

"I know what you're thinking, Hala. I'm wondering the same things," he said. By now, I was physically exhausted and emotionally drained.

"Why don't we call it a day?" said Steve, looking at me with concern. I was determined to press on.

"There are lots of Alis now," I said, "but we still need to find ours."

I ASKED TO BE TAKEN to the Shawader hospital, where I had last seen Ali, thinking the little girl I was seeking might be located here. I could not visit Ali that day, but opposite his ward, which was grandly styled as a burn unit even though it had no specialist capable of containing septicemia, was a bed containing three small children. A boy, Ahmad Farhan, lay snuggled up to his injured sisters, Wassel and Amira.

Ahmad, Wassel, and Amira came from a family with eleven children altogether. Of these, ten had been injured when an American missile demolished their home. The eleventh and youngest, a three-month-old baby named Zeina, had disappeared.

Their mother, Tashara, was torn between soothing Ahmad, whose foot had been amputated, and searching for Zeina. Perhaps she knew deep down that her baby was dead and buried in the rubble of the house. Perhaps that was why she was at the hospital with her other children. But for now, she preferred to believe that Zeina had been rescued and was in the care of a kindly neighbor who had decided to look after her until her brothers and sisters were better.

"She's only missing," Tashara stressed to me when I sat beside her.

I did not say that her brother had already told me he had knocked on every door in the area and none of the neighbors knew anything about the baby.

Tashara started to cry. Not only had Ahmad lost his left foot, but his right leg was severely broken and blood was seeping through the bandages wrapped around his thigh. "All the other children have got shrapnel in the head or the abdomen," she said. "I've lost my home and I've got nowhere to go."

I did not know how to console her.

Nor was I of any comfort to Marwa Falaj, an eleven-year-old girl whose leg had been crushed when another missile had dropped on her house. She was very pretty, with large eyes, long brown hair, and smooth skin, but in the three days she had been lying in the hospital, gangrene had begun to set in one of her legs. The doctors had cut it off above the knee, and she had lost two pints of blood. I looked at the sweet face of this poor girl, who was just a few years younger than Lara but not yet a teenager, and my mind emptied of words. Unable to think of anything better to say, I asked: "How do you feel?"

Marwa looked down at her stump, covered her eyes with both hands, and burst into tears. I realized that this was not just an innocent child coming to terms with the loss of a limb. She had also lost any prospect of a happy marriage one day. In a poorly educated community in Baghdad, there would be no suitors, no falling in love, no netting a nice young husband. If she married at all, it would be either to a much older man looking for a younger second or third wife, or to a cousin who would have to be talked into it as a favor to the family. More likely, she was destined to become an unwanted spinster. Marwa was grieving not only for her leg but for her future.

As I gently smoothed her hair, my sadness turned to anger at those who had ruined this young life and so many others. I did not care about the liberation of a people from its monstrous regime. My only thought was that Marwa would be lonely and confined for the rest of her unhappy days. Rafed asked whether I wanted to carry on.

"Yes," I said curtly.

He tried to cheer me up by suggesting that the next hospital, the Kirkh, would be the last one that day.

A young doctor greeted us there with tea and cigarettes. He had been working at the hospital for more than ten years, he told me, but the last few weeks had changed him.

"I've seen injuries I've never come across in my life," he said, faltering as he spoke. "Women and men searching for their children and their parents . . . not knowing who's alive and who's dead after their homes have been destroyed . . ."

And then he was sobbing unashamedly. "It's difficult for me to watch a child die in front of my eyes," he went on. "I know I'm a doctor and I should be used to this by now, but I've left the operating room and cried so many times these past few weeks that you wouldn't believe it."

It was after this that he told me about Zahra.

YOU MAY THINK THAT if I had not been overwrought at the end of my long day with Seif, Ahmad, Wassel, Amira, and Marwa, if I had not seen the charred bodies of the children in the morgue and prayed by the glass-bottle grave of the little girl in the white cotton trousers, if I had not wept with the young doctor whose heart had been broken by the deaths of his young patients, my reaction to seeing Zahra for the first time would have been less overwhelming. I am not so sure.

When I look now at the pictures Steve took as I stood stunned into silence at Zahra's bedside, I can almost make sense of what I felt. I see why I was powerless to quell yet more tears, why I was seized with a longing to save her, why I vowed that nothing would stop me.

The photographs show Zahra lying on her side on a thin mattress with her head resting on a rough brown blanket for a pillow. Much of her hair has been burned away and cream has been smeared over the scorch marks on her scalp. The ointment applied to her cheeks and ears is too little to cover the red-raw sores beneath. Her face is so badly seared that the bottom of her nose seems to have melted. She is sedated, but the corners of her mouth are turned down as if she has cried herself to sleep.

Zahra's right hand and left leg are swathed in thick bandages, and although her shoulders are bare, much of her body is shrouded in gauze to protect the parts of her skin that are less severely burned. She has wrapped her arms around herself, as if to provide the comfort her mother cannot. Beneath the chipped metal frame that supports her blanket, she has drawn her knees up in front of her like a baby in the womb.

The pictures instantly recall her words.

"Cover me up, Mama . . . Baba, where are you? I'm cold."

It was because there was no mother to weep at her bedside, no father to take charge, that Zahra touched me more deeply than the other children I had encountered. All day long, I had tried to contain my emotions: if I had cried, I could not have completed my assignment. But as the strain had built up, my defenses had come down. The howls of the children and the pleas of their parents reverberated through me until I could hardly bear them. Now I was confronted by a burned little girl who had been thrown to safety from a blazing car by a mother she would never hold again. The sight of Zahra and the sound of her voice provoked an overpowering urge in me to take care of her. The maternal instinct I had worked so hard to suppress was surging back, and I had no defense left against it.

Steve usually stays calm when I am going crazy, but in a small way his reaction that day reflected my own. I noticed that his eyes swelled with tears until his vision was so blurred that he had to switch his camera from manual to auto focus.

It was not the first time that day that we had been struck by the contrast between the obscenity of an injury and the innocence of a child whose beauty was still plain to see. Yet no matter how much I wanted to protect Zahra, the shuddering of her limbs suggested that her hold on life was precarious. Even though she was surrounded by people trying to help her live, she appeared remote from us. She had entered a semiconscious world where she would have to summon what strength she could for her solitary struggle.

When Steve placed a hand on my shoulder, he felt me trembling as I tried to make sense of this. My mother would have called it profane, but I was questioning Allah's wisdom once more and I craved answers. How could He allow a tiny girl to suffer so greatly? Why did He bless some couples with children, only to snatch them back? What lessons were we supposed to learn from all this?

"Do not question Allah's will," my mother always said. But that afternoon I thought, "How can I not, Mama? How can I not?"

Zahra's grandmother, towering over her, muttered verses of the Koran, recited prayers and Allah's words of consolation. For once, I took no comfort from them. But when the old woman introduced herself as Um Ali and informed me that she was a Shi'ite, I revealed my sect, as I do when I believe people will relate better to one of their own.

"May your day be blessed with Allah's goodness, my daughter," she said.

I supposed that she believed I was heaven-sent. She had heard me tell Zahra's doctor that my newspaper was looking for a child whose picture and story would bring in money to help the victims of the war, and she knew that her granddaughter needed a miracle.

"May Allah grant you protection," she said. "May He protect the souls of your parents. May He grant you the ability to make a pilgrimage in your lifetime. Please don't let her die. You mustn't let her die. Please make her better for me."

I thought of the love my mother had for Lara as her grandchild and of how she had explained that she doted on her more than she ever had on Rana and me. "There is nothing more precious to a parent than one's own child—except the child of their child," she would say.

That was why I told Grandmother I would make sure Zahra received the treatment she needed, whatever it cost. That was why I made the big promise: "Your granddaughter will live." Yet I did so without a moment's thought about how I would fulfill my pledge.

Outside, the Americans were preparing to impose the nightly curfew.

"Steve," I said quietly, "Zahra's our case. Let's go back to the hotel now before it gets too late."

I bade Grandmother farewell, promised to return the following day, and took one last look at the sleeping child.

"Hang in there, baby. Hang in there," I muttered.

I GOT STRAIGHT ON THE PHONE to my foreign editor as soon as we reached our room. My resolve was strong, my purpose clear, but Sean would never have guessed it from my hysteria. I started by speaking so fast that he could not understand what I was saying. Then I cried for a bit and begged him to help. Finally, I demanded that he do so—all before he had the slightest inkling of what I was talking about.

"We're a large newspaper, we have money," I raved. "I beg you, we must help this little girl even if we have to pay for her evacuation."

It was just as well that I had a special rapport with the boss. He let me blow off steam, then cooled me down with a few calm words and told me to start at the beginning.

"It's about a little girl, Sean. We must help her."

When he had heard Zahra's story, he said exactly what I needed to hear. The paper would do everything it could to help Zahra and as many children like her as possible. It had already linked up with Merlin, a medical charity based in London. Merlin's team of doctors would be arriving in Baghdad the next day.

"Take them to see Zahra," Sean said. "Get their view on what needs to be done."

There was more. The paper was devoting its fund-raising appeal to Merlin, Sean explained. Zahra's story could launch it that weekend. As the face of the campaign, Zahra would be the first of many beneficiaries.

"Let's get her assessed and write a really emotive piece," Sean said.

I dropped into bed, exhausted but exhilarated. I had found a child who needed me and a way of supporting her, even if I could not help all the others. Zahra was on the critical list, but I was arranging for her to receive the gift of life. Her family's sorrow knew no bounds, but I would make that grandmother smile again.

"This was meant to be," I thought as my head hit the pillow. "Tomorrow, I will save Zahra."

IN THE MORNING, I returned to the hospital with a spring in my step and a bag of sweets in my hand. But when I saw Zahra, I realized how stupid I had been. She looked even more fragile than she had the day before. The shaking had worsened in her limbs and she was racked with pain. The last thing she needed was the chocolate I had brought.

In the eyes of Zahra's grandmother, however, I could do no wrong. She greeted me like a long-lost daughter. Here was a woman who had been robbed of her son, daughter-in-law, and five grandchildren all in one day, and who had not had time to mourn them because she had been left with Zahra and the baby, Hawra. Yet when I walked into the ward, her eyes sparkled with the hope I had given her when I made my big promise the previous evening.

With great excitement, I told her about the medical team arriving that day, about how we were going to help Zahra and make her better.

"You swear it's true?" Grandmother asked me.

"Yes, it's true, Hajieh," I said, using the term of respect for one who has made the hajj, or pilgrimage to Mecca.

Zahra's moans pulled us both back to reality.

"Mama!" she cried before drifting back to sleep. I sat and watched her as any good mama would. I felt like taking her in my arms and holding her delicate body against mine while I kissed her head and nuzzled her hair. I wanted to make her warm and stop her shivering. I wanted to whisper in her ear that there was a life ahead of her and that it would be good. I willed her to not let go, but to seize that chance. I promised her silently that I would do my best to make sure she and Hawra had whatever they needed to thrive. I would never replace their mother, but in some way I had yet to clarify in my own mind, I would try to make up for their loss and ease their pain.

"Live on, little one," I murmured. "Hang on." She opened her eyes for a few seconds and cried out when she saw me. At least her grandmother knew how to soothe her back to sleep. Then she told me about her dead son and all the grandchildren she had hoped to enjoy for the rest of her life. She could not understand how they had been killed in the name of "liberation," she said. What would she tell Zahra when she was older? How could she, a poor Shi'ite woman worn out by years of toil, bring up not one little girl, but two? What would the future hold for them now?

I had no answers for her there and then. I was scribbling down everything she said, reminding myself that I was working here, that I had to write an article that would raise many thousands of pounds. But the bond between Grandmother and me was becoming personal, not professional. She was looking to a fellow Arab, a fellow Muslim, and a fellow Shi'ite for something more than the money to save her granddaughter. I could not yet define what it was, but a thought that excited and frightened me was beginning to form in my mind.

Six

TWO LITTLE GIRLS

I sat on the floor next to Zahra's bed, willing her to live and wondering if I might be destined to play some part in her future. There was so much to consider and so little time to come to a conclusion. Merlin's doctors would be arriving in a few hours, and if I had my way, they would get her out of there fast. I felt compelled to make decisions about Zahra while she was still with us in Baghdad, because I knew it would be harder to think clearly about her once she had gone. That left me a day—two at the most—to resolve whether or not to take one of the most important steps of my life. I gazed intently at her shivering form, looking for inspiration.

Grandmother excused herself, saying she had to tend to Hawra, Zahra's baby sister. I was curious to know more about Hawra. She was the only member of her family to have emerged unscathed from their obliterated car, and she had not needed to spend a single day in the hospital. By her family's account she smiled when she woke, sucked contentedly on her bottle, and slept soundly for her age, oblivious to the shadow that had fallen over her life. So when

Grandmother said she was expecting a stream of visitors to pay their condolences, I seized my chance to see this miraculous child for myself.

"I'll drop by later," I said, embracing Grandmother. Steve saw that I needed some quiet time and went outside to smoke some cigarettes with the driver.

Resting my back against the wall of the ward, I shut my eyes and searched my brain for a sensible idea about what to do next. When I could not find one, I tried to understand the feelings I was having about Zahra as she whimpered in her sleep at my side. My desire to pick her up, hold her gently to me, and softly kiss her made no sense, but I had to face the fact that I wanted to mother this child. I had not sought her out for that purpose, but now that I had discovered her, I wanted to look after her, make her better, enfold her in my love.

I could not think of a logical way to explain this to Steve. I had come to regard myself as tough enough to compete on hard news stories in the most demanding places, and I assumed that was how Steve saw me, too. But now that I was forty-three, I was beginning to wonder about the cost to my life of this relentless drive to report on so many deaths from Beirut to Baghdad.

My reverie was interrupted by a nurse checking Zahra's bandages. I noticed her looking at me, but she barely spoke: she must have seen that I was too deep in thought to exchange pleasantries.

My family had always thought journalism an odd departure from my first career in accountancy. I had been working for Price Waterhouse when I first walked into a journalists' office in Beirut to audit their expenses. It was immediately obvious to me that their jobs at Associated Press, the international news agency, were more exciting than mine. They were constantly rushing in and out to bring the latest developments in the war to the world's attention. I merely sat in a back room poring over invoices.

If I spoke to them, it was in clipped tones about trivial details. They spoke to me with passion about the major events they witnessed and the consequences they believed would follow. So when the bureau chief, Terry Anderson, called me into his office one day and asked me to monitor the English-language radio stations for him at night, I jumped at the chance. Before long, Terry was kidnapped at the start of what would become the longest ordeal of any hostage in Lebanon. Western staff were withdrawn and I filled one of the vacancies. I swapped ledger books and balance sheets for car bombs and street fighting in the best school of practical journalism to be found anywhere on earth.

This had been the perfect professional preparation for the Iraq war nearly twenty years later. But had my familiarity with suffering made me aloof and hard when children did not materialize? Perhaps it was because I had built a carapace around me that I was a good journalist, capable of writing the distressing stories of injured children without yielding to emotion. Or perhaps what Zahra was showing me was that I could be a better journalist if I cast off my shell and let my feelings show. Objective reporting was all very well, I reflected. But to write with humanity might not be such a bad thing after all.

I allowed my thoughts to drift back to the early years of my marriage. Had dedication to my job diverted me from creating a happy home as a younger woman, when I might have stood more chance of conceiving a child? I had never been in any doubt about what I wanted. Not long after my wedding, my mother and sister came to see me in England. One night, we were joined by my Lebanese journalist friends, Diana and Lena, who had also moved to London, and as we sat around the table over a glass of wine,

Mama asked each of us her habitual question about our ambitions for the years ahead.

"I want to be the best war photographer the world has ever seen," Lena said, with a determination that made us certain she would succeed.

"I'm going to spend my days riding horses and writing novels that will make me a famous author," said Diana, smiling as she conceded that to acquire the horses, she might be obliged to marry an American rancher.

Rana, as ever, refused to take my mother's question seriously. Besides, she was newly divorced and preoccupied with personal matters. "I want to find a millionaire tycoon for a husband and jet from city to city, shopping and generally being a lady of leisure," she said, laughing.

Mama giggled and turned to me. "So, Hala, what's your dream now? You've found the man you were looking for, but what do you want next?"

I did not hesitate. "Mama," I said, "I want to be a great journalist, but the one ambition that supersedes that is to have a huge kitchen full of small blond boys and girls running between my legs, shouting and screaming and laughing as I bake them cakes with flour all over my head and an apron round my waist. That's my dream."

Staring at Zahra now, I saw that this old dream, which I had been forced to throw out when I did not conceive, had returned.

I thought of how, in my anger on seeing Zahra's swollen, blistered skin for the first time, I had questioned Allah's wisdom. Yet had He not led me to this hospital and this special child? I deliberated for a while. Had it been Allah's wish all along that I take responsibility for Zahra? Was I bound to her by fate in some way that had yet to be revealed to me?

I SAID NOTHING IN THE CAR. I just thought and thought about what to say. Steve was a pragmatic man with a practical outlook. I would have to appeal to his sense of reason if I was going to win this argument. But where was the logic in what I was about to suggest? There was nothing rational in tracking down a wounded orphan in the first place, let alone in deciding in two days flat that Zahra should be more than a picture story in a newspaper, that her needs coincided with my desire to provide support and that she should start a revolution in our lives.

Glancing at Steve as we drove through the city to pay our condolences to Zahra's family, I saw a husband content to be far from home in the midst of the war Saddam had called "the mother of all battles." However grueling it was for Steve to photograph Baghdad, it surely beat commuting to an office in London. Besides, he had given up his desk job to work at my side. The two of us had made a triumphant team. A child would terminate that: one of us would always have to be at home.

The harder I thought, the more difficult everything seemed. An Iraqi child would require elaborate arrangements to ensure that bonds with relatives did not fray, but our home was thousands of miles away. A badly injured child would need meticulous medical attention, both surgical and psychological, and we would not know where to start looking for the best. An orphaned child would need exceptional care in a family home of the kind we had no experience of making for ourselves.

By the time we arrived at Grandmother's, I had failed to come up with a single coherent argument for the proposal I was going to make that night.

GRANDMOTHER GREETED STEVE POLITELY in the doorway of her house, a single-story concrete dwelling like the others in her street, with a patch of ground at the front that would have been just big enough for a car. She pointed him toward a room where her two remaining sons were standing, dressed in black mourning shirts and jeans. I was welcomed with embarrassing reverence and taken into a tiny sitting room with whitewashed walls and no furniture. This was a mourning day, and in accordance with tradition, the mourners were to be segregated, with men and boys in one room, women and girls in the other. A cleric was reciting verses from the Koran in melancholy fashion for all to hear.

It was clear from Grandmother's expression that, from her perspective, everything was simple. I had promised Zahra would live. I had money. I had connections, influence. What could go wrong as long as I kept my word? After a few niceties, she directed me to a mattress on the floor, sat cross-legged opposite me, and came straight to the point.

"So, Hala, what exactly are you going to do about my Zahra?"

I explained that we were going to have to move her to a hospital a long way away. "She needs treatment that isn't available here at the moment," I said. "Zahra is very sick, and the doctor believes that we should take her somewhere else to try and make her better."

The tears trickled down a face lined by decades of unthinkable hardship and two weeks of unimaginable grief. I held her hand in mine to comfort her and waited for her to recover some poise.

"Where's Hawra?" I asked, to take her mind off her other grandchildren. Grandmother regained her composure. "She's a baby, Hala, and she needs to feed on the breast. Since her mother is dead, a lady across the road who has a baby of her own is breast-feeding Hawra during the day."

"Oh, I so wanted to see her."

"You will, Hala," she replied, and called for one of her sons to fetch the child from across the road.

The son disappeared briefly, then stepped gingerly over the threshold as if afraid that he might drop the delicate bundle in his arms. Hawra was wearing short-sleeved cotton pajamas and had evidently just been woken from a nap. Her uncle lulled her with tender words as he brought her over. For a moment, he tickled her and her toes curled. There were baby dimples in the chubby flesh of her elbows.

Grandmother took Hawra from her son and placed her lovingly on my lap, then went to make some tea. I cradled her head in the crook of my elbow and rocked her slowly. I gazed at Hawra and she gurgled back at me. So far, so good.

"God, she's adorable," I thought as I touched her skin and smelled the baby fragrance of her soft black hair. I bounced her on my lap with the gentle motion that had always brought a smile to the face of my niece, Lara, when she was that age, and ran my finger across her temple, where there was a slight bruise from her fall. I saw no other injuries.

"Subhanak ya Rab, subhan hikmitak," I muttered—an Islamic phrase that translates roughly as "God moves in mysterious ways." Here was a small miracle, an infant unmarked by an inferno that had scarred her sister for life. As I pictured the blazing car, the urge to help both girls became irresistible.

Grandmother appeared with a tray of tea served in the Iraqi style that I love: strong and sweet in tiny glasses called *istikana*s. While I held Hawra, she showed me photographs of the parents, brothers, and sisters the infant had lost without knowing it.

"It will be difficult for me to raise two young girls," she said. "It will be hard for Zahra and Hawra here. I don't just mean this district—I mean the country as a whole."

There, in summary, was the case for an alternative future: this poor old woman would struggle to bring up the children in the fractious capital of a dangerously divided country. I asked whether it would be okay for Steve to join us.

"Of course." She smiled.

Steve crouched beside me on the mattress and I held Hawra out to him. "Here she is, Stevie. This little one is Zahra's sister."

His reaction astounded me. He held her gently for a moment, looked lovingly into her eyes, then kissed the crown of her head before handing her straight back to me and leaving the room without another word, apparently overcome.

I POURED STEVE A BEER in our hotel room and persuaded him to leave his cameras alone and settle onto the sofa. Since I had been unable to construct a rational argument for taking our lives in a new direction, I did the only thing I could do. I spoke from the heart. I came straight out with it.

"Steve," I said, sitting at his feet and resting my elbows on his knees. "What do you think of asking the grandmother to let us adopt Zahra and Hawra?"

I was looking up at him, but he was inscrutable. He did not speak. "It's been on my mind since we first saw Zahra," I went on. "I know it doesn't make sense. I know things like this should be thought through in depth. But in many ways it feels like I've been thinking about it for the last few years since we put babies aside. I believe I finally have my answer."

Once again, I examined his face for some sign of what he was thinking, but in vain. Although friends of ours had brought up the topic of adoption on many occasions over the years, Steve and I had rarely discussed it. I believed that to consider adoption would be to accept that I would never conceive. I had seen many doctors, but none had said it was impossible for me to get pregnant. So for a long time after my head told me it would never happen, my heart cried out to me that it might yet. To have applied to adopt, I would have had to resign myself to my infertility, and I was too stubborn to do that. It was too painful a thing for me to acknowledge inside, whatever I told my closest friends about having come to terms with it.

"I needed time to get myself back up emotionally and professionally, Steve. I needed time to feel good enough about myself. Well, I'm ready now." I had promised myself I would not cry, but as I heard my voice wavering, I saw tears in my husband's eyes.

"I seriously can't turn away from these two little girls, Steve. I know it'll be a huge endeavor, but I'm truly committed. I know it's the right thing to do."

"Oh, Hala," he sighed, kissing the top of my head just as he had Hawra's. "I've been waiting for you to ask me this for a very, very long time."

It was the first time Steve had hinted that he might be interested in becoming the father of another man's child. I jumped up onto the sofa and rested my head on his chest as he wrapped me in his arms.

"You," he said, "will be the mother of all mothers."

BY MORNING, Merlin's medical team had arrived. It was led by a handsome, kind French doctor, about thirty years old, who liked to be known as JB. Over coffee, I described the desperation I had seen in the hospitals he had come to help. In turn, he set out his plan to spend the *Sunday Times* fund on medicines, medical equipment, and specialist care. JB had it all worked out, right down to the psychological casualties who would need help after the war. To me, that seemed a long way off. I was more concerned about the pressing needs of the day. I told JB the story of Zahra.

"I want her helped now," I told him. "Future plans are meaningless for her. She won't live to see them put into action if we don't deal with her case immediately."

JB looked doubtful. His priority was setting up a system to help lots of people rather than coming to the aid of a single child.

"Please," I insisted. "Let's start with Zahra right away. My driver's here. We can take you to the hospital where she is. It's a big hospital. I'm sure you'll benefit from talking to the director. He can give you a better assessment of the needs than I can."

Perhaps out of sympathy for me, perhaps out of deference to the newspaper whose money would be paying for his projects, JB relented.

"Okay, I'll visit her immediately, check on other patients, and gauge conditions in the burn unit and the rest of the hospital."

We arrived at the Karameh to find the director dazed and distressed. He had just heard that his anesthetist had been killed at an American checkpoint.

"I can't make sense of it all," he said, a comment I had heard from so many doctors and patients in the past few days.

His account was horrifying. The anesthetist had been driving to the hospital for his shift. He slowed down as he approached the checkpoint, but like many Iraqis who could not read the long instructions posted in English by the American soldiers, he did not know what to do. He was waved through one barrier, and thinking he had been cleared to complete his journey to work, he accelerated. What he did not realize, the director said, was that he was supposed to slow down for a second check a few hundred yards farther along the road.

When he drove toward this at normal speed, a soldier mistook him for a suicide bomber and opened fire.

"I just can't comprehend it," the director said. "He survived weeks of bombardment and now he's been killed by the men who liberated him."

I could barely register the number of innocent victims we were hearing about, day after day. But the fact was that while nothing could be done for the unfortunate anesthetist, we could still make a difference for the children we had come to visit. Every minute counted. We moved as quickly as we decently could to the burn unit.

Here, JB fell into intense conversation with the doctor who had first described Zahra's condition to me. Grandmother was back at her side. When I introduced JB as the French doctor who had come to help Zahra, she simply nodded and looked at me with shining eyes as if I had performed a wonder.

Zahra was no better than she had been the day before. She lay on her side, shaking on sheets stained yellow by the cream that had been applied to her burns. Her eyes remained tightly shut even though she was moaning sporadically, and I guessed that she was drifting in and out of sleep. I felt the anguish in those tremulous limbs as acutely as if I had been racked with the same pain. I ached to relieve her suffering.

It was just as well that Grandmother could not follow the briefing that ensued as the Iraqi surgeon summarized the case to JB. He enumerated the treatments Zahra had received. He emphasized that he had used all the resources at his disposal. He explained that her infection was spreading, her condition deteriorating.

I watched JB's face as Steve photographed the doctors. If our French friend was shocked, he hid it well. He was speaking in language devoid of the emotions that filled me. Before I knew it, they had moved on to other patients when I wanted them to concentrate on Zahra. I would have this out with JB later, I thought, struggling to subdue my outrage.

As it turned out, I need not have worried. I had misread JB's clinical manner on the ward. No sooner had we reached our car than he was on the phone to colleagues in Jordan. He was pleading with them to act fast and help him save Zahra.

AT THE HOTEL, we asked JB to come to our room. Just as Grandmother had placed her faith in me, so I had pinned my hopes on him. My hands trembled slightly as I prepared coffee and cheese for lunch and waited for him to tell me what would happen next.

"You drink too much coffee, Hala," he began gently. "Not to mention the smoking. It's not good for you, you know."

"You're right," I said. "But after three months here, I probably need more than my average intake of caffeine and nicotine. Can we talk about Zahra, please?"

He had several things to tell me, and they were not easy for him to say or for me to hear. First, he was worried about me.

"You're overtired and overly emotional. You're incredibly stressed out. You're living on your nerves, Hala."

"Come on, JB," I countered. "That's normal. I haven't had a day off for weeks. I've nearly been blown up in my own room. I've seen dead and injured children day after day. What do you expect? There are plenty of other journalists living off their nerves by now."

Yes, JB said, but he thought I might be identifying to an excessive degree with some of the Baghdadis whose stories I was writing. He likened it to Stockholm syndrome, but what he really meant was that I was getting too close to people.

"Take the case of Zahra. You're not objective anymore. You're too emotionally involved. You have to distance yourself slightly."

JB was right, up to a point. The Reuters bureau chief who had poached me from AP and trained me to be detached from my subjects would have been appalled. But it was too late now. I was inextricably connected with Zahra, and in any case that was positive, not negative: I was helping her. My story about Zahra had had a huge impact. Within a few days of publication, £50,000 had poured into *The Sunday Times*, enough to help her and dozens like her. That was just the start. The total quickly shot up to £150,000 and beyond as readers glimpsed the suffering through our eyes and responded with a kindness and warmth that astounded me after all the thoughtless brutality I had witnessed. My tattered faith in humanity was partially restored.

JB's second point was much harder to accept. He had examined Zahra and spoken to her doctor. She would not last much longer in that hospital. "Hala, her chances of survival are zero if she remains in those conditions. We're talking a few days."

"But she won't stay here, right?" I said obstinately. "You'll arrange for her to be flown out, correct?"

I looked at Steve for reassurance but saw only a frown. "Please, JB, we need to help her, please." I was begging him, as Grandmother had begged me.

"Hala," he said, and he paused, aware of the sensitivity of what he had to say next, "you need to understand that even if we take her over the border to a hospital with fine facilities and specialists, her chances of pulling through will still only be fifty-fifty."

This came like a shock of a thousand volts. I took a deep breath and nodded. But inside I was thinking he could not be right. If Zahra was taken away and given the best treatment, she would surely live, I told myself, cursing my ignorance of medical matters. She was badly burned, yes. But that was not like having an injury to the head or the heart, was it?

JB was moving briskly on. I should be frank with the grandmother about Zahra's prognosis, he said. I should stress that no doctor could make any promises about her granddaughter's prospects.

"I can't do that," I said. I was very alarmed now. "She's suffering. She's lost too much. How can I tell her this?"

"You must, Hala. She must be aware. I know it's hard, but whatever you do, don't promise her miracles. Tell her the truth so that she's prepared."

I did not confess the promise I had already made to Grandmother. I simply said I would try to talk to her.

THAT EVENING, there was good news at last.

"Steve!" I screamed as I scanned my e-mails. "They're going to take Zahra to Jordan!" I was shouting as if he were in the parking lot below, when in fact he was standing right beside me, reading over my shoulder.

Not only had Merlin agreed to take Zahra to the Jordanian capital, Amman, where burn specialists could provide the treatment she needed, but the government of Jordan was offering to pay.

I was elated. It was Friday, and JB had warned that if Zahra did not receive proper care that weekend, she would be dead by Monday. We had to get her out of Baghdad on Saturday morning to give her a chance.

"Oh, Zahra," I whispered. "Hang in there a little longer, hang in there, baby. Help is on its way. The cavalry are coming."

I rang Merlin's representative in Amman, as I had been instructed to do.

"Great news, Hala," he said. "Everything's shut down because it's the weekend here, but we managed to contact the necessary people and we have the green light to bring her here."

I could barely contain my excitement as he explained that he would send a fully equipped ambulance to his side of the border. It would wait for Zahra and rush her up to Amman as soon as she was through the border controls.

Then came the bad news.

"All you have to do, Hala, is arrange for an ambulance to take Zahra to your side of the border, where she can be transferred to our vehicle. Oh, and Hala, it has to be clear to all concerned that no member of Zahra's family can escort her. She must come alone. Permission has been granted for her to enter Jordan, but not her relatives."

As if that were not tough enough, there was worse to follow. "Zahra must have her passport and documents so that she can get an entry visa at the border," he said. Now I was deflated. Arrange for an Iraqi ambulance to drive her from Baghdad to the border, a journey of ten hours? Had anyone in Jordan been reading the newspapers? I wondered. Did they not know that most hospitals had been looted, and that if any ambulances remained, they had been stripped of the equipment Zahra would need on such a long journey?

No family member? Were they serious? I could not ask Grandmother to send a child of three alone on a journey that would drag on for fifteen hours, including the leg from the border to Amman.

Zahra did not have a passport anyway. Her parents had been too poor to travel abroad. And any documents Zahra might once have had would have turned to ash in the car where her family had burned.

By the time I hung up the phone, my spirits were sinking as fast as they had risen an hour earlier. By midnight I had pleaded with everyone I could think of to produce a vehicle, but none were available. I had tried everything possible to get some documentation for Zahra, in vain. It was out of Merlin's hands. They had tried their hardest, but this was the best they could offer and it simply would not work. Each extra hour that Zahra remained in her own country was one less for her, and I was running out of options and ideas. All I could do that night was pray.

It was then that I met an American angel.

Seven

ANGEL OF MERCY

I was close to tears as I started writing my article about Zahra at the bleak little desk in the corner of our hotel room. It was a few minutes after midnight and I had just paused to wonder how the story would end when my phone rang. Jon Swain was on the line from his room two floors below: a routine call to exchange information about the reporting we had done that day. He knew immediately that something was terribly wrong.

"What's up, Hala? *Qu'est-ce qui se passe, chérie?*"

I tried to be calm and professional as I told him Zahra's story, but my distress kept bubbling to the surface. As I described the danger she was in, I started to think it could not be averted. I tried in vain to hold down a rising sense of panic.

"We can't get her out in time, Swainy," I said. "I'm terrified she'll die." Swain hesitated for a moment. Then, in a soft but resolute voice that told me my emotion had moved him, he said he had an idea. A few minutes later, he rang back with questions. He wanted Zahra's full name, her date of birth, the hospital she was in, and the precise nature of her injuries. He had a friend, he explained—Marla Ruzicka, an American girl he had met in Afghanistan. She had helped some of the innocent casualties of that conflict and had come to Baghdad to succor the victims of this one. Not only that, but she happened to be right there, right now, in Swain's room. She would go to the hospital first thing in the morning.

Marla was twenty-six when I met her, but she had the face of a teenager. Blonde and beautiful, with a luminous smile that belied the grimness of her work on the wards, she would not have looked out of place among the surfer girls of her native California. There, she had been known at school for her twin passions of rollerblading and salsa, and for her determination to go out into the world and make a difference. In Afghanistan, she had done precisely that.

The way Swain told it, he had met her in the Afghan city of Jalalabad when, weary and disheveled from traveling, he had checked into a guesthouse where three Western aid workers, all women, were camping in sleeping bags in the room next to his. Before he could introduce himself, one of the women, dressed in pajamas patterned with cartoon animals, had flung out her hand and said, "Hi, I'm Marla. You look tired. You need a massage." Without further ado, she had placed him on the floor and pummeled his back with a pair of tiny fists.

Together, they had gone to a hospital where dead and wounded civilians had been taken after a misdirected American air strike. The sight of the bodies and the cries of the injured affected Marla deeply. From that moment on, she set out to see that ordinary men, women, and children caught in the crossfire of America's wars were counted and compensated for their losses.

Marla always traveled with very little money and never found this a hindrance. She slept on the floors of journalists' rooms and hitched rides with their drivers. Her admirers in the media not only adored her company but appreciated her amazing skill at puncturing inflated officialdom. Besides, she made good copy.

She had once staged a demonstration outside the American embassy in Kabul with a father and daughter who were the only survivors of a U.S. bombing that had killed eighteen members of their family. Although the Marines guarding the embassy did their best to intimidate the demonstrators into silence, Marla stood her ground. She stayed with the grizzled, bearded Afghan tribesmen, telling their story to the American papers and ensuring that their plight received international publicity.

The same combination of charm and tenacity was displayed in Baghdad, where she was nicknamed "Bubbles" by journalists because of her infectious giggle, and "Cluster Bomb Girl" by American forces for the way she hounded them to clear civilian areas of hundreds of lethal bomblets they had dropped. In the battle to save Zahra, she could not have been a more potent ally.

MARLA LEFT OUR HOTEL EARLY that Saturday morning without fuss or fanfare, while Swain and I stayed in our rooms and raced to meet deadlines for the Sunday edition. My instructions were to put so much power into my piece about Zahra that readers would feel compelled to give generously to the fund-raising appeal we were launching that weekend. It was not difficult to capture the sadness of her story, but I did not know how it would unfold as I wrote, and that was hard.

Arriving at the Karameh, Marla found it surrounded by American tanks and GIs guarding against mobs of looters who might be tempted to go in, as they had done at Ali's first hospital. Marla had only to smile at the soldiers to be sure of their full cooperation. Some of them had hung around for weeks on the border to the south in a fog of testosterone while the invasion forces built up. Most of them had seen virtually nothing but the porn-plastered interior of an armored vehicle on the slow, tense, tortuous journey up to Baghdad. None of these men had laid eyes on a California surfer girl for a long, long time.

Once inside, Marla made her way to the burn unit and then to Zahra's bedside. By now she had seen scores of blameless individuals hurting and wailing in wards such as this during her short career as a one-woman aid organization. She had adopted a practical attitude to her work, focusing simply on how to help. But she was driven by the same raw emotional reactions that motivated me. She was transfixed by the sight of Zahra, just as I had been. Without hesitation, she resolved that the child shivering beneath her bandages and puckering her burned, swollen face in pain would be given a chance to live by those who had killed her family. Marla would summon the American military to the rescue.

First, however, there was an unexpected hurdle to overcome. Zahra's grandmother was standing there with her arms folded and a defiant expression on her face. She did not like the look of this pretty young American.

"Where's Hala?" she demanded to know.

"Hala sent me," said Marla, beckoning over a doctor to translate. "Hala asked me to help Zahra. I'm going to do everything I can to help."

Grandmother was not convinced. She had promised that Hala could take her granddaughter away, and only Hala had the right to do that, she said.

"I have given Hala my word," she said. "Besides, I'm expecting her this morning. Everything will have to wait until Hala arrives."

Try as she might, Marla could not persuade Grandmother to

deal with a stranger. In any case, Grandmother said, why should she believe that Hala, who knew the Arab world and understood what the Americans had done to this city, would send an American in her place?

Marla told her everything I had said about Zahra, but it was no use. She did not have a phone with her, so she scribbled a note for me and asked a taxi driver to take it to my hotel. The note begged me to stop what I was writing and come immediately.

In the meantime, Marla concentrated on organizing an evacuation. She commandeered a radio and set about finding someone with the authority to order transportation. Further and further up the chain of command she went, but she still could not secure a commitment. So she tried something that no one other than Marla would have dreamed of trying.

She marched outside to the cordon of tanks, found the senior officer, gazed into his eyes, and pleaded. Taking his arm, she pulled him away from his post and into the hospital. She almost pushed him to Zahra's bedside.

"There," she said. "That's what we've done. Now we're going to put it right. Or are you just going to leave this little girl here to die?"

Grandmother was impressed. Less than two hours later, Zahra and two other patients on the ward were on their way to an army field hospital in a helicopter.

THE BLONDE BOMBSHELL BURST into my room to break the news of her single-handed triumph an hour before her note arrived saying she needed help.

"Zahra's out!" she shrieked, jumping up and down in her excitement as I went to hug her.

It was the first time I had met Marla, and what an introduction. It was hard to believe that this slender girl had taken on the U.S. Army and won her battle so swiftly, but then I did not know Marla yet. Her youthful looks belied an iron determination. I would soon come to appreciate that the combined power of her passion and compassion was a force of nature that no war-weary Marine could resist. All she had to do was flirt a little and flash her wide smile and they would obey any order she cared to give.

I hardly dared celebrate at first, so gloomy had I been all afternoon about Zahra's prospects. But for Swain, Steve, and me, deadlines had passed, stories and pictures were going to press, and another turbulent week was ending. It was time to relax and unwind before the next one started in the morning. This was happy hour, and as we cracked open a bottle or two, the life and soul of the party was Marla, Cluster Bomb Girl and angel of mercy.

As she raised her glass and asked us to drink to Zahra's good health, I knew I had found a friend and ally. She giggled with me when I recounted the strange demands from the office for secret intelligence files and special orphans. She wept when I recalled the most pitiful patients I had encountered in my rounds of the pediatric wards. But when I pressed her for details of her mission on behalf of Zahra, she resisted at first, fearing she might seem boastful. When she finally spoke, she made her astonishing achievement sound like a routine day's work.

"I left here with the names of Zahra Kathem and her doctor," she said. "The hospital was surrounded by U.S. tanks. I talked my way into the ward where Zahra was."

"Marla!" I cried. "You know we won't be satisfied with that. Come on, we're journalists. We want the full story. . . ."

Marla paused and shook her head, tears welling. "Hala, she looked so sad and ill. The girl was dying slowly and I knew this wasn't right. I made some calls to the U.S. military and explained the situation and said we needed to help evacuate."

I pressed for more details.

"All the responses were negative," she went on. "Everyone was on operations, there were no guys in the vicinity to check the hospital, there were no spare helicopters to move the girl. By midday, I was pretty angry with the stalling. I was frustrated just waiting for calls back. So I had to do something different. I went back to the tanks outside and asked as many soldiers as it took until eventually I got to see their commander."

"And you persuaded him?" I asked. "How?" The room was very quiet as we sat round Marla, picturing the scene.

"I pleaded with him to come inside with me and take a look," she said. "When he saw Zahra, he was very emotional. He said he had kids of his own and one of them wasn't much older than her. We went outside and he got on his radio and made the calls to order the evacuation."

However casually she spoke, none of us underestimated the forcefulness of the personality that had been brought to bear on the defenseless commander.

"He spoke to the hospital director about two other patients who needed treatment they couldn't get in the burn unit. He arranged for them to be flown out on Zahra's helicopter," she concluded. "I told him, 'You should be proud of what you've done today. I'm going to tell your mom!' "

Zahra and the other two were headed for Camp Dogwood, a U.S. field hospital that had been set up little more than a week earlier. According to Marla, this hospital was not only treating wounded coalition forces but had begun taking Iraqi patients, including burn victims. It sounded ideal: Zahra had been spared a torturous journey by road to Jordan, and even as we spoke she was safely in the care of experienced physicians.

As the drink flowed, Marla and I laughed and cried in each other's arms. This amazing woman had achieved something I had come to regard as almost impossible. She had rescued three helpless victims of this crushing war by making the U.S. Army take responsibility. She had saved Zahra.

Eight

ADOPTION

"Steve, wake up," I said quietly. "There are soldiers outside our room with guns pointing at the door."

I had woken to a loud banging and jumped out of bed, thinking the hotel cleaning crew must have come back to work. We had not seen them for a month.

"Thank God—this room really does need a good cleaning," I had thought. "Finally, some decent washing." But as I reached the door, the banging became distinctly aggressive, and I could hear American voices raised in anger outside. Nervously, I peered through the peephole.

The American soldiers were screaming at us to open up, but I was wearing a ridiculously revealing nightgown and I wanted to make myself modest first. Steve told them to hang on a minute. A split second later, the door flew off its hinges and several hulks with big guns charged in, roaring.

"On your knees," they shouted, pointing the guns at us.

"Dear God," I thought. "Have we survived a war, only to die at the hands of a search squad?"

"Passports!" they demanded, even though we were still kneeling in our nightclothes. They looked young and nervous, and their fingers were stroking the triggers. I was not sure I liked this at all. Eventually, I was allowed to stand up and present them with my British passport.

"How dare you barge into our room like this? How dare you treat us like criminals? How dare you point your guns at us?" I cried, my outrage distracting me from the danger of their weapons. "If you don't know we're journalists, you should. We've been holed up here for weeks on end and everyone who is anyone knows that this has been the hub of the media throughout the war. What are you doing, harassing us like this?"

The soldier inspected my passport. "We're looking for the terrorists, ma'am," he said.

"Well, you won't find them in our rooms. These rooms are occupied by journalists," I snapped as I showed him the door.

As the last soldier left, I knew it was time to take a break. This was the second argument I had had with American troops that week. There had also been an incident at a checkpoint when Steve, Rafed, and I were trying to get back to the hotel.

My blond, blue-eyed husband was of no interest to the soldiers who stopped us, but Rafed and I—the Arabs—were questioned with extreme suspicion. When the soldiers informed Rafed that he would not be allowed to continue the drive back to our hotel, even though he had been staying there for weeks in service to Steve and me, leaving his family to face the bombing of Baghdad alone, I exploded.

The Arab in me was furious on behalf of my Iraqi friend being insulted and degraded by these Western soldiers on our territory. The

Western journalist in me was embarrassed and guilty: it was because of me that Rafed had been separated from his family and was now being subjected to abuse.

"He's an Iraqi and this is his country," I shouted uselessly. "He's one of the people you came to liberate, if you recall. How dare you try to prohibit him from driving down this road?"

Of course all this did was convince the soldiers that I needed to be searched, too. I was asked to lift my trousers so that one of the soldiers could check my shoes. The question was put politely, but I was incensed.

"If you want to check my shoes, you do it on your own," I said. "I'm not bending down to lift my trousers for you. Bend down yourself."

The American soldiers courteously ignored my rudeness. One of them duly bent to check my shoes and Steve, Rafed, and I were all permitted to pass. I was still enraged as we left the checkpoint behind, not least with myself. I knew I had been foolish to lose my cool like that. Yet I could not help it. Everywhere I went, I saw not only the soldiers themselves but the victims of their mistakes: charred families and limbless, motherless children who had broken my heart. I was struggling to separate personal emotion from the politics of the conflict. These soldiers were swaggering when I thought they should be deferential after all the suffering their country had caused, especially to infants such as Zahra.

In the end I decided I had used up all my luck. If I was not careful, I would get myself shot for the sake of a petty argument. I was so focused on Zahra and Hawra that I was losing my journalistic perspective. I had also been in Baghdad for too long. It had been more than three months and we had endured surveillance, threats, bombardment, sleeplessness, and the sight of families being torn apart. I was physically and mentally exhausted.

I knew I would want to be back on the story soon, but for now I needed to be taken off it. I phoned my boss and told him so.

"Good call, Hala," he said. "Time for a holiday."

A FEW DAYS BEFORE OUR DEPARTURE, Steve and I returned to Grandmother's house to ask whether we might form our own family from the remnants of her son's. We felt it best to put the proposition to her then in the hope that she would think about it while we were away: Would she allow Zahra and Hawra to live with us in London? There were arguments for and against, but we believed the advantages to the girls outweighed the disadvantages. The prospect of seeking Grandmother's permission and the potential impact of the children on our lives filled us with trepidation.

The warmth of our welcome seemed to bode well. Grandmother was elated that Zahra had been flown out of Baghdad, and my own euphoria drove JB's warnings about the child's prognosis out of my mind. As far as Grandmother was concerned, I had promised that Zahra would receive vital treatment, the pledge had been fulfilled, and her granddaughter was recovering. The way I saw it, Zahra had been rescued from the Iraqi hospital that could not save her and been placed in the hands of skillful American specialists who were providing the best treatment available. Her burns would be tended to, the infection overcome, the skin repaired. I had willed her to survive, and so she would live. I saw no reason to tell Grandmother that in spite of all my assurances, Zahra might yet die. I did not believe it, whatever the French doctor had said.

"Your granddaughter is making progress," I assured her, relaying the bulletin Marla had received that morning from her American contacts. "She will most likely be coming back to you when she has totally recovered."

Grandmother beamed with anticipation. "Can I visit her?" she asked.

"I'll check and see what the possibilities are," I said. "She's in an American field hospital somewhere and it may not be possible to get you there. But I promise you she will be back home soon."

When tea was served, we sat together on the floor while Grandmother showed me happy family photographs of the parents and brothers Hawra and Zahra had lost. The girls' father, Ali, had been a taxi driver, and their mother had raised their sons and daughters, from Muntather, the eighteen-year-old son, to three-month-old Hawra. Ali's earnings would have been less than $10 (£7.50) a day, enough to feed his wife and children but not enough for any luxuries at their sparsely furnished, single-story home. Far more important, Grandmother told me wisely, was that the family was rich in love.

We dwelt for a while on the girls' prospects in Baghdad. I understood that had it not been for the war, they would have had opportunities. Iraq's children had long been among the best educated in the Middle East. Zahra and Hawra might have hoped to follow the example of their aunt and become a teacher. As orphans, however, their options would be more limited. Grandmother came from a poor background. She was religiously conservative and traditional in her outlook. However much she doted on her granddaughters, it was unlikely that she would encourage them to pursue a career. Her priority would probably be to secure their future by seeing them married as young as possible.

I knew Grandmother would do her best to ensure that suitable husbands were found, but Zahra would be scarred for life and her chances were as dismal as those of Marwa, the girl whose leg had been amputated. The Arab world is not a land of opportunity for children with defects and disabilities. Zahra would be lucky if she became the second wife of an older man who would make her feel that he had done her a favor. I could not bear the idea that she might never be able to fall in love, to believe in herself, to make her own choices.

"Hajieh," I said slowly. "I need to talk to you about something."

She looked at me intently. I felt so nervous that I could hardly bring myself to ask the question that had been in my mind since I had first seen Zahra and heard her story.

"Would you let me adopt Zahra and Hawra, and take them back to England?"

Grandmother looked stunned. If I had thought her talk of how tough it would be for her to raise the girls might be a hint that I should take her place, I had been seriously mistaken. The thought had obviously never occurred to her. I exchanged anxious glances with Steve, who could not follow our Arabic but knew what I had just said from the reaction.

"I promise you that I would give them a good life and bring them back to you every year," I pressed gently. "I have no children of my own, but I know I would be good for the girls and I could offer them a great deal if you'd agree to my plan."

Grandma paused, a look of the utmost concentration on her haggard face. Then came the questions.

"How would they be brought up?" she wanted to know.

"What languages would they learn?"

Devout herself, it was natural for her to ask: "How much religious awareness would they have with you?"

Not the least of her questions was: "How would I be able to see them as often as possible?"

I said I could not deal with all these points until the three of us had thought them through together. "I don't have all the answers yet," I told her. "But I'm sure we can work every one of them out."

I knew in my heart that Zahra and Hawra could never be completely "mine." I would not wish to sever them from their roots and cut them off from their home, their family, and their country. Given the enormity of their loss, it would be especially important for these two girls to know that their grandmother, two uncles, aunt, and various cousins remained devoted to them. I knew from a lifetime's experience the importance of keeping such bonds firm across international borders. Having been born and raised in Africa, and then living in England since my marriage to Steve, I have found that my strong contacts with family in Lebanon have given me stability in turbulent times. I have always had someone to turn to for love and support. I would never wish the girls to be deprived of this.

"I'm not suggesting I take them away and pretend to be their real mother," I assured Grandmother. "I sincerely believe that they should never lose touch with their family. I've lived abroad for much of my life, but I could never do without my true home, Lebanon. It's enriched me in so many ways. So, knowing this, I could never cut the girls off from you."

Without warning, Grandmother wailed. Heartrending sobs filled the room as she rocked backward and forward, locking her arms around herself. I knew why: she saw that the girls would have a better chance in life if they came away with me, but she was imagining the day she would have to say good-bye to the last two members of her son's family. The girls were all that was left of him.

She took both my hands in hers and kissed them profusely. The gesture signified gratitude, but she needed a great deal of time before she could make any commitments about the girls' future.

"This is a hard request, Hala, let me think about it," she said. "Promise me you will save Zahra first. Promise me you will. I know you can."

I wavered. The words of JB were reverberating in my ears. "No promises," he had said. Now was the time to tell Grandmother there were no guarantees that Zahra would live. I owed it to her to make this clear. But she was still talking.

"Only you can make sure Zahra stays in the good hospital," she was telling me. And then she looked me in the eye, as she had done at the Karameh. "Hala, make sure she gets the treatment she needs, but promise me now you will bring her back to me safe, sound, and recovered."

I opened my mouth to tell her that I could not make this promise, but the words would not come. Unable to bear her anguish, unwilling to compound it, I heard myself telling her what she needed me to say. I promised her hope, life, and a bright future for her granddaughter.

God forgive me.

Nine

FALLING FROM A GREAT HEIGHT

During the final few days of our most arduous assignment, Steve and I were reinvigorated by the news that Zahra's condition had stabilized in the field hospital. Marla brought bulletins, Swain brought wine, and we celebrated together each night. Not only that, but checks were arriving by the sackload in the *Sunday Times* mail room. Zahra's appeal was going to help countless other children, and JB, the French doctor, joined us in drinking to her health.

As for the complex question we had put to Grandmother, it would be weeks before we could ask for a simple yes or no. While she was thinking about it, mulling things over with family and talking through the pros and cons with friends, there was nothing more we could do. We would return in a month or two, refreshed and hungry for the challenge of children. The mere possibility that Grandmother might agree to let them leave this benighted place for brighter prospects in London was electrifying.

All that remained for us was to pack, arrange drivers, fixers, and accommodations for colleagues coming to relieve us, ask our contacts to help the new arrivals, set up some stories for them, and put our files in order. We had created a news factory, and transferring it to new management would be a tedious job. Nevertheless, I felt so happy to be leaving that I could not stop humming a favorite dance tune: "I'm coming up, I want the world to know. . . ."

To mark our departure, I decided to throw a grand farewell party that Marla and my newspaper friends would never forget. We had a decent venue in the form of the two interconnected suites Steve and I had been using, one for sleeping, the other for working. We also had a makeshift kitchen that I had created by rigging up camping stoves in one of the bathrooms. From here, I had already produced meals of jarred frankfurters and cheese for Swain, with whom we had sat out late on our seventeenth-floor balcony to watch bombs rain down on the city. Now that the bombardment had ceased and the shops were reopening, I wanted to put that stove to more ambitious use and fill pots, pans, and plates with the finest food anyone could wish for in a bombed-out Middle Eastern capital. If the food was horrible, we would wash it down with as much bad wine as a party of journalists could drink in one night, and my culinary humiliation would be forgotten by the morning.

Rafed was dispatched to scout for grilled chicken while I checked out my special ingredients for the pièce de résistance. All I could find were some chicken tikka and *jalfrezi* sauces that I had swept off a supermarket shelf before the war without knowing whether I would ever need them.

I deboned the chicken, fried chunks of it in butter and onions on the stove on the bathroom floor, and added curry powder to the mixture to spice it up. Then I poured in the supermarket sauces with some water and let the whole lot simmer for a while. On a second stove, I added saffron to a huge pot of rice to make it fragrant and golden.

When that was done, I cooked a heap of frankfurters and what can only be described as an industrial quantity of French fries.

All the food was kept out of the sight of our Saturday night guests when they arrived. None knew what was on the menu and most were probably expecting tinned tuna since we had largely existed on the stuff for weeks. As the suite filled with the sounds of jokes and laughter, wine bottles and beer cans were strewn around our candlelit table and the frankfurters and fries were served as nibbles. If it had not been for the crackling of distant gunfire and the odd explosion, we could have been anybody, anywhere.

I was especially happy to see a wonderful *Sunday Times* colleague who had come up from the south in a tank with the U.S. Marines. He was Italian and fond of his food, but had had only army MREs (meals ready to eat) to keep him going for weeks. He looked famished. An elegant American correspondent with a penchant for Prada had been embedded with the makeshift army of an opposition leader returning from exile to the north of the country. The poor woman had lived rough in hangars and sheds. She deserved to be spoiled, too.

Such was the fug of cigarette smoke that even the most discerning partygoers failed to notice the aroma of spices. So when Rafed brought out the great pots of chicken curry and rice, followed by dishes piled high with tuna, sausages, and cheese, there was bewilderment, then laughter. Where had this banquet come from?

"See, we girls do have our uses after all," I said. "War or no war, I can still be domesticated and take care of my boys. This is *The Sunday Times*'s top team and we are all alive and kicking. Thank God."

Everyone drank to that. But as I caught Marla's eye, I knew that her mind, like mine, was on another survivor far away from those who loved her. Together, we raised our glasses in a silent toast to Zahra.

THERE WERE TWO LAST VISITS I had to make before I could leave. One was to my injured friend Samia, who had been released from the hospital but was still languishing in the hotel, awaiting a medical evacuation. She was asleep when I slipped into her room, and she looked too drugged up to wake. I sat with her nurse for a while, staring at the bandages wrapped around her head and praying that the next time I saw her, she would be restored to her vivacious, immaculate old self. Samia did not so much as stir when I kissed her good-bye.

THE OTHER VISIT WAS to Grandmother's house among the narrow streets of the Hay al-Shuhada district. She was waiting for me at her gate as usual in the black chador that covered her from head to toe. Flashing a toothless smile, she gave me her usual ecstatic reception but no clue as to what she was thinking about the proposal I had put to her. She merely led me inside to the small living room where she and Hawra slept at night beneath a photograph of the child's father, its frame still draped with black ribbon.

"The hospital says Zahra's improving. She's doing well," I said, passing on the latest bulletin. I explained that Marla would keep her in touch with all the news from the field hospital while I was out of the country.

"I've been in Baghdad for three months without a break, and I need to go and see my mother for a little while," I added. "When I return, Zahra will be back with you. Then you and I can talk about the girls' future."

Grandmother, who looked much older than her fifty-four years after a lifetime's poverty compounded by the grief of recent weeks, nodded gravely. I gave her some cash for Hawra, who was fast asleep, and begged her not to be embarrassed but to buy whatever the baby needed. So captivated was I by Hawra that I needed to feel I was looking after her even when I was far away.

"This isn't charity," I assured Grandmother. "This is from me to Hawra—a little present I want her to have before I go."

It was not only Zahra I would miss during the coming weeks: the baby sister with the big brown eyes would be gazing at me in my dreams until I came back. Then, if Grandmother was persuaded, I would take her home, tuck her up in a crib at my bedside, and wake next morning to the dawn of a new life for all of us.

I bade Grandmother good-bye, and she prayed that Allah would protect me and provide me with success.

"You were sent by Allah to me," she said, enfolding me in a tearful embrace. "Thank you. We will always be grateful to you."

I assured her that it was to Marla that the family owed any gratitude. It was Marla who had made it her mission to help; Marla who had gone into that ward and eased the suffering of three of its patients; Marla who had brought salvation where without her there would have been death and despair.

The war had drawn us together—Zahra, Hawra, Grandmother, Marla, and me. As I stepped out of Grandmother's house into the sunshine, I could never have imagined how the insurgency that was to follow would tear us apart.

AT THE END OF THAT WEEK, we set off on the desert drive that would take us out of the war zone and back to the peaceful normality of our everyday lives. Swain, Steve, and I chatted away in the car but avoided looking back on the surreal horrors of Baghdad. Instead, we focused on the delights that awaited us in the real world. What I had missed most, I realized, were a long soak in a hot bath, fresh towels and crisp clean sheets, and drifting off to sleep without having to wonder whether I would be killed where I lay.

In between banter, my thoughts returned again and again to Zahra at the field hospital. Marla had mentioned as we left that my girl might be transferred to a specialist unit in Saudi Arabia when she was well enough to travel. I pictured her undergoing skin grafts and myself rushing to her side to comfort her through her convalescence. It would be a hard time for Zahra, and I was not sure what scars would be left in the end. For now, all I knew was that I wanted to help these two girls. I prayed to God that I be given the chance to do so.

The border officials brought me back to earth with a bump. Had we stolen the carpets we were carrying? they wanted to know. No, we had bought them before the war and had kept the receipts to prove it. Had we plundered presidential palaces for artifacts? Certainly not. Had we taken any of the treasures from the museums that had been looted? No, no, no.

When the officials removed some files from Jon Swain's luggage, I lost my temper and demanded to see the senior official, who duly felt the full force of my frustration that, after three months in Baghdad, it looked as if we would not make it to Amman before nightfall.

"You are Lebanese, no?" he asked.

"Yes. What's that got to do with anything?" I snapped.

"Which part of Lebanon do you come from?" he demanded to know.

Take a deep breath, I told myself. Do not let him rile you. Calm down and get this over and done with.

"The south," I said sweetly.

"See?" he shouted, slamming his fist on the desk and smiling at the underlings standing around him. "I knew it. This woman is feisty. She is not only Lebanese, but from the south. They're all fighters there, including the women. They drove the Israelis out after twenty-two years of occupation."

He looked at me. "You have their spirit," he said.

"Well, sir," I said in my least feisty voice. "Now that we have established all this, may we please have our things and get going?"

"Of course," he replied. "In the meantime, have tea with us."

WE REACHED BEIRUT THE NEXT DAY, but I knew on the first evening that it would take a while for me to adjust to ordinary life, even in my home city. Steve and I stayed with dear friends, a doctor and his wife who laid out a traditional Lebanese dinner with a multitude of meats, sauces, and salads. It was a sumptuous meal with all our favorite dishes, from eggplant dips to big bowls of tabbouleh salad with flat parsley tossed in lemon juice and olive oil, but we could hardly eat a thing. We had not noticed how much weight we had lost, but our friends did. There was not much chance of fattening us up fast, either: our stomachs seemed to have shrunk.

Leaving most of our feast in the fridge, we went to a nightclub. It was a place I usually loved, but I did not enjoy it that night. The music was loud when all I wanted to do was to sit quietly. People were dancing on tables where I would have preferred just to talk. The more exuberantly they swayed, the sadder I felt. The ghosts of the forgotten world we had come from were spooking me. Did these people boogying the night away not realize that there were widows out there who would never dance again? Mothers who could not even cry for the sons and daughters they had lost, let alone smile? Children who would have to learn how to eat and drink without hands? Did they not know that Zahra was alone in an American field hospital with no family to comfort her as she grappled with pain? Did anyone here really care?

I looked at Steve on the other side of the bar and frowned. He understood. It was too early for us to be in the middle of all this. The pressure of the past few weeks had got us down. We were in a cold, dark place and we needed to come up slowly, like a deep-sea diver avoiding the bends on his way back to a sunlit surface. I began to cry. My doctor friend did not need any explanations: he had worked it out. He took me in his arms, gave me a hug, and said, "Let's take you home, Hala."

MY MOTHER WAS STAYING in Cairo with my sister, Rana, and that is where I went next. It was not enough to tell them on the telephone that I was fine. They needed to see the evidence for themselves.

The first to greet me at the airport was Lara, my darling niece, now a bright and beautiful sixteen-year-old. She ran up and threw herself at me so hard that I almost toppled over.

"Lollie!" she said, using the name she had bestowed on me as soon as she had been old enough to talk. "I'm so pleased to see you." Then, as if to warn me, she whispered confidentially: "They've been incredibly worried."

My mother and sister were close behind. As they embraced me in tears, I realized they had made themselves ill with anxiety. Rana cried like a child, telling me how she and her friends in the office had fretted and sweated over every bulletin from Baghdad for weeks, dreading that they would hear terrible news of British journalists killed in crossfire or massacred by a wayward missile. Mama hugged and kissed me over and over again, sobbing her thanks to Allah for keeping me safe.

Then suddenly my mother stopped crying and fixed me with one of her looks. "You're too thin, Hala!" she exclaimed.

I did not mind. I was overjoyed to have the brusque Mama I had missed so much on one arm, with Rana on the other and Lara hopping backward and forward in front of us, trying not to miss a word.

"Your face looks tired," Mama said as we reached the car. She touched my skin and recoiled. "In fact, it is dry," she said, genuinely horrified. "Rana, you will book her an appointment at that new spa and beauty salon. It's very important, you understand. A full facial is what she needs."

Rana and I looked at each other and giggled.

"Does she ever change?" I asked as Mama continued with a list of instructions.

"Nope," said Rana and Lara in unison.

Mama admonished her disrespectful daughters. "Make fun of me, both of you," she said, wagging a well-manicured finger. "But one day when I'm dead and gone, you'll thank me."

"We sure love ya, Mama," we said, and she smiled.

"Oh, and Rana, don't forget," she said, "Hala needs a manicure and a pedicure. Her nails look like a man's . . ."

THE ONLY WAY I COULD REASSURE THEM was by enjoying myself while I was there, so that is what I decided to do. Rana, with her insatiable appetite for fun, took me out every evening with her friends to restaurants, clubs, and pubs. I spent the days with Mama, seeing the sights and talking at home while Rana worked. I had put them through a lot, I realized. They were worried sick about me. But if they saw me sunbathing by the pool with a glass of wine and a book, if they heard me laughing and joking, they would know I was my old self. I owed them that.

And so it was for a few, blissful days. We ate, drank, shopped, lazed, and chatted. I kept the conversation light, carefully avoiding any mention of tank rounds coming through the hotel wall and soldiers' guns pointed at my head. There was only one serious topic I needed to raise.

I spoke to my sister first. I explained how Zahra's crying for her mother had drawn me to her, the terrible suffering she had endured, and the sorrows that lay ahead. But I did not hide my excitement at the latest news, that the doctors had fallen in love with her and the nurses' tender care was speeding her recovery. I said that nothing was certain and if I was permitted to adopt, it would be hard at first for Zahra and Hawra to adjust to England. Nevertheless, I was allowing myself to hope that one day we might finally share the magical family Christmas we had always wanted, Rana with her daughter and I with my two.

Needless to say, Rana was wildly enthusiastic. "Finally, you'll have girls, Haloul—girls that I can teach to be crazy like me, not conservative like you."

She thought for a moment, cocking her head mischievously to one side. "What fun they shall have with their auntie Rana," she teased.

Then, solemnly, she said: "It will be great for you. I will be so happy for you. Oh, Sis, just go for it."

I was more apprehensive about telling Mama of the burned little girl and her infant sister with no mother or father to love them, and the plans Steve and I were making to give them a home. I suspected she might disapprove for some reason or ask whether I had rushed into a decision when I was too run-down to think clearly. I wondered if she might make me doubt myself. I needed her approval.

"Do you think you could love the girls, even if they were not mine?" I asked her one evening after dinner. "Could you feel affection for them, or would you always regard them as strangers?"

My mother seemed surprised by the question.

"I will love them because they are innocent children," she said. "I will love them because they are with you and they make you happy. I think you should do this, Hala. A good mother isn't just someone who gives birth to children. A good mother is someone who raises children well and gives them love and security."

IF I HAD BEEN A GOOD MOTHER, I would not have been gaily shopping for trinkets when the call came. We were strolling through the affluent district of Zamalek, where Rana lived, and we had dipped out of the hazy late-April sunshine into her favorite jeweler's. Arab women have a weakness for jewelry, and I am no exception. My eyes gleamed at the sight of diamond rings, pendants, and earrings in glittering display cases.

"Treat yourself, Hala," my mother said when she saw me entranced by a set of two white gold rings encrusted with diamonds. "You deserve it."

Part of me wanted to be pampered. Another part felt guilty that I should even be contemplating such extravagant self-indulgence when so many people in Baghdad were deprived.

"Should I be wasting money like this, given where I have been and what I have seen?" I asked.

"Oh, Hala," my mother sighed. "You cannot save the world and you cannot punish yourself like this."

I succumbed to vanity and bought the rings. The shame of it remains with me to this day, like a self-inflicted scar.

The two of us were walking toward Rana's flat. Looking back on that afternoon, it seems indecent that I was deriving such pleasure from the buzz of Cairo, a city that had never failed to send my pulse racing. The atmosphere was always febrile because everybody wanted to rush from A to B, but gridlock forced them to sit still, honking their horns in exasperation beneath a big black cloud of pollution. I loved the frustrated energy of the place. I could feel it coursing through me.

It seems even more obscene now that I should have been happy for the first time in months—so happy that I startled my mother by suddenly giving her a hug in the middle of the street.

"Thanks, Mama," I told her with a big grin. I did not need to say any more. She had seen me quiet and down, and had known I needed some time. Now I was chirpy and cheerful, and she was reassured.

Not for long. My cell phone trilled as we were crossing the road, arm in arm.

"Hala, ma chérie, comment vas-tu?"

"Hey, Swainy *habibi*, how are you? I miss you so much." I giggled, thinking he was phoning for a bit of flirtatious banter to cheer himself up. But then his tone changed.

"Hala, I need to talk to you."

"Sure—shoot," I said, assuming that he was feeling low, as he sometimes did after a big assignment.

"Well, it's about Zahra," he said.

Still, I did not get it.

"How's my little one doing? Don't tell me someone's beaten me to it and adopted her," I joked.

"No, nothing of the sort, I'm afraid," he said. He was speaking so softly that I had to stop and strain to hear him amid the bustle all around me.

"Marla's just called with bad news, Hala. I'm so very, very sorry, *chérie*. Zahra has died."

The sensation I had was of falling from a great height. I was plummeting from heaven to hell; from a vision of Zahra running toward me with outstretched arms, fully recovered and bursting with life, to the reality of a three-year-old orphan wrapped in white muslin and laid out in a lonely coffin; from hope for the future to a terror of the here and now. As I plunged, I panicked. I could not even see my mother at my side. All I could do was scream: "No!"

Swain was trying to say some words of comfort. I was not listening.

"No, Jon. Please tell me it's not true. You said she was fine. A few days ago you told me Zahra was doing fine. You said so. Marla said so. How can she be dead now?"

I was sobbing. Oh my God, I thought. I have killed her. I have let her down. I have abandoned her by leaving the country. "I promised her life, Swainy. I promised her grandmother I would bring her back, safe and well."

My mother had her arm around me now and was guiding me along the street to my sister's apartment. Swain was explaining that Zahra's condition had deteriorated suddenly. Her infection from the burns had flared up and she was too frail to fight it. This was all they knew. Marla was trying to find out more. He would let me know.

"I was buying stupid jewelry," I said. "Zahra was dying, and that was all I could think of."

Ten

LOST IN THE MAELSTROM

The years that followed that dreadful day were filled with sadness, not only for Zahra's few surviving relatives but for thousands of families who suffered similar losses in wave after wave of sectarian violence that engulfed Baghdad.

I lost count of the widows who poured out their grief to me for husbands snatched from the street and bound, gagged, shot, and dumped for no other reason than their families' religion. However hard I tried, I could not shrug off their suffering when the interviews were over: I suffered with them. It was harder still to sit with the husbands of murdered women, striving to write down their stories in a dispassionate, professional way while my mind raced and my imagination ran wild with images of the victims' dying moments. Hardest of all was to hear mothers and fathers sobbing for children who had been caught in cross fire or car bombings and whose lives, like Zahra's, had been stolen and wasted.

No matter how many of these stories I heard, I felt them in my heart for days, weeks, or months afterward. I sensed an obligation to remember every one of them, for Zahra—and for myself.

Yet it was not only the victims but also the perpetrators of violence that I came to know. I introduced myself to the militias fighting the insurgency and allowed them to draw me into a netherworld as far away from the paradise I had planned for Zahra, Hawra, Steve, and myself as it was possible to imagine. I befriended insurgents, sitting with them in the dead of night to glean insights into their killing. I even cooked for a small army of insurgents preparing to defend their city from the overwhelming firepower of the U.S. Marines.

I was drawn to Iraq's men of violence in part because they gave me what journalists call "scoops" that were beyond the reach of my Western competitors. But I also needed to see inside their minds to understand the war. The shooting and bombing were destroying so many families like Zahra's who were not interested in fighting the Americans, but were simply trying to survive. Everyone knew the Americans' motives through their public statements and private briefings. Few in the West understood the religious zeal, patriotic ardor, and sheer bloodlust that drove the militias to confront the occupiers, let alone slay one another. I felt it was my duty to shine a light into the dark corners of embattled streets and offer a little illumination.

The fighters, in turn, were drawn to me, partly because I gave them a voice in the propaganda war and partly because they assumed that, as a Muslim, I was on the side of those resisting the occupation. My job required me to remain open-minded and objective in my reporting. Yet having narrowly avoided being blown up by an American tank, having been threatened by American soldiers, and having seen the burns inflicted on Zahra by an American missile, I admit that there were moments of weakness when my neutrality may have wavered.

The militias detected this in me. Some of the commanders regarded me as an ally. They trusted me to an absurd degree and expected the same trust in return. One, close to Al-Qaeda, came to me with the proposition that I allow Steve and myself to be kidnapped, saying we would all benefit from the publicity. I politely declined.

It was not easy for a woman to invade the overwhelmingly male terrain of the insurgents. To do this required a certain machismo on my part. As I developed a facility for making small talk with the big guns of the insurgency and learned to tell an M16 rifle apart from an M18, my desire to be a mother, which had burned with a new intensity in the days before Zahra's death, began to flicker and fade. Looking back, I can see that I coped with my grief by working myself into the ground in a barren underworld devoid of reminders that, had things turned out differently, I might have been bringing up two small daughters in London. That dream had been buried with Zahra.

THE DAY I LEARNED of Zahra's death was the bleakest of my life. I wept for her, thinking of the family ripped from her, the agonies she had endured, and the efforts of so many people to save her, which had all turned out to be in vain. I sobbed for her grandmother, who had already lost so much and now had to face another jarring shock: the realization that of her son's seven children, only Hawra was left. And I shed bitter tears of self-recrimination. I had made a big promise. How could I have been so stupid as to tell that poor woman that Zahra would live, when I had known there was a fifty-percent chance she would die? How could I have left the country for rest and recreation when Zahra was in the throes of a mortal struggle with septicemia? Would it have made the difference between life and death if I had gone to that field hospital, held her hand, and harried the doctors? I would never know. And I would take that doubt to my own grave.

Apart from Steve, the only other person I rang that day was Sean.

"Mrs. Matey!" he boomed, using his jovial nickname for me—something to do with my being, in his eyes, a particularly friendly soul. "What are you doing calling the office, Mrs. M.? You're supposed to be on holiday."

"Oh, Sean. Zahra's dead," I cried. "She's dead and it's all my fault."

His voice changed immediately.

"I'm so very sorry, Hala."

Through tears, I ranted about having tried to save her and raved about having killed her by leaving.

"You haven't killed her, Hala—you did everything you possibly could have done to help her," Sean said, doing his best to comfort me. "Zahra had you to fight for her, which is more than a lot of badly injured children have had. If you couldn't save her, she was beyond saving—we just didn't know it at the time. Look at it another way. Zahra's story has raised a fortune for our appeal. The money will help a lot of other children. Because of Zahra, they'll get a chance to live."

Inconsolable, all I could say was: "But Zahra is still dead, Sean."

That night, I sat alone in my room for hours, staring through my tears at the two rings I was wearing and berating myself for my extravagance earlier in the day. Children who had seen Zahra's story in the paper had sent their £1 pocket money to the appeal. Retirees with nothing to spare had mailed £5 with heartfelt apologies that it could not be more. I, who was supposed to care more than anyone, had just squandered a small fortune on shiny baubles to show off to well-heeled friends and family. I had never been so disgusted with myself.

So I made a vow. I would keep those rings on my finger as a constant reminder of my shame until I found the dignity to face Zahra's grandmother and the courage to tell her how cowardly I had been when I failed to give her Zahra's true prognosis. After I had begged Grandmother for forgiveness, I would try in some small way to redeem myself and give the rings to Hawra. The gold and diamonds would pass to her in memory of the precious sister she would never be able to treasure.

IT WAS SIX WEEKS before I returned to Iraq in the prickly, sweltering heat of summer. After a month of mourning, it seemed the only solace for me might lie in a return to work, and my editors gave me approval to track down some insurgents, with the aim of gaining information and insights that might come more easily to an Arab reporter than a Westerner. As Steve and I crossed the Iraqi border, however, my thoughts kept coming back to Zahra, Hawra, and Grandmother. Had things worked out differently, this might have been the journey on which Steve and I collected the girls. I might have been embracing the family life I had coveted since my own childhood. The prospect of going to their house to offer my condolences now filled me with nausea and dread. I preferred the idea of burying myself in my reporting of the war. The more dangerous the assignments, I told myself, the more distracted I would be from my pain and guilt.

The arrival of a new fixer to greet us at our hotel was a welcome distraction. Ali Rifat was a sharp-witted but soft-spoken young man who smiled and bowed slightly as he entered our hotel room and introduced himself. Steve and I took him down to the hotel dining room so that we could get to know one another, and as we ate, I caught sight of Marla moving between the tables. Such was her popularity that she was too engrossed in the greetings of other guests to notice me at first. Then she gave a squeal of delight and scampered over. We hugged long and hard. The last time we had been together, there had still been hope for Zahra.

Marla and I shared more in common than the fight for Zahra's life. We had both been weighed down by guilt over her death. Just as I could not forgive myself for abandoning Zahra to go home, so, too, Marla was burdened by a sense that she could have done more to save the child. Yet while I had been unable to drag myself out of bed in London, Marla had gone to Grandmother's tiny house, breaking the awful news and sitting with her as the old woman howled in horrified disbelief. She had attended the family's mourning ceremony and feast for relatives, friends, and neighbors on the seventh day after death and its Arba'een, a similar function to mark the end of the forty days' mourning traditional in the Islamic world. Marla had offered Zahra's grandmother and two uncles my sympathies in the war-torn west of Baghdad while I merely cried into my pillow in London.

I had also encouraged Marla to extract more information from the American field hospital about Zahra's death, to help the family bring back her body, and to make sure our little girl could be buried with her parents. Marla had battled away on all these fronts while waging a simultaneous war on the Coalition Provisional Authority, which was running the country. She was determined to secure compensation for every widow and wounded child in her casebook. Her superhuman efforts humbled me, yet she punished herself every day with the thought that she was useless if help did not materialize immediately.

"It's great to see you," she said finally, searching my eyes for some clue as to how I was feeling.

"It's good to be back," I reassured her.

As she sat down at our table and shot Ali a radiant California smile, a waiter asked if she would be eating her usual vegetarian dish.

It had already been prepared: a plateful of raw carrots and peppers, chopped into sticks and stacked in neat piles interspersed with heaps of cucumber, lettuce, and tomatoes. Between mouthfuls, she helped herself to my chips and Ali's rice.

"Grandmother would really like to see you," she said eventually. I looked at her and she read my thoughts.

"She doesn't hold you responsible, Hala," she said. "I go to them when I can, but I know it's you she really wants to see. She's constantly asking about you. Go visit them, dude! I know you'll feel better afterward."

"I've got a few things to do," I told her. "Then I'll go and see them." Marla smiled again.

When I thought about it later that evening, however, I realized that it was not that simple. I knew I should go, of course. For one thing, religion and custom obliged me to pay my respects in person. For another, I owed Grandmother not only an apology but an explanation for having misled her about Zahra's chances of pulling through. I had allowed hope to blind me to reason, with the result that a woman already suffering the strain of unimaginable loss had been unprepared for the shock of her granddaughter's death.

And yet, as I pictured myself arriving at the house, I felt a panic rising inside me. I realized that I was afraid of seeing the grief I had compounded with my foolishness and the reproach I was certain to detect in Grandmother's eyes. More than this, I was terrified of seeing the infant Hawra. The thought of holding her made my hands clammy with cold sweat. I had idiotically allowed myself to believe that I would raise this baby as my own, but it was too late for that now. Having let one granddaughter die, I could not ask the old woman for the other. All that was left to them now was each other.

I was still lamenting my own rash judgment in having permitted myself the renewed hope of a child to care for, educate, and send out into the world. But the heartbreak I felt at losing this dream for the final time was nothing compared to the losses Grandmother and Hawra had suffered, and I was embarrassed that I could not be stronger. I had thought I had come to terms with all this when I stopped trying for my own baby. But now that my last chance of motherhood had gone, I found it so hard to imagine cradling Hawra again and kissing her soft scalp, knowing that she could not be mine. I realized that it might not be possible for me to go to the family on this trip after all. Staying away would be rude, unkind, and unspeakably selfish. But my fragility scared me. I sensed that to hold myself together, I might have to keep myself apart from Hawra for a while.

I was so ashamed of my feebleness that when Marla turned up a day or two later with some photographs of Hawra, I could not bring myself to explain how I felt. I cooed, smiled, and promised to see Hawra soon. When Marla had gone, I cried for a long time, then turned my thoughts to the work of the week. I had coped before by losing myself in reporting. I would do so again.

OVER THE FOLLOWING MONTHS I concentrated on writing about the stupefying disintegration of the country's security and its impact on ordinary families. I put myself in harm's way to meet some of the killers, and found that the domains of execution squads and snipers represented safe territory for me because they made no emotional demands. Strange though it seems now, it was easier to confront the insurgents than to comfort Zahra's grandmother. I avoided her while I studied them. It was during my first encounter with the insurgents in the calm of a date grove under the stars that I saw the early signs of the almighty storm that would follow. The masked men of Iraq's Islamic Jihad had different motives but were united in their hatred of the occupation. They staged a discreet show of guerrilla firepower.

They described how they had ambushed an American convoy. They spoke of their determination to protect their nation's oil.

As Steve finished taking his pictures of the insurgents and we said our good-byes, I did not know how long this motley crew would last in the face of sophisticated American weaponry, but I was certain that if men who loved Saddam were fighting side by side with those who hated him, they would not be quelled as quickly as the Americans believed. This was going to be a long war. I was going to need all the strength I could muster to cover it. I could not afford to show weakness in front of groups such as this. I would have to impress them with courage if they were to become my sources for stories that would set me apart from my Western colleagues.

Between clandestine meetings with the men fighting this war, I remained preoccupied with the women and children who became its most pitiful casualties. Every child's death reminded me of Zahra, and the fear that gradually paralyzed family life in Iraq made me wonder how Hawra's household was faring.

No street seemed untouched by tragedy. A sixteen-year-old boy was blown up by a car bomb as he opened a kiosk outside my hotel one morning. A few days later, I found his mother with her six younger children in an apartment block nearby.

"I wake up at three a.m. and sob my heart out remembering him," she cried. She had taken two daughters out of school because she was terrified of losing them as well. "If they were kidnapped, where would we get ransom money from, and if they were killed in an explosion, what would we do?"

On the floor below, I was introduced to her sister-in-law, who was living in a state of ceaseless anxiety. Her husband, a taxi driver, took their two boys, aged six and nine, to school every morning, and she dreaded the thought that they might not come home for lunch.

"Every time I hear a gun or an explosion, I put on my abaya and run out to the street, expecting bad news," she said. "I worry about my husband and cry. What if he's caught? What if he's blown to pieces? Every night when he returns home safely I kiss his hands with joy."

The adults' terror was transmitted to their children. One father told me his boys slept on his wife's lap every night because they were too afraid to go to their beds. A mother said her sons had glimpsed an execution on someone's cell phone and asked: "What does it mean to behead someone? Can humans be beheaded like sheep?"

Not the least of people's worries was money. There was little work to be had, but hunkering down at home was hard with power cuts for up to twenty hours a day, and many couples could barely afford to feed their children, let alone fuel a generator for air-conditioning. On summer nights, they sprayed the rooftops to repel mosquitoes and cockroaches and laid their little ones there when it was too hot to sleep inside.

The longer the fighting lasted, the more children were kept indoors. A day in the park was a thing of the past and outings to restaurants, friends, and even relatives stopped. I saw panic in the eyes of Ali, my fixer, if his wife did not immediately answer her phone. He invariably imagined the worst.

"It's continuous, twenty-four-hour stress," he said simply. "I'm constantly afraid of car bombs, kidnappings, and sectarian killings. Each day I leave the house, it feels like the last time I'll see my family."

Ali compensated his two young boys for their confinement with sackloads of toys, video games, and DVDs. I asked whether he ever worried about spoiling them.

"But Hala," he said. "They have nothing else, poor things. We need to make up for the way they're having to live."

What of all those families who could not afford such luxuries? I wondered. What of Grandmother and Hawra? I tried to visualize the drudgery of their routine in the little concrete house and felt the tears prick my eyes. I could have spared her all this had fate not decreed otherwise, I thought. Yet as things stood, I could not even bring myself to see her. I was afraid that if I went to visit, I would fall to pieces. Whenever I brooded about Hawra, I convinced myself that all I needed was a little more time to recover from the shock of Zahra's death; that I might be less brittle the following week or perhaps the following month; or that it might be on the next trip that I would finally be strong enough to go and visit.

Eventually, as the violence intensified and the risks of driving to her district increased, the promise of being reunited with Hawra seemed more distant. Everything was changing, for Iraq and for me. I was obliged to affect a certain swagger in the face of the perils around me. I realized that my outlook would have to harden and some of my sensitivity would have to melt away. I had to push Hawra to the back of my mind, I told myself. I would have to work like a man to stop thinking like a woman.

Eleven

SUPPING WITH THE DEVIL

If Marla disapproved of me for coldly keeping my distance from the family, she was too warmhearted to show it. That is not to say that she approved of all my comings and goings. Marla understood the risks of operating in Iraq and knew what could happen when somebody's luck ran out. So as I gambled my life and Steve's on increasingly daring forays into territory any sensible woman would have shied away from, Marla became more and more concerned for our safety.

"Think about what you're doing, dude," she would say. "Got to be easier ways of making a living!"

She also understood that my work was not primarily about making a living, any more than hers was. Since Zahra's death, I had been seized with a sense of mission, a duty to bear witness to the havoc wreaked by war on the lives of innocents. I believed that the perpetrators of atrocities on all sides would thrive in the shadows and that some indefinable good would come of highlighting what they were up to.

Marla was on a more practical crusade to find money and aid for sufferers, pure and simple. She thought that when I wrote about victims, it helped her to procure compensation. So if I was heading out to the scene of a siege, an outbreak of sectarian fighting, or a strike by a stray missile, she invariably had her own briefing for me.

"Find out about the state of the women," she said again and again. "The victims, Hala—they're important. Get me names if possible." And I would do my best to add to the caseload of deserving women and children for whom Marla was seeking redress.

In April 2004, one year after Zahra had died, Ali and I drove to Fallujah, a stronghold of Sunni insurgents that was besieged by American forces. We slipped into the city with the help of insurgent contacts and soon found ourselves sharing a lunch of rice and stew with some fighters, no more than two hundred yards from American positions. They were talking about a twelve-year-old boy who had apparently shot an American sniper. I asked to be taken to him.

That night, two guides led us to a narrow alleyway where we parked Ali's navy blue Buick and knocked on the door of an ordinary little house in a nondescript row. Sitting on a mattress in the living room with one of his comrades was the most extraordinary child I have ever met. It was easy to see why he was the talk of the town. He spoke in a piping treble but talked like a man about love and loss, pride and patriotism, destruction and death. His name was Saad and he was scarcely four feet tall.

When he peeled off the checked scarf that covered his face, I saw that although his cheeks were still smooth and his smile childlike, he already had the makings of an attractive teenager, with wide brown eyes, a firm jawline, and strong white teeth.

Boys grow up fast among the tough tribes of the Sunni Triangle of cities to the west of Baghdad. Saad explained that his thirteen-year-old brother had already been married with a child when he died, fighting to defend Fallujah from the Americans. Saad himself had been superficially wounded by a bullet to the leg on the first day of the battle, he said with a shrug.

When my preliminary questions were punctuated by explosions in the distance, followed by one nearby, Saad showed no sign of nerves. His angelic appearance contrasted oddly with the diabolical tale he went on to tell.

The story began when he returned to the fray several days after his injury. That afternoon, a group of his fellow fighters was pinned down by an American sniper in the north of the city. Hiding his AK-47 automatic rifle behind his back, he defied orders to keep away and walked toward the building from which the sniper was shooting.

"I knew the soldier would think I was only a child and wouldn't fire at me," he said.

He was right. As he approached the American position, the sniper turned away. The boy promptly knelt in the road, lifted his rifle, and took aim.

"I kept on firing until I saw smoke coming out of his body," said Saad.

I wondered how he had felt about taking a life at his tender age, and would have asked him had a series of blasts not rocked the alleyway and forced us to flee. When Ali and I finally escaped to his beloved Buick, we found that it had been destroyed by helicopter fire.

I NEVER TOLD MY PARENTS what I was doing in Iraq. They were only too aware that I was reporting the news along with hundreds of other journalists. But they were oblivious to the unconventional methods I used to gain insights into the insurgency. For instance, I would never have dreamed of mentioning to Mama or Baba that I had driven to a remote farmhouse at dawn without any security to interview a highly educated, multilingual geek who had filmed an Italian hostage being executed with a shot to the head beside a shallow grave.

Although my mother would have preferred me to be changing her friends' lives as a cosmetic surgeon, a corporate lawyer, or at least a tax accountant, she took a certain pride in the recognition I was beginning to receive. My father just worried and could not stop himself from telephoning the foreign desk of *The Sunday Times* for news of me.

"Good morning, my dear," he would say to Sean in his overfamiliar English. "I haven't heard from Hala. Is she well?"

One day when he was recovering from a cataract operation, he asked my mother to bring a copy of *The Sunday Times* with her to the hospital. He had thought I was in Baghdad, so he was alarmed to see my picture byline staring back at him from the page beside the dateline of Najaf, the holy city, where American forces had surrounded the rebellious troops of the Shi'ite Mahdi Army. Imagine his horror if he had known that I had crossed from American to Mahdi army lines by walking slowly toward them in a bulletproof helmet and a black chador over my twenty-two-pound flak jacket, my arms in the air and my mouth dry from a combination of 50-degree-Celsius heat and pure terror.

Another thing I kept from the family was my sense that the harder the assignments became, the easier I was finding it to live with myself. It was not just that the danger saved me from introspection; in highlighting the horrors of the war, I was also paying homage to the little victim who had been closest to my heart. It was as if covering the conflict gradually absolved me of the guilt I felt for letting Zahra die.

The trouble was that as I put myself in more and more frightening situations, my courage began to desert me. The illusion that I would be safe in Iraq as an Arab, a Muslim, and a woman was diminished by the deaths of others like me, including journalists, as the bombings and beheadings intensified.

In some nightmares, I would find myself frantically trying to escape from kidnappers who could run faster than me. In others, I would be kneeling with my hands bound, staring at the lens of a video camera in which I could see the reflection of a masked man coming up behind me with a long, curved knife. I had watched too many videos of hostages' heads being jerked up by the hair so that their throats could be cut with the sawing motion that precedes decapitation. I had heard too many screams and the high-pitched wheezing of too many dying men trying to suck in a last breath through a severed windpipe. Would they do such things to women? I asked myself. Frankly, yes. These butchers were capable of anything.

Yet I could not allow my fear to control me. If I did, I would be powerless to fulfill my obligations—not just to my newspaper, but to the people in my articles. The increase in violence had reduced the number of reporters willing to cover it. There were fewer and fewer of us to give the victims a voice. I believed it was vital to keep writing about the Zahras of the war, because otherwise they would become mere statistics. As Marla always said, "Each number is a story of someone whose hopes, dreams, and potential will never be realized, and who left behind a family."

RATHER THAN TAKE A BREAK FROM IRAQ, I not only pressed on with my work, but proposed the most daunting and dangerous assignment of my life. Fallujah had become a bastion of Al-Qaeda. Foreign fighters were pouring in from all over the Middle East and from Muslim countries beyond. They were killing American soldiers, European hostages, and any Iraqis who stood up to the fundamentalist regime they wanted to impose. Everyone knew that coalition forces were going to have to storm the place. The Americans even had a code name for it. This was to be Operation Phantom Fury.

Western journalists bravely volunteered to be embedded with U.S. forces on this most fearsome of offensives. But I wanted to cover the story differently, so I asked to embed with the insurgents instead.

I believed that this would allow me to report on the ordinary inhabitants of Fallujah, not just the fighters but the residents who were intent on protecting their property or were simply too old or ill to move. These were my own people, I reasoned. They shared my origins and my faith. Leaving them to their fate would be tantamount to abandoning them.

Naturally, I did not put it in these terms to the office. I argued that reporting from a city with no other media would provide a scoop and that I would be as well guarded as I had been the last time Fallujah was under attack.

"But the Americans weren't about to pulverize it then," said Sean, "and this is where all the head-choppers are now."

"They won't be interested in me," I countered with more confidence than I felt. "They wouldn't touch a woman. Anyway, even if they wanted to, my friends wouldn't let them."

The argument went to and fro, and in the end it was left up to the editor, who took the view that I should be allowed to make my own judgment on the ground.

ALI AND I HAD ARRANGED to bed down in a mosque that had been turned into a clinic, but at the last minute were diverted to stay with some men who, I was told euphemistically, had "remained in the city to look after their homes." It was Ramadan and the condition of our lodging there was that I would cook every evening so that the men could break fast. I was putting my life at risk to do the most professional job I could, and my hosts still thought my place was in the kitchen.

"Okay," I said, smiling as if I had been granted a privilege.

We were briefed on the move. Three hundred foreign fighters had volunteered for suicide bombings against the American invaders, we were told. Some would be used in 118 vehicles that had already been rigged with explosives. Others would be waiting in booby-trapped homes. Bridges, a railway line, and several narrow alleys had been mined.

It was impossible to know how much of this was true, but I saw thick black cables running across roads in the city center, indicating the sites of "improvised explosive devices"—homemade bombs intended for American convoys.

By the time we arrived at the house where we were staying, only one hour remained before the men would break fast. A swift inspection of the kitchen confirmed my worst fears. It was filthy. The twisted pots and pans were smothered in a thick layer of old grease. Most of the rings on the cooker did not work. I found salt but no herbs or spices. This was the ultimate kitchen nightmare.

While the men went in search of ingredients for the feast they had somehow been led to expect, I sat outside on a discarded mattress, smoking a cigarette and thinking.

The men reappeared, looking pleased with themselves. They dumped some bags on the kitchen floor, hooked up a single cooking ring to a bottle of gas, and left Ali and me to our work. But when Ali pulled ten pounds of "meat" from the bags, I saw to my horror that all he held in his hands was fat, which wobbled like Jell-O when he set it down. I could not even bear to touch it.

"Okay, Hala, I'll cut this into chunks while you prepare the rest," Ali said brightly. "Deal?"

"Thanks, *habibi*. But Ali, I'm not used to working in a full abaya and scarf. Do you think they'd mind if I took it off while we're standing in this suffocating kitchen?"

He went to warn them so that nobody would come into the kitchen and be offended by the sight of my hair. I mixed rice with fried onions, finely chopped eggplant, and tomato paste, and left it to simmer in a large pot. Then I fried the fatty mutton that Ali had hacked into lumps, adding sliced potatoes, black pepper, and turmeric borrowed from a neighboring house. Fifteen cucumbers and tomatoes were scrubbed and chopped into a salad bowl, with only vinegar and salt for dressing. I finished the job by the feeble light of an oil lamp after the electricity failed, and I have to say the meal looked better in the dark. From the men's reaction, however, you would have thought they were in a Michelin-starred restaurant, savoring the subtleties of a meal prepared by Gordon Ramsay himself.

It was not long after the meal that the first bomb fell. The men were amused to see how the shock of it jolted me in my chair. Then came another and another, and soon I was as accustomed to the sound as they were. I counted thirty-eight bombs in the first half hour. The Americans were softening up their targets from the air for the imminent ground assault.

The after-dinner entertainment was not entirely to my taste. When the power came back on, the men watched videos of "resistance actions," starting with footage of a Mahdi Army fighter aiming a rocket-propelled grenade at an American position. As he crouched on the ground, a bullet from an American sniper hit him in the leg. He paused, then aimed again. This time a bullet struck his head and he slumped to the ground.

"This Shi'ite is an amateur," said my Sunni host. "Our fighters are professionals. The Americans will soon learn their lesson."

To prove his point, he insisted I watch clips of Al-Qaeda suicide bombers ramming their cars into American convoys in bursts of orange flame.

In the early hours of the morning, I checked my e-mails. There was one from Steve, who had stayed behind in England at my insistence, because Iraq had become too treacherous a place for a blond, blue-eyed British photographer.

Hi Habibi,

I do love you so much!

You are the strongest person I know. You have every right to be worried but don't forget you have your own strength and you also have mine. Take whatever you need.

He attached a poem from one of my favorite Lebanese writers, Kahlil Gibran, describing a union of two devoted but independently minded lovers.

It took just a few seconds for the high drama of my Fallujah escapade to descend into farce. As the men explained how the leading lights of the Sunni insurgency were preparing to martyr themselves, I suddenly found myself distracted. From the way I continued nodding solemnly at their evocations of heroic sacrifice, they would never have guessed that my period was starting. Such was the religious conservatism of these young men that they would not have been able to comprehend my horror at the realization that in all my meticulous planning for the assignment, the one eventuality I had failed to prepare for was this. In short, I was stuck with nothing more than wet wipes in a city that viewed tampons as sinful. All I could think as I searched for a solution was that it was a good thing I was wearing jeans under my abaya.

No matter how hard I tried to be macho about my time of the month, I concluded as I tossed and turned on a lice-ridden cushion during the night that I was not man enough for this job. The next morning, when Ali suggested he return to Baghdad to buy a generator that might sustain us through the offensive, I snatched at the opportunity to accompany him.

He did not understand why at first. For weeks, I had demanded to be taken to Fallujah. Now, having reached the heart of the city against all odds, I was suddenly intent on leaving. Not until we were on the road to Baghdad did I blurt out the truth.

"Thank God you didn't ask them to get you anything, Hala," he said, reminding me that tampons are prohibited by fundamentalists. Then we imagined Al-Qaeda hearing about a crazy foreign woman looking for tampons in the middle of Fallujah, and dissolved into giggles.

I telephoned Sean to say we had left Fallujah to fetch a generator, and although I could tell he did not believe my explanation, I had no intention of enlightening him. By the time I was equipped with everything a modern woman needs, Fallujah was sealed off and its destruction had begun. I was reduced to covering it, like every other journalist, from a vantage point miles from the action. It seemed a depressing way to end the saga. I had been unable to help Zahra, and now I could not even see my own assignment through.

Only in hindsight did Ali and I learn how lucky we had been to leave Fallujah when we did. Much of the city was destroyed in the blitz that followed, and the insurgent who had arranged our stay told me he had been forced to run from one hiding place to the next with no food or water for days.

"You would never have survived it," he said. Some of those we had stayed with had been injured, and others had been killed.

So in the end I was grateful for my departure. If I had learned anything in Fallujah, it was that I could not escape being a woman. It would soon be time to start thinking about what I could do for Hawra.

Twelve

ANGEL IN HEAVEN

It was my great misfortune—and, I believe, Hawra's—that by the time I felt strong enough to go to her, events conspired to bar my way. Each new development increased my desire to seek her out, but each made it more difficult to find her.

No single factor persuaded me that I was ready to see Hawra again. The shock of Zahra's death had subsided after two years; a certain amount of praise for my work had made me feel better about what I was doing and who I was; and a glorious long lunch with neglected friends had reminded me that we should hold special people close during difficult moments in our lives, not turn away from them.

I returned to Baghdad in the early part of 2005 acutely aware that I had missed Hawra's second birthday, just as I had her first. I thought of all the changes she had undergone since I had last seen her, at three months, and it hurt to know that they had eluded me. I imagined that she would have sat up at six months and crawled a few weeks later. At eight months old she would have been introduced to solids in the form of vegetable soup. At ten months, I could see her begin to dip her fingers into hummus, stews, and rice. She would also have relished *tashreebs*, bread soaked in stew sauce with rice on the side.

Then, at one year old, when she had started walking and talking in quick succession, she would have progressed to *marak* dishes—stews of chopped meat with eggplant in tomato and garlic sauces—and even started tasting stuffed vine leaves, dolmas. It was doubtful, however, whether her grandmother could have afforded the kebabs for which Iraq is renowned in the Arab world. How I would have loved to prepare these for her.

Yet the sectarian fighting in Baghdad had become so ferocious that even Marla, who took more risks than most Westerners by driving around in a car with no armor and no guard, had ceased to visit the family. Entire districts were disappearing from view because it was no longer safe to drive into them. Shi'ite death squads stalked the streets, and marketplaces shuddered from the impact of Sunni car bombs. I filed my reports from a city paralyzed by terror, constantly thinking of Hawra and wondering how her grandmother would protect her. Gradually, my anxiety about seeing them—and the effect this might have on me—diminished. All I wanted was for the danger to pass so that I could help them. But I knew there was no way of reaching the family in a suburb teeming with militias and strewn with the corpses of unwelcome visitors.

What could I do but wait for this maelstrom of violence to pass? Only when the massacres dwindled and the explosions eased would I be able to make my peace with Grandmother.

In the meantime, Marla pursued her compensation claims as vigorously as the checkpoints, road closures, and curfews allowed and did not hesitate to put herself in danger if it helped her gather the evidence she needed. She eagerly traveled between injured children and the military she blamed for their wounds, even though her routes took her along roads notorious for bombings, sniper fire, and abductions.

Like all Marla's friends, I worried about her willingness to take risks, but I admired her courage, too. She returned the compliment with warm words about my determination to report from some of the most hazardous of the many trouble spots around us.

"Hala," she wrote in a scribbled note she left in my pigeonhole at the hotel. "You are a woman I want to be. Amazing. Thanks for all you do and being the coolest person around, Dude."

I might just as easily have written the same to her.

AND THEN, EARLY ONE MORNING in April 2005, the phone rang at my bedside at home in London, where I was resting between stints in Baghdad. It was Jon Swain. I knew immediately from his soft, sad voice, echoing the call he had made to me about Zahra's death two years earlier, that once again, somebody we both cared deeply about had died.

"I have terrible news, Hala," he said as I sat bolt upright. "Marla is dead. She was killed yesterday."

He was almost choking on the words. "It's just too awful, Hala, too terrible. She died in a car bomb."

I searched for something to say but could not find my voice. My tears were flowing very fast. My heart was beating hard but my breathing had stopped. There was silence on the other end of the line, as if breaking the news had exhausted Swain.

"I can't talk, Jon," I whispered eventually. "Oh God . . . I'll call you later."

Where was Steve? I had to find him. I walked slowly down one flight of stairs after another, following the sound of voices to our kitchen in the basement. Images of Marla standing over Zahra's cot, hugging Grandmother, playing with Hawra, flashed in front of my eyes. I was dazed and disorientated.

I saw Steve's mother, who had come to stay, mouthing "Morning," but I did not hear her.

"You're up early. Coffee?" Steve asked. I did not answer. I walked straight up to him, rested my forehead on his chest, and started to cry. I could not bring myself to say the words.

"Hala," Steve said urgently. "What's the matter? Talk to me. Is it your parents? Say something."

"Marla's dead. Oh God, Steve, Marla's dead," I wailed, slumping to the floor and shaking uncontrollably.

Steve sat on the tiles beside me, talking gently. "Tell me, Hala. Speak to me. What happened?"

"Please, please," I begged. "Go call Jon. Find out more. I couldn't talk to him."

Steve hugged me, rocking me back and forth to soothe me and kissing my hair, but he was too stunned to speak. All I could say between my sobs was: "Oh God, why?"

IN KEEPING WITH HER LIFE'S WORK to aid the helpless victims of war, Marla had spent her last morning with the family of an injured child. She had died on her way to an American base to ask for compensation.

The route took her onto Baghdad's airport road, perhaps the most dangerous stretch of highway in the country. Unlike the Western contractors who paid $5,000 for armored vehicles and security guards to take them along it, Marla was in an ordinary, battered, soft-skinned car. Traveling as ever on the cheap, her only protection was the black abaya she was wearing to disguise herself.

Using the same procedure I had seen in the videos in Fallujah, a suicide bomber rammed his vehicle into a convoy that happened to be traveling in front of Marla. It ignited a fireball and Marla's car was engulfed. American soldiers pulled her from the wreckage, but ninety percent of her body was burned. She regained consciousness just long enough to say, "I'm alive," then died of shock. She was twenty-eight, or as she had liked to put it in her characteristically ebullient way, "twenty-great."

Marla had achieved so much in her short life. After Zahra's death, she had returned to America to lobby lawmakers and cajole donors. She inspired Congress to appropriate $17.5 million for civilian casualties in Iraq and Afghanistan, and persuaded the George Soros Open Society Institute to fund her fieldwork.

Then, even though she was physically and mentally exhausted and had seen more death and sorrow in her twenties than most of us ever will, she had returned to Iraq and stayed. As my colleague Catherine Philp of *The Times* put it, "Her holiday in Thailand could wait; the little boy with his leg blown off could not."

Catherine, who was one of Marla's closest friends, read a eulogy at her funeral in California. "She found something to love in the most unlikely of people, but the person she found hardest to love was herself," Catherine told the one thousand mourners. "Every morning she said to herself in the mirror, 'Today I will be a better Marla.' She didn't know she was better than all the rest of us already."

FOR DAYS, I COULD NOT STOP CRYING. I cried when I went to bed late at night and I was still crying when I woke up in the morning. I burst into tears in supermarkets, bookshops, and with family and friends. It was as if I had blocked all my emotions for two years and now the dam had burst. My tears poured forth in a flood of grief for

Marla and Zahra, fury that they had been killed so recklessly, and fear that I could be next.

My nightmares returned, more terrifying than ever. In one recurring dream, I was stuffed into a body bag and stacked with the luggage on a plane from Baghdad to Beirut, where my family was waiting, struck dumb by the news of my death. It was not so unreal a fantasy: on my last flight out of Iraq, my bag had rested against the coffin of a Canadian bomb disposal expert at the back of the aircraft.

Soon the night terrors were haunting my days as well. The vision of the body bag and the sound of the zip as I was enclosed in darkness clung to me despite my best efforts to shrug it off.

It took a certain courage to confess my cowardice to the office. "I can't go back there now," I sobbed to Sean. "I can't face it. Maybe in a little while."

"Take your time," he said. I took no comfort from his support. Instead, I was tortured by self-recrimination. I had a job to do in Iraq. It mattered. Shutting myself up in my house in London meant letting down people in Baghdad, not least Grandmother and Hawra. What right had I to shy away from the dangers they confronted every day?

Ali, my fixer, evidently thought I was losing my mind, and perhaps he was right. We talked for hours on Skype. He reminded me of the Islamic faith we shared. He told me how strong I was. He tried to inspire me with plans for great work we would do together when I returned. All I could think was that I lacked the faith, the strength, and the drive to cope.

I read and reread Marla's simple note, over and over again, searching for some deeper meaning. She had said she wanted to be the woman I was. I knew she would not have thought much of the mouse

I had become. But how was I going to regain the nerve and spirit she had loved in me?

I called up an e-mail I had sent her when I heard she was going back to Baghdad. "The situation there has really deteriorated compared to the old times," I had written. "Marla, please be very careful, no more risks." Yet of course she had run more risks. Her work gave her no choice and mine was the same.

"We are helping lots of kids with medical care," she had written to Swain just before she died. "This place continues to break my heart—need to get out of here—but hard!"

MY BREAK FROM BAGHDAD gave me more time to spend with Lara, my niece, in London. My sister, Rana, had sent her from Cairo to an English boarding school and she was desperately missing home. I became her substitute mother.

I brought her to stay with us on weekends and we shopped, cooked, and watched movies together. We talked about everything from her applications to British universities to my work in the Middle East. Picking her up from the station became the highlight of my week, and the low point was taking her back. So close did we become that I started speaking to her on the phone every weekday as well.

Lara's dislike of being separated from her family reminded me of how much I had detested it as a child. When she came home to us, she would hug me and say: "Lollie, you smell like Mami." It reminded me of how Rana would come to me when we were young boarders, how she would sit on my lap and tell me: "You smell like Mama, Hala. I miss her so much."

Lara's presence in our lives and the love I felt for her eased my pain to a degree I had never imagined possible. The bond between us seemed so strong that it was almost as if she were my own. She made me think more and more about Hawra.

Would it be possible to feel this close to Hawra one day? I started to believe I could love Hawra even if she were not living in my house. I needed to show her how I felt in person and give her some practical help, rather than pointlessly fret about it all thousands of miles away.

It took six months, but in the end I realized that it was as hard for me to stay away from Iraq as it would be to return. Marla had discovered that for every victim she found in need of compensation, there were dozens more who were desperate for help. That had kept her going. For every victim whose story I told to highlight the horrors of the war, there were dozens whose suffering had yet to be illuminated. That, I decided, should be enough to keep me going, too.

EVERYONE HAS A FAVORITE AIRLINE. Mine was the Flying Carpet, operating between Beirut and Baghdad. How could anyone fail to enjoy the joke? For someone who had dreamed of being whisked away by a magic carpet as a child, it was perfect. But on this occasion the carpet would transport me to a nightmare. I dreaded every minute of the journey and every day in a city convulsed by violence that had claimed first "my" child, then my friend. Would I be able to face my fear?

The sole comfort was knowing that the eighteen-seater aircraft had a tall, dark, handsome pilot, one Captain Hussam Taweel. I sat on my bag and waited for him to appear, beaming at his passengers as he always did and hugging regulars like me.

"You still here, you crazy woman? Come on, follow me," he said.

On arrival in Baghdad, I bade him farewell at the bottom of the aircraft steps, saying: "Whatever happens, promise me you will keep on flying in, week in, week out, until you pick us up again. You dropped me here. You will make sure you take me out of here no matter what."

"I will come get you. Just promise me that you will take care and not do anything crazy," he said. "No more Fallujah madness, Hala."

Little did the good captain know that Fallujah loomed large in my plans. I wanted to find out whether I could reach Hawra, but first I had to report on how the so-called City of Mosques was faring a year after the offensive that had largely destroyed it. I was delayed by a slight hitch: an insurgent contact told me that one of the factions had heard I was coming and planned to kidnap me so that I could be sold to Al-Qaeda in Iraq for $50,000. Fortunately, we found another faction willing to guarantee our security and smuggle us through checkpoints in disguise. Steve, wearing full traditional Arab dress, ended up tottering madly about on a pair of platform slippers (the equivalent of high heels in the West) in a moment that strangely combined fear and humor.

Soon afterward we thought we had come under attack, only to learn that the shots were being fired in celebration of a 4–3 victory over Syria, which secured the Iraq soccer team a gold medal at the West Asian Games. It was a rare moment of release for a city where gunfire usually meant the return of a desperate cycle of rebellion, retaliation, and revenge.

Such was the violence in Baghdad, however, that there could be no question of tracing Hawra and her grandmother. At the city's main morgue, hundreds of bodies lay unclaimed, some with holes drilled in their faces, others dismembered by bombs.

A doctor's account of two children found strangled with a piece of green cloth showed me that anyone could be targeted. But I had no way of contacting Grandmother to make sure she and Hawra were safe. I did not even know which street she lived on because the address had been given to the driver who had taken us there and I could not find any sign of him.

After four difficult, dangerous, and frustrating months we were instructed to leave Iraq for Christmas. I found it hard to plan a holiday knowing that the insurgents were intent on inflicting ever greater suffering on those around them. It was tougher still to drive to the airport past the spot where Marla had died, because she had put her responsibilities to the Iraqi people before her desire to take a break.

Steve and I did not feel safe until we were inside the airport. It was only as we were waiting for our flight that I allowed a pleasant sense of anticipation to build inside me. It seemed an eternity before Captain Taweel appeared in the distance, and the excitement spread up and down my body. He strode purposefully toward us, beaming at the thought of transporting another eighteen passengers from the frenzied fighting of Baghdad to Beirut, which had embraced the pleasures of peaceful coexistence, at least for a while. I beamed back, knowing that the sanctuary of my family home was just a couple of hours away. We hugged.

"You still here, you crazy woman?" he said, as usual. "Come on, follow me, let's get you home."

Shortly after takeoff, Captain Taweel glanced at me over his shoulder from the cockpit and cried: "Hala, Fallujah below you." As I looked down from the sky on the dots that denoted the city's landmarks, it felt as if Fallujah existed in another dimension of space and time. Finally, the captain announced that we had left Iraqi airspace.

"No dancing in the aisle, Hala," he said. "My little plane could not take it." Then he invited us to share a cigarette with him and tell him about our latest adventures.

Once the high of being flown out of Baghdad in a passenger seat rather than a body bag had worn off, my mood sank fast. I always felt low at Christmas, but the thoughts of children I had failed to conceive overwhelmed me that year. I knew that if I spent the holiday in London, I would imagine Zahra and Hawra opening presents while Steve and I looked on lovingly. I could not bear it. The house would seem empty, no matter how many friends I invited for drinks.

Something else was gnawing at me, too. I was tired of living in a man's world, worn down by dealing with the hardest of the hard men, exhausted by incessant talk of driller killers and marketplace massacres. What I needed more than anything was a spell of unadulterated, unashamed frivolity with my old girlfriends in Beirut. I craved gossip, giggles, and a good hairdresser.

"I just can't do it this year, Stevie," I said. "I don't want another Christmas of pretense. I want to stay home with my family in Lebanon and be a girlie for a change. I just want to talk about manicures and pedicures, not politics."

Ever understanding, Steve flew on to London alone to indulge his family, while I indulged myself.

AT THE TURN OF THE YEAR, my thoughts were fixed on Hawra. It was January 2006, and she would be three years old. I imagined her playing with dolls, imitating her grandmother, asserting herself. But I also wondered whether she was cowed by the danger that loomed throughout the city. Did the sound of a gunshot make her jump? Did she run terrified to Grandmother if an explosion rocked the neighborhood? Marla had been my only link to the family, and I knew she would have wanted me to check on them now as she had done.

By the end of the holidays, I was hungry for news. But Hawra's family had no telephone I knew of. I could not just call them and say, "Happy New Year." Nor, if I discovered their address, could I take the risk of asking someone to go to Grandmother's house on my behalf: another surge of sectarian killing prompted *The Sunday Times*'s security advisers to warn us against any travel around Baghdad unless it was essential.

Steve and I returned in January anyway, only for me to break my foot and find myself grounded for months. It felt like a never-ending, infuriating cycle. I went back in June, determined to find Grandmother after completing my assignment for the paper, but this time I received a call that chilled me to the marrow.

It came from a trusted contact whose advice on how to keep safe had often been a source of reassurance. On this occasion, the urgency of his tone was as alarming as what he had to tell me: my name had been placed on a hit list.

"A decision has been taken to liquidate you and your colleagues," my informant said. "You are to be the second Atwar Bahjat."

Atwar had been a star of Iraqi television and a friend of mine until she became the first Arab female journalist to be kidnapped by the death squads. Since her murder four months earlier, I had thought about her every day.

"You have been named as a target—there is a specific danger," the voice said. "Do not go outside."

I could not help thinking of the Baghdad morgue I had just visited. More than six thousand corpses had passed through it since the start of the year, many of them horribly disfigured. We would have to act fast to stay alive. I felt angry, vulnerable, helpless, and frightened. In short, I knew what it was to be an Iraqi.

The difference, of course, was that I had a safety net that ordinary Iraqis lacked. Steve was already on the phone to our security team. Within an hour, ten former Royal Marines led by an ex–Special Boat Service officer arrived to move us to Baghdad's international Green Zone. The next day we were on the Flying Carpet, heading for Beirut, and our dreams of being reunited with Hawra and Grandmother had been abandoned for the unforeseeable future.

FOR OVER A YEAR I covered Iraq as well as I could by Skype and e-mail from London and Beirut. My best work, as ever, focused on children. One article related the anguish of a woman whose baby had died at birth because she could not make it to the hospital during a curfew. Another was the story of a young father who had kissed his three-year-old daughter good-bye, strapped an explosive belt to his waist, and blown himself up at an American checkpoint to avenge the accidental shooting of his wife by U.S. soldiers.

I will not pretend that it was easy to find these stories from afar. Nor did it give me any pleasure to write them when I was stuck on my own in the silence of my study, staring out at the rain drenching our garden in London and yearning for the blue skies and bustle of an Arab capital.

My restlessness intensified after telephone interviews with two women, one Shi'ite and one Sunni, whose husbands had been murdered for no reason other than their sect. One of the women had been preparing to welcome her husband home from an academic posting abroad to see their new baby for the first time. She told me he had been kidnapped and killed before he could reach her.

"The tale of these two women has left me pretty depressed," I told a dear journalist friend in an e-mail. "I felt so callous pushing them for details, though I shed a lot of tears for each one of them after each interview. I don't know if I can do this kind of stuff anymore. It's all too sad."

"Get a grip," my friend replied. "You are one of their hopes. If you don't tell their stories, who will? It's not that hard . . . I know you think of what they have and what we have so keep going. Think of them . . . x."

That was the problem. I thought of them all the time.

Somewhere, somehow, I seemed to have become a part of them and they a part of me. I could not hear of someone's bereavement and shrug my shoulders, as a hard-nosed hack should. I grieved for every person whose death I reported. After receiving another award for my reports from Iraq, I gave a little speech in front of some of the best writers and broadcasters in the country but could not muster much joie de vivre. They must have thought me a little crazy when I asked: "Is it right to benefit like this from other people's misery?"

I thought long and hard about my friend's e-mail as I agonized over what to do next. I did not know whether I brought hope to any of those I interviewed, as my friend had suggested, but I certainly gave them a voice that made their suffering impossible to ignore. And the more I thought about this, the more I realized that Zahra's story was reason enough to carry on working in Iraq. It had made waves, raised money, helped others. But it had been forgotten, even by the readers who had been so inspired by her torment and given money to our appeal to ease other children's pain. To me, Zahra represented the anguish of the past four years. Her sister Hawra, the sole survivor of the terrible air strike of April 4, 2003, stood for resilience and hope for the future. I had to return to Baghdad. I had to see Hawra.

MY DECISION COINCIDED with a lessening of the violence, although it was still at giddy levels. It was the end of 2007 and the American troop surge had restored a measure of order. Sunni militias outraged by Al-Qaeda's indiscriminate killing were driving the foreign fighters out of their strongholds. The Shi'ite Mahdi Army had largely ceased fire. Conditions in Baghdad were starting to improve. But how could I track down Grandmother when I had no address and Marla, our go-between, was dead?

I looked at Marla's last letter to me:

Faiz can help you find Haiwa (?)
Or if he is not back
call my other driver Shutait (?)
(I'll ask to leave a note)
Give love to Steve & Ali

XXX
Marla

PS I can't wait for Sunday
For you

Marla was guiding me. Her driver Faiz had died with her, but perhaps this "Shutait" could take me to Grandmother's house.

I e-mailed a close friend of Marla's who had run her organization after her death. She did not know Shutait but suggested I speak to another of Marla's friends, a magazine journalist in New York. The journalist in New York referred me to an Iraqi reporter who had since moved to London. She finally traced two numbers for a man whose name was not Shutait, but Shawkat. The first number was unobtainable. When I rang the second, Shawkat answered.

He knew where Grandmother lived. I begged him to go and see her, to hire a local driver who would be able to take him there safely.

Three days later, Shawkat called me.

"Hala, it was incredible," he said. "She didn't remember me at all, even though I have visited her several times, but the minute I mentioned your name her eyes lit up with recognition. But Hala, let me warn you. She said she was disappointed that you'd abandoned them and never asked about them. So prepare yourself for some recriminations."

Then he surprised me. When I had last seen Grandmother, there were no cell phones in the country, but she had one now. He gave me her number.

ONLY TWO OBSTACLES NOW STOOD between Hawra and me. The first was *The Sunday Times*. My foreign editor was worried that I might still be under threat. But when we consulted the security company that had removed us from Baghdad, it advised that since a year had passed, the hit men would have other targets by now. I could return for a short visit, I was told. If there was no trouble, I could go for longer next time.

The second obstacle, my niece, Lara, was a different proposition altogether. Now a student in London, Lara was living with us while she studied for her degree. When did Lara become an adult? Not so long ago, she had been asking me for "oudi," her baby word for milk, and I had cradled her in my lap while she sucked on her bottle and stared up at me with wide brown eyes. Now she still called me Lollie, as she always had, but she was in college, with opinions of her own—about the Palestinian cause and the plight of street children in Brazil, about democracy and saving the world. Not the least of her opinions was that I should not set foot in Iraq again.

Lara's presence in our home filled me with a joy I had never felt before. Even at twenty-one, she needed a lot of tender love and care. I learned how it felt to wait for her to return from lectures, when we would talk about her day, and from nights out, when I would stay up to make sure she was safe. I loved cooking her favorite Lebanese dishes, taking her out for treats, and providing a little extra cash when she needed it to buy that special dress.

It is possible that "mothering" Lara—and making a good job of it, if I may say so myself—relieved some of the guilt I felt at having failed Zahra. More than that, Lara's unconditional love showed me that I did not need to be her sole guardian to feel motherly toward her. I wondered if the same might apply to Hawra. Would I perhaps look on her one day as I did on Lara—with the same pride and love that any mother would feel for a daughter on the cusp of adulthood? I could not know for sure. What I did know was that my plan to return to Baghdad would make Lara deeply unhappy. Steve and I decided to tell her as we were preparing dinner. The smell of garlic and coriander filled the air as I cooked away on the mother of all stoves, my red Lacanche. Lara chopped sweet peppers, radishes, and tomatoes for her favorite salad dish, a Lebanese *fatoush*.

Steve looked on, bracing himself for an outpouring of emotion. While we would worry about leaving Lara behind to fend for herself, every day we spent in the danger zone would make her more desperately anxious. Such was her phobia of Iraq that she refused to utter the word, referring only to "that bad, horrid place." So when I broke the news, I spoke in a matter-of-fact tone but watched her face with the utmost apprehension.

"What if something was to happen to you?" she asked immediately, eyes brimming. "I don't want you to go there. Why can't someone else go?"

"Because it's my job," I explained patiently. "Because I'm needed there. Because my newspaper wants me to go."

I did not say what I was thinking: "Because it's time I faced my guilt."

Lara looked me in the eye.

"Lollie, you promise me you'll come back? You promise me nothing will happen to you there?"

I hesitated. Another big promise was being asked of me. Not only was I warier than ever of making promises, having broken mine to Hawra's grandmother, but I knew that no journalist bound for Iraq at that time could be certain of staying safe. Yet she needed to hear me promise, just as Grandmother had.

"Everything will be fine," I said, hoping she would not see any sign of the fluttering in my stomach, that she would not hear the pounding of my heart. I promised to come home safely. I promised to attend her graduation. I promised to come to her wedding.

"Of course I'll be back," I told her. "Our time together is far from over."

In the meantime, I reminded her, there were errands to be run in the house, the weekly cleaner to supervise, the mail to check for anything important, the doors to lock.

"Oh, and don't forget, no wild parties—and no boyfriend staying over. I'm very strict and traditional about that, and don't forget to study hard. . . ."

At last Lara was giggling, but the tears still glittered in her beautiful brown eyes.

Thirteen

"ARE YOU AFRAID OF DEATH, HALA?"

It was a warm May morning in Beirut when Steve and I boarded the Flying Carpet for the final stage of our journey. My spirits had risen with the sun that brightened the windows of my parents' apartment at dawn. The fragrance of gardenias and roses heightened my anticipation of the sweetness that lay in store. As my mother anxiously hugged and kissed me good-bye, I could not wait to greet my little girl with the same ardor and fold her in my arms. I wanted to stroke her hair, gaze into her eyes, and—at long last—fulfill the promise I had made to look after her when she was three months old.

In the taxi down to the airport, I trembled inwardly at the realization that by the time we drove back up this road I would have assumed an awesome responsibility. I had let Hawra down on every trip to Baghdad in the five years since I had last seen her. Once we were joined together, I would never be able to ignore her again. She would look to me for simple things in the short term—clothes, sweets, and the like—and perhaps eventually for help with her education. In the longer term, she would understand that an affluent woman in London could offer a girl from a poor part of Baghdad a great deal more: foreign travel, a perspective on the world, a passport to a brighter future. Such weighty expectations could never be taken lightly.

Everything was changing and the Flying Carpet was no exception. When Steve and I had flown from Beirut to Baghdad in the past, the aircraft had not been much bigger than an executive jet carrying its handful of dedicated diehards under Captain Taweel's personal protection. Now the captain had been replaced by an impersonal pilot and crew on a much larger plane filled with businessmen and shoppers heading home to austerity with booty from their raids on lavish markets and shopping malls. The talk among passengers was no longer about militias and murders, bombings and blast-proof vehicles, but about imports, exports, and the cuts and colors of the season. It could have been any commercial flight.

I closed my eyes, shut my mind to the banal chatter around me, and drifted away into my own special world.

When I thought about it, there was something different about me, too, that day. On so many previous journeys to Baghdad, I had been filled with mortal dread. This time, there was no racing of the heart, no knotting of intestines as I contemplated the weeks ahead. We had accepted a wealthy Baghdadi's offer of accommodation and security. We would be met by his guards at the airport and made comfortable in his private compound. The danger of kidnapping was lower these days. Our risk of coming to grief was remote. Instead, there would be the joy of embracing our family. I pictured the excitement that would light up Hawra's angel face as I helped her to unwrap the gifts I had brought with me from London.

But how would Grandmother react to me after so long? I wondered. Marla had always said how much Grandmother wanted to see me, but it had been difficult to speak to her on the phone.

IT HAD TAKEN ME a whole day to pluck up the courage to make that call a month before I flew to Baghdad. My hands were shaking like a frightened child's as I dialed Grandmother's number.

I began, hesitantly: *"Al-salam alaikum, Hajieh"*—Peace be upon you. "It's me, Hala."

"Wa alaikum al-salam"—And peace be upon you—she replied. "Hala, where are you?"

I explained that I was calling from London, that Shawkat had given me her number. "I was worried you'd forgotten me," I said.

"No, Hala, I haven't. But where have you been? What happened to you?" The tone was reproachful. I feared that recriminations would follow.

"Listen, Hajieh," I said to preempt them. "This is not the time to discuss all this. I'm calling to let you know that I'll be coming to Iraq soon and I'm hoping to visit you and see little Hawra. . . ."

There was a moment's silence on the line.

"How is she? Will you accept my visit?"

"Hawra is fine, grown up, nearly six now. She'll be going to school this autumn," Grandmother said. "But Hawra is all alone, Hala. Things are hard. I was expecting you to help her over the years and you disappeared."

I could hardly bear it.

"I know I did, Hajieh, and for that I'm truly sorry, but I'll explain it all to you if you let me visit."

I tried to lighten the mood.

"Will you offer me an *istikana* of tea, Iraqi style?"

She softened.

"Oh, Hala," she sighed. "You will be welcomed and we will be honored to receive you."

I needed to visualize Hawra, so I asked how tall she had grown and whether she was thin or chubby. Remembering how my mother had nicknamed me "Radio Station" at that age for my incessant chatter, I asked whether Hawra was talkative or quiet. I particularly wanted to know what kinds of clothes she liked and was relieved to hear that she had developed a taste for sleeveless dresses and jeans. This was significant: it seemed highly unlikely that she was being brought up strictly like so many girls of her age in Shi'ite districts under the sway of fundamentalists. Sleeveless dresses now could mean a greater likelihood of education, a career, independence later in life, I thought.

"Hawra has a sense of fashion. I can't keep up with her," Grandmother said, and I smiled.

Then she asked me something I had not dared to expect.

"Do you want to speak to her, Hala? She's standing right beside me."

I could not begin to make her understand how much I wanted to speak to Hawra.

"Yes," I said gently. "Please put her on."

Suddenly, a polite little girl was saying, "Peace be upon you, *Khala*"—Auntie—and I was infused with a sense of serene tranquillity. Hawra was shy, as any girl her age would have been, and I could hear Grandmother prompting her to ask where I had been, whether I would visit, and when she would see me.

"Tell me, Hawra," I said. "What would you like me to bring you? Dresses or jeans?"

"I like pretty dresses, T-shirts, and jeans," she informed me solemnly.

I realized that my Lebanese accent must make me sound like an alien to an Iraqi of such tender years, so I asked her to put Grandmother back on the line and said my farewells.

"Before I go, Hajieh, I just want to tell you that I'm so pleased I've found you," I said finally.

My concern was that I did not know what would happen next. Grandmother finished by telling me we had much to discuss. I could not guess her thoughts, but even more worrying was that I would not know my own mind until I was actually holding Hawra.

Would I be filled with regret at the lost years, consumed with bitterness that I could not have her as my daughter, afflicted by a terrible urge to take her home when I knew this would be impossible? Or would I find, as I hoped, that the passage of time and the suffering I had witnessed in my work had destroyed the old preoccupation with myself, restored my sense of proportion, and left me with a simple wish to help this child?

Grandmother and I arranged to meet a week after my arrival in Baghdad. First, I had to return to Sadr City to report on a military offensive that was beginning there. The assignment would take me back to some of the hospitals I had visited five years earlier, the places where my story began with the search that ended with the discovery of Hawra's captivating sister. More than anything, I wanted to see life on the ground, not for the fighters, not for the politicians, but for ordinary families. This was the world in which Hawra would grow up.

NO SOONER HAD OUR SECURITY CONVOY—an armor-plated car with three jeeps to the front and three more to the back—set off down the infamous road from the airport to the center of Baghdad than I noticed another stark change. The thousands of palm trees that had always lined this route in two neat rows, greeting visitors with a vision of orderliness and verdant vitality, had disappeared.

Date palms had stood proudly to attention here ever since the road had been laid. Thirty feet tall, with roots that ran twice as deep under the ground, they had proved as tough as the generations of soldiers who passed between them. But since 2003, their trunks had concealed a new type of fighter. Insurgents would peer out from behind them, waiting for an American military vehicle to pass so that they could detonate the lethal explosives they had planted in the dead of night. Suicide bombers would lurk in the shade of the foliage until a suitable target presented itself in the form of U.S. soldiers gathering at a checkpoint. So the Americans had decided the safest course of action would be to take their bulldozers to every one of these majestic trees. Generations of resilient beauty had been flattened in less than two years.

I could see why the Americans had done it. What I could not see was why so much destruction had become necessary in the first place. These trees had withstood decades of neglect, but they needed care to flourish and bear fruit—rather like Iraq and its people, I thought. The country had cried out to be nurtured in its time of crisis. The response had been annihilation.

"Something else is different," I said, turning to Steve as we sped toward the city center. "What's new?"

I often prompt Steve in this way. I make him open my eyes to what I cannot see around me. As a reporter, I concentrate on the people I am interviewing. I reconstruct the plots of their lives. I look to Steve the photographer to color in the scenery for me. His observations and insights are splashed across nearly everything I write. Yet Steve did not have to say much that day: as we entered the heart of Baghdad, even I could not miss its transformation.

This once unified city of 6 million souls had become a labyrinth of concrete blocks and barriers, bricked-up windows and walls up to twenty feet high, dividing Sunnis from Shi'ites. The Americans had turned it into a maze complex enough to confound the most sophisticated sectarian killer. Each enclave was guarded by armed men assigned to repel intruders—to keep Baghdadis from one another's throats.

"Dear God, what have they done?" I said out loud.

In their anxiety to keep out terrorists, they had turned the metropolis of the mighty Tigris River into a city of concrete and shadows. Colleagues and cousins had been separated for fear they might knife, shoot, or bomb one another to shreds.

Communities had been cut off from mosques and schools. They had been left to contemplate new cityscapes in isolation. On some gray walls, artists had painted garish scenes portraying green pastures, fun fairs, or the glory of the ancient Mesopotamian civilizations, all equally far removed from twenty-first-century Baghdad.

Others were plastered with posters proclaiming attractions that ranged from the local kebab joint to a university degree in Ukraine. Others still bore graffiti hostile to the United States, Israel, Iran, or, more ominously, Iraq's own prime minister. Most were just ugly slabs that had sliced through communities to provide a short-term fix to the security crisis. It seemed to me to be storing up long-term problems for the future. This was the so-called Balkanization of Baghdad that I had read about but never believed until I saw it for myself. For me, there was a parallel closer than the Balkans. I had seen segregation like this in my home city, Beirut. Even in a seventeen-year civil war, however, Beirut had never resorted to anything quite so extreme. I knew from my own experience that this was no way to heal divisions between communities. The lesson of Beirut had been that when an entire community was driven out of an area and separated from its neighbors, the hatred did not go away. Sooner or later, divided communities had to be reconciled. The barriers erected in Baghdad would only prolong the divisions that had provoked its maelstrom of murder in the first place.

NOWHERE IN BAGHDAD were the divisions being felt more acutely that month than in Sadr City, the teeming slum of 2 million neglected people whose resentment of the Iraqi government's failure to improve conditions had found expression in support for the largest Shi'ite militia, the Mahdi Army. My return to Baghdad coincided with a drive by the official army, backed by the Americans, to seize control of Sadr City from the Mahdi militia. Hundreds of people were dying in this test of strength between Nouri al-Maliki, the prime minister, and Moqtada al-Sadr, the radical cleric leading the Mahdi Army.

Fitted with a black abaya that covered my entire body except for the face, hands, and feet, I was driven to a rendezvous just outside Sadr City with a Mahdi Army commander called Moqtada. I wished Steve could be with me. It had been decided by all concerned that he should stay behind, at least until I had gauged the level of danger in Sadr City for a white British male with blond hair. Five British hostages seized from the finance ministry in Baghdad a year earlier had not been seen since. Most observers believed they had been taken by supporters of the Mahdi Army, and some thought they were being held in Sadr City. Whether or not this was true, we did not want to risk turning Steve into hostage number six. Leaving him safely in our host's compound made me feel more vulnerable on our drive toward the battle zone.

Little had changed since I had last come into Sadr City, just before the death threat that had driven me out of Iraq eighteen months earlier. Junctions were clogged with cars and horse-drawn carriages, while sheep grazed on weedy patches of wasteland. Piles of rubbish littered even the narrowest streets. Raw sewage bubbled from broken pipes and streamed down innumerable alleyways. If anything, the infrastructure had deteriorated. So much for the coalition's aim of winning hearts and minds.

I did not have to wait long for sights and sounds that would make excellent copy for the paper.

"Come on, Hala—it's your lucky day," said Moqtada as he came off the phone. "Get ready, we need to move now."

Moqtada had received word that an attack was about to be launched on Al-Quds Road, the dividing line between the Mahdi forces to the north of it and the Iraqi Army to the south.

As both sides exchanged equally heavy machine-gun fire, the noise reached a crescendo with an exchange of mortar rounds that smashed shops on either side of Al-Quds Road, showering the whole area with shards of debris. The cacophony faded, only to be replaced by the whizz of snipers' bullets shooting up the street. It was time to take cover.

My escort hammered on the gates of the nearest house and a woman ushered me into her courtyard, introducing herself as Salma Jamila, an unmarried teacher, aged forty, who lived with her elderly parents. When she heard that I had come to report on the fighting, she fetched a small plastic chair and propped it against the yard wall so that I could peep over it to see what was happening. Evidently a cool hostess in a crisis, she disappeared into her kitchen and returned beaming with bottles of orange juice on a tray as mortar rounds crashed onto the road less than one hundred yards away.

Stranger still, another guest arrived, a cousin and Mahdi Army commander named Abu Ali, who was enjoying a day off. He hugged Jamila, explained that he had come to visit her father, and chatted away about how he had been arrested a few days earlier.

It was around six p.m. on that first day, as we were driving toward the center of Sadr City, that another call came through on Moqtada's cell phone, and we headed back to the front line. This time Mahdi fighters were trying to push back Iraqi Army and American forces to rescue several people who were said to be buried under some collapsed buildings.

Driving along more roads with open sewers, past children playing soccer in winding alleys and old women peering out from their doorways, we reached a point where men on street corners were handing cold water to fighters taking a break from the front line. The thump of artillery fire was coming close and I pleaded with Moqtada to stop the car. We were becoming perilously conspicuous on a road with no other vehicles, which seemed to be leading straight into the line of fire.

"But it's a long walk, Hala," Moqtada protested.

"I know it is, but at least it will be safer," I replied. "I do not need door-to-door service—at least not on the front line."

I did not tell Moqtada that I had had a peculiar horror of being shot in a car since my sister Rana, then newly married, was hit while driving home with her husband after visiting us one evening in Beirut. A dumdum bullet fired by a sniper had shattered the windshield and wounded Rana in the face, neck, and arm. She was fortunate to have survived: one fragment of bullet shrapnel had missed her artery by a millimeter.

Moqtada parked and we moved forward through ranks of Mahdi Army fighters who had lined an alleyway with rocket launchers, rifles, and machine guns. The sound of sniper fire intensified, but while my heart pounded and my legs shook, the hardened militiamen accompanying me paid no attention.

As we rounded a corner, I noticed a school one hundred yards ahead on the right-hand side. I was wondering how long it would be before the pupils could return, when an explosion almost knocked us off our feet. An artillery shell had landed in the playground and the classrooms were shredded by shrapnel. I froze with fear and crouched on the ground, catching my breath and covering my head. Someone shouted to me that I could not go any further.

"Go further?" I thought. "Are you kidding me?"

For the second time that day, a fighter rapped on the nearest gate and I was beckoned into a secluded courtyard. So shocked was I by now that my legs barely carried me into the house. While Moqtada and some of the other men stood outside, smoking casually, I headed for the back of the building in search of sanctuary. I identified what I assumed was the safest wall in the place and squatted against it with my eyes closed, breathing heavily.

Three spinsters who lived here took it upon themselves to calm me down, though I cannot say I was particularly soothed by the fuss they made. It turned out that they ran a shop from this house. How they expected to attract any customers on the front line was beyond me, but they produced a large bottle of 7Up, which was welcome. They then showed me their collection of shrapnel, which was not.

"Where did this come from?" I asked, gazing in astonishment at the heap of lethal metal shards.

"Oh, it comes into the courtyard every day," said one of the spinsters casually, as if this were the most natural thing in the world. "Sometimes it sprays into the house when we have the doors open."

I needed a cigarette.

Moqtada was calling for me. He must have noticed my apprehension as I stepped outside, acutely aware that the whizzing of snipers' bullets was as close as ever. Then he laughed at me.

"Are you afraid of death, Hala?"

I stared at him blankly.

"As a Shi'ite, you shouldn't be," he informed me lightly. "If death comes to me, I will be a martyr, following in the footsteps of the Shi'ite imams."

"Great," I thought. "My life is in the hands of someone who doesn't care if he dies."

I took a different view. I have never hidden my fear in a scary situation. Bravado leads to mistakes. It encourages people to take unnecessary risks. I have always feared and respected the gun.

"I am not pious," I told Moqtada. "What use is a dead journalist?" Then I realized that we had hurried out to the action so fast that I had forgotten to put on my flak jacked under the abaya.

"And another thing," I said. "I don't have my vest on. My foreign editor will not be happy with me if I get killed without it."

Moqtada beamed. "Okay," he said, calling over a friend. "You walk in the middle and we'll cover you from either side until we get back to the vehicle. I'm a big man and any bullet that comes this way will have to go all the way through me to get to you. I think you'll be safe."

When we finally made it back to his house, we discussed the day's fighting while his children played peacefully around us. His wife served fried chicken and tomatoes followed by strong, sweet tea. I was ready for bed.

ZAHRA'S DEATH HAD TAUGHT ME to cover not only the conflict but its victims. By the time I arrived in April 2008, the death toll in a month of fighting had reached 935. Of these, about 700 were civilians, according to officials at the various hospitals. I asked Moqtada to take me to Sadr General Hospital so that I could see for myself. It had been in such places in 2003 that I had found Ali Abbas and later Zahra. This was where I would bear witness to the real victims of war, irrespective of statements by political and military officials.

On a bare patch of ground outside the entrance to the general hospital, fifteen women clad from head to foot in black were squatting in a sandstorm, wailing and waiting for their dead. Lightning flashed, thunder rolled, and the women's robes were spattered with mud falling from a sky filled with rain and sand. They did not even notice.

"Ya'mma, Ya'ba"—Oh Mother, Oh Father—cried Amira Zaydan, a forty-five-year-old spinster, slapping her face and chest as she grieved for her parents, Jaleel, sixty-five, and Hanounah, sixty, whose house had exploded after apparently being hit by an American rocket.

"Where are you, my brothers?" she sobbed, lamenting Samir, thirty-two, and Amir, twenty-nine, who had also perished along with their wives, one of whom was nine months pregnant.

"What wrong have you done, my children?" she howled to the spirits of four nephews and nieces who completed a toll of ten family members in the disaster that had struck the previous day. "Mothers, children, babies, all obliterated for nothing."

The keening of Zaydan and her distraught circle of friends was drowned out briefly by sirens shrieking as ambulances sped through the hospital gateway with the latest consignment of casualties. Doctors and nurses with pinched faces darted out of the dilapidated hospital to greet the wounded and dying, while administrators stared at the weeping women and saw that they were beyond comforting.

Zaydan had hardly moved from the hospital for twenty-four hours since her family's home had been demolished as she and her sister Samira, forty-three, prepared lunch. Neighbors were trying to dig bodies out of the debris when another rocket landed, killing at least six rescuers.

Apart from the two sisters, the family's only other survivor was their brother Ahmad, twenty-five, who arrived at the hospital with leg injuries and in shock. "I lost everybody," was all he could say.

Zaydan was still waiting for seven family members to be disinterred from the rubble and delivered to Sadr General. The other three were in the morgue, among them a nephew, aged three, lying on a gurney in a puddle of blood from a head wound. Even by the callous standards of Iraq's cruel war, this was a ruthless struggle, I thought. So many of the dead and wounded were children.

Beside Zaydan sat her neighbor Um Aseel Ali, who had lost her husband and three boys, aged six, four, and two, when their house was blown up by a rocket.

"As I ran to them, the second rocket dropped," she cried. "I started shouting their names. I looked for them and tried to dig through the rubble. What fault did we commit for this? What wrong have we done to [Prime Minister] Maliki?"

While she spoke, another woman, Um Marwa Muntasser, wept softly. Her pregnant daughter, Marwa, survived the same attack but was being kept under sedation, unaware that her husband, Samir, her four-year-old son, Sajad, and her two-year-old daughter, Ayat, had all been killed.

"Was my daughter a fighter?" asked Muntasser. "My daughter was not a fighter. She and her family were innocent civilians minding their own business and now they are dead." The toll in the row of six houses inhabited by these families climbed to twenty-five.

I found Lina Mohsen, twenty-four, walking in a daze at the hospital, her face covered in brown dust. One minute she had been watching her eighteen-month-old toddler Ali play in the courtyard of their home, she said; the next, a rocket had struck.

"I began screaming for him, shouting his name, trying to find him, but I couldn't see him for dust and smoke," she said. Eventually, she saw that he was dead.

"I blame Maliki and his government and all those who are sitting in power and letting this happen," she said. Then she burst into tears and walked away.

At another hospital, the Imam Ali, I stumbled across the case of

Moqtada Raed, a two-year-old boy who had never stood any chance of recovering from the shrapnel wound to his leg. He writhed on his thin plastic mattress and whimpered to his father, Ahmad, who knew that nothing could be done to save him.

The child's thigh had been cut deeply when the family home was struck—also by a U.S. rocket, it seemed. He was bleeding profusely. Eventually his eyes fluttered and began to close, and doctors rushed to his bedside, gently slapping his face to keep him conscious. He died that evening.

IT WAS INEVITABLE THAT as I went about my wretched search of Baghdad's hospitals for stories to put in the newspaper, my thoughts should be drawn back to 2003.

When I saw what the shrapnel had done to Moqtada Raed's leg, I remembered finding Ali Abbas without his arms so vividly that it was as if he were stretched out in front me, explaining that "a missile cut them off, you know." I longed to see him again.

When I heard that Moqtada had died, I thought of the day I had received the news of Zahra, of how I had screamed in the street and sobbed in my room and cursed myself for dressing my fingers with diamonds as my child lay wrapped in her shroud.

Fourteen

ALI, THE SEVENTEEN-YEAR-OLD STATESMAN

The Hunting Club in the affluent district of Mansour was a haven of tranquillity in a city laid to waste by sectarian violence. Its fortress walls and armed guards concealed a place of peace and pleasure that was highly prized by the secular middle classes. Nowhere else in the city could they work up a healthy sweat on clay tennis courts, then choose between a sauna and a swim before lunch. The small talk over their aperitifs was not of the otherworldly grind of daily life for ordinary Baghdadis deprived of work and cash, but of bright business opportunities in the reconstruction of the city and of children being educated abroad on the proceeds. In Saddam's time, this club had been a haunt of Uday, the psychopathic son. Uday had once drunkenly fired his pistol over the heads of fellow members and was said to have installed a bed in an upstairs billiard room on which to rape young girls who took his fancy as he gazed out of the window at parties on the sleek lawn below. These days, the club was simply the most elegant rendezvous in town. That was what worried me.

I had chosen this oasis of gushing fountains and lush trees for a reunion with Ali Abbas because it could not have been more different from the squalid hospital room in which, five years earlier, he had asked me to bring back his severed arms. Yet when I heard that he was on his way here in a car, I had a sudden horror of embarrassing the boy. Would the chandeliered banqueting hall of the Hunting Club, with its refined atmosphere and ostentatious good manners, really be such a pleasing environment for a teenager who ate with his feet?

"What in God's name was I thinking?" I asked Steve as I paced up and down the marble entrance hall.

My husband looked at me with one eyebrow raised, as if to say, "You don't seriously expect me to answer that, do you?"

I had been astonished to find that Ali was in Baghdad in the first place. I knew he had been fitted with prosthetic arms in Britain because I had read as much in the papers. It had always been in my mind to catch up with him there sooner or later. When I decided to track down Hawra, I thought it was time to find out what had happened to Ali, too. I had put out some feelers just before I departed London, only to learn soon after my arrival in Baghdad that he was here on an extended visit. My contact even had a phone number for him.

So while I was waiting for security arrangements to be made for me to see Hawra, I dialed Ali's number, hoping he might spare me an hour or two. It was not just that I wanted to satisfy my curiosity about his fight for survival and the more complex struggle he must have endured to adapt to his injuries. Ali had played a pivotal role in my story. If it had not been for this brave little boy, my office would never have made me go in search of "another Ali" for its fund-raising appeal. It was Ali who had set me on the trail that led to Zahra; Ali who had prepared the way for me to meet Hawra. It seemed appropriate for me to start with Ali all over again on my return to Baghdad.

"Alloo," he answered in a singsong voice resonant with confidence and charm.

"My name is Hala Jaber," I began far less confidently, wondering if he would remember me. My name meant nothing to him, of course. "I'm a journalist with *The Sunday Times*, currently in Baghdad, and I would very much like to meet you if you have the time."

"You're from London?" he asked, and I knew instantly that he was interested enough to meet.

As the car swept up the Hunting Club drive with Ali inside, I thought of the frightened child whose world had fallen in when his bedroom ceiling collapsed and the furniture went up in flames. I remembered the bewilderment in those long-lashed eyes as he looked down at the stubs where his arms had been. I heard again the shock in the shrill voice saying, "Will you take me with you?" and the grim-faced doctor's prognosis of near-certain death.

The handsome young man who sprang from the rear passenger seat when his uncle opened the door could not have been further from this vision. Ali exuded vitality and self-assurance with every step toward me. He was wearing a soccer shirt in the exuberant red of Manchester United Football Club, a passion of his, as I was about to discover. You would not immediately have noticed that the short sleeves flattened by a faint breeze were empty, because your eye would have been drawn, as mine was, to his dazzling smile. Since we could not shake hands, we greeted each other simply by beaming. My grin was as broad as his.

"How you have grown!" I exclaimed vacuously, fussing over him like a doting aunt who has been absent for too long. I admired his impressive height, strong bone structure, and broad shoulders. Steve realized that I was in danger of embarrassing myself as well as Ali and gruffly complimented him on the shirt. As a Manchester man by birth and a fervent United fan since he had been old enough to say "ball," Steve soon found plenty to talk to Ali about. The two of them strolled into the restaurant together, chatting amiably about their team's triumph in the European Champions League final the previous week. I brought up the rear with Ali's twenty-seven-year-old uncle, Mohammed Ali Sultani.

"Ali needs help," Mohammed confided as we were directed to our table. "He won't go back to school in Britain without me, but I can't get a visa to enter the country."

That story had to wait while we ordered. At first Ali accepted only water, and Mohammed held up his nephew's glass whenever he wanted a sip.

As he looked from Steve to me and back again, Ali's face lit up in a flash of recognition. "I remember you guys," he said. "When I was in the hospital here my aunt Jamila told me a British photographer had given some money for me. He brought a bag of sweets and chocolate."

Ali smiled at Steve: "It was you."

That was my cue to recall how Aunt Jamila had been sitting at his bedside, flicking away flies and flapping a piece of cardboard over his head to cool his burns. I repeated his words to me—"Have you come to give me my arms back? What about my hands?"—and saw in his face that he remembered this, too. He sat very still and quiet as the weight of my recollections bore down on him.

Steve saw that it was time to lighten the mood. He often does this when he thinks my questioning has become too intense for my poor interviewees. He interrupts to give them a break, knowing I will get more out of them if I come back to my questions later.

"Don't take any notice of the dwarf," he said—an old joke of his that has worn thin with me over the years (I am five feet, two and a half inches tall and very particular about the half-inch), but that somehow gets a laugh every time from the person it is intended to relax. "She's just a journalist who writes and writes and writes about nothing. Let's talk about something serious." With that, he changed the subject back to soccer.

Ali gave a throaty giggle and the two of them launched into an animated analysis of the Manchester United striker Cristiano Ronaldo—his perfect skills and flawed temperament—until I could see that our guest was happy to answer some more questions.

I wanted him to tell his remarkable story from start to finish, and Ali was a willing raconteur, for reasons he would save for the end of his account. But as he sipped from his glass and braced himself to relive the traumatic events of 2003, I could see that he was troubled by flies, just as he had been when we had met him in the hospital. It was as if they sensed he was defenseless. He shook his head and shoulders vigorously to scare them off.

"Why don't you have your arms with you?" I asked.

"I left them in London," he replied, matter-of-factly. "They're heavy, so I decided to take a break from them. I thought I'd be here for two months. Instead I've been here for nearly a year. By the time I get back I'll probably have forgotten how to use them."

The last remark was accompanied by a mischievous smirk, so I smiled back at his joke.

"Anyway, I prefer to use my feet to eat, brush my teeth, write," he explained. "I can type with my toes. Also, I'm unbeatable at PlayStation even though I use my feet for that, too. For one year at school, no one could beat me at PlayStation." That smirk again.

Yet being stuck in Baghdad when he should have been taking important exams in London was no laughing matter, I thought. I resisted asking how he had ended up here, when people in Britain thought he had settled into a new life there. It seemed best to start at the beginning and come back to that later. Gently I coaxed him to tell us what he could remember of the day he was hurt.

IT WAS MARCH 31, 2003. He had been on a family visit to relatives nearby and returned home, late and sleepy, to the hamlet of Arab al-Khrsa, thirteen miles southeast of Baghdad. For a house with only two bedrooms, a lot of people lived there. His father Ismaeel, a farmer who grew palm and raised cattle and poultry, had two wives. With his first wife, Leila, Ismaeel had had six daughters and a son. They shared one of the bedrooms. In the other, Ismaeel slept with his second wife, Azhar, and their younger son, Abbas, who was ten, and Ali, who was two years older. Azhar was five months pregnant with their third child.

Ali fell asleep with his family all around him.

"The next thing I knew, I felt the roof crash down over us and the heat of a blazing inferno," he said, with such intensity that it seemed the fire was burning in his eyes.

Ali was conscious of being soaked in blood, but worse than that, both his arms were on fire. He saw the flames coming out of his forearms and felt his flesh being burned away from the hands to the elbows. In this moment of profound anguish and unfathomable horror, Ali thought he was having a nightmare. The reality of it struck him when he heard a neighbor rushing in to rescue Leila and her children, who escaped with cuts, and shock.

"The neighbor didn't see me. I was under all the rubble. I had to call him and tell him where I was," Ali said, "My arms were on fire as I lay under the rubble."

Several other people had arrived by now and together they pulled him out. He heard screaming—probably from Leila shrieking that he needed to be driven to the hospital—and cried out for his mother.

"The neighbor drove me in his car to the hospital. I was conscious, but I don't remember feeling much pain on the journey," he said. What he did remember was hearing a doctor at the Kindi hospital telling someone there was no hope for him. Then he woke up to find that he had had an operation, that his incinerated arms had been cut off, and that he would never be the soldier he had dreamed of becoming. He was inconsolable.

Ali interrupted his narrative at this point and glared around the table.

"There was no reason to hit our house," he said. "My father raised cows and chickens." I nodded silently.

Assailed by painful memories, he resorted to a little black humor in self-defense. "One house was not enough for them," he continued with a bitter laugh. "Oh, no. They had to hit the next-door houses of my relatives as well, and so fifteen people were killed."

What Ali could not have known at the time was that in and around the neighboring town of Za'Faraniya were several prime targets for American bombers. Quite apart from two factories that were suspected—wrongly, as it turned out—of producing biological weapons, a nuclear research center and a missile-manufacturing plant also stood nearby. The hamlet surrounded by fields of broad beans and radishes where Ali's father had thought the family would always be left to themselves in Saddam's time was in the eye of the firestorm when war came.

Lying in the little hospital room where Steve and I had found him under the crudely constructed cage with the torn blanket draped over it, Ali did not dare to ask his aunt Jamila why his mother, father, and brother were not coming to see him. The truth—that his uncle Mohammed had found them charred to death where they lay and had buried Ali's arms with his father—was far too shocking for him to absorb when he was already suffering so much. So Ali was left to wonder what had happened to his parents, where his arms were, and who would bring them back to reattach to his bandaged stubs. He could not conceive of life without them.

The immediate dangers to Ali were not the inability of the Kindi hospital staff to treat burns or blood poisoning properly, but the breakdown of law and order that ensued when American forces took control of Baghdad with no orders to curb looting. According to Ali, the doctors and nurses gradually decided that it was too dangerous to come to work.

"Only one male nurse who lived nearby returned every day to wash my burns and cool me down," he said. This nurse visited him twice a day, then returned home to his own family. For the rest of the time, Ali's aunt was left to care for him as best she could, alone. Eventually, the nurse put Ali and his aunt into an ambulance and drove them to a safer hospital in Sadr City.

THE SHORT TIME Steve had spent photographing Ali had a prolonged impact. No sooner had the pictures appeared on one front page in Britain than the beautiful child whose mutilation encapsulated the ugliness of "collateral damage" became an icon of the war. My Lebanese friend Samia Nakhoul interviewed Ali the day after I did, and her story on the Reuters wire was published around the world. Ali's incongruous instinct for poignant sound bites—"If I don't get my arms back, I will commit suicide," he told Samia—helped to turn him into an international celebrity. More than £1 million was donated to British newspaper appeals set up in his name. But although the money was distributed to worthy charities, most of it was earmarked for projects rather than individuals, and most of the journalists covering the story did nothing for Ali, whose risk of succumbing to septicemia was growing by the day.

It took the intervention of a bighearted reporter who had not met Ali and who had made no more than a passing reference to him in print to ensure that he left Iraq in time to be saved. Peter Wilson, of the *Australian* newspaper, was contacted by a philanthropist who wanted to know how he could help. Wilson responded by asking the authorities in Kuwait whether Ali could be admitted to a specialist burn unit there. Ten days after Steve had taken his photograph, Ali was airlifted out of the country.

Finding himself in a strange place without even the company of the journalists he had fleetingly come to know, Ali missed his mother and father more than ever.

"No one had told me at the time that both my parents were dead, but I felt inside me that they had died. I knew it within me," he told us solemnly. When he was finally deemed ready to know the full extent of his loss, the few remaining family members who would have been in the best position to comfort him were far away. He cried alone at night, not only for his parents but for himself.

"I would think to myself, what am I going to do now? I realized I wouldn't be able to do all the normal things in life that I was able to do when I had my arms," he said.

Yet even at that time of crisis, Ali behaved with a maturity beyond his years, showing early signs of the self-sufficiency that had stood him in such good stead ever since. He decided to put on a brave face, he said. He chose not to burden his caregivers with his grief or his fears for the future.

"They wouldn't have been able to do much about the issues that were upsetting me then," he explained softly. "Could they have brought my dead parents back to life? Could they have given me back my real arms? I knew the answers to those questions were no, so there was no point in complaining."

Instead, he knuckled down to the grueling process of regaining his health. Four painful operations followed in as many months, including skin grafts to his chest and back. He coped with the help of Ahmed Mohammed Hamza, a fourteen-year-old Iraqi boy he befriended in the hospital. Like Ali, Ahmed had survived a bombing but would live with the consequences forever. His right arm and left leg had been amputated.

Aware that his celebrity status had resulted in offers of further treatment from Sweden to Spain and from Canada to California, Ali resolved that his newfound friend would benefit from all the opportunities that came his way. If he was going to receive first-class care in some exotic, far-flung location in Europe or America, then so would Ahmed. When it finally came down to a choice of rehabilitation in Canada or Britain, Ali challenged his prospective benefactors on his friend's account. The Canadians could not take Ahmed, too. The British—in the form of a charity called the Limbless Association—were willing to help both Ali and his friend. That settled it. The Kuwaiti prime minister put his private jet at Ali's disposal and he arrived in London in style.

Yet for reasons that Ali had yet to explain, all these efforts had somehow culminated in a strange reversal of fortune. As he put it with another of his bitter little laughs: "Ahmed is in London and I am in Baghdad. I took him there and I got stuck here."

NOW THAT ALI HAD RECOUNTED the more unpalatable parts of his story, Steve asked whether he had gotten his appetite back. Sure enough, he was starving. Anxious to avoid making him self-conscious with a formal lunch at the club, I suggested we order at our table but eat at the house we were staying in just down the road, where we could be more comfortable. Ali agreed, and our guard arranged a takeout of grilled chicken and minced lamb kebabs.

While Steve and Ali resumed their soccer talk, I spread out the meal on a low coffee table in the sitting room, thinking this would make it easier for Ali to eat with his feet. Ali then surprised me by asking for the food to be transferred to a dining table, presumably thinking this would make it easier for the rest of us to eat with knives and forks. As lunch began, Uncle Mohammed started spooning morsels into Ali's mouth.

Such was his devotion to the task that he did not take a bite himself until Ali's keen teenage appetite had been sated with a second helping.

At one point, Ali stopped munching and stared at me as I lit a cigarette and pored over my scribbled notes.

"Don't you eat?" he asked. I giggled.

"Sometimes I do, but generally I'm not a big fan of food," I said. Steve chimed in with another of his well-worn jokes. "Of course she doesn't eat—look how skinny she is," he exclaimed.

Ali paused to observe me for a moment, then said solemnly: "I wouldn't say she was skinny. I think she's just right, perfectly healthy and exactly as she should be."

There was a moment's silence while we digested the fact that Ali had taken a shine to a woman old enough to be his mother. Then we all burst out laughing. Ali joined in, savoring his role as the comedian who had brought a little light relief to a day of tough talking. There was more of that to come as he told us what had happened to him in Britain.

Ali had evidently received the best the British health service and education system had to offer. With a free place generously provided at the private Hall School in Wimbledon, where fees would normally have come to £10,000 a year, Ali began his rehabilitation not far away at Queen Mary's Hospital, Roehampton, whose pioneering expertise in prosthetics is renowned worldwide. For a boy with no English and a daunting disability, neither school nor therapy could be anything other than hard. Rehabilitation was especially demanding.

First Ali learned how to perform many of the routine chores of daily life with his toes, from typing to using a teaspoon, from undressing to unlocking a door. Like every other step on the path to independence, it required painstaking practice and inexhaustible patience. Then a mechanical right arm was strapped on, complete with elbow, wrist, and hand. Ali learned how to eat and drink with it but also to limit his expectations of what he would be able to achieve with any artificial limb. Finally he was equipped with electric arms. He was delighted to see that they had been stamped with the Manchester United tattoo he had requested, but was dismayed by their weight: just over three pounds each. As time went on, he began to think that the benefit of being able to maneuver three fingers on each hand of these arms was counterbalanced by the cumbersome burden they represented to an energetic boy entering his teenage years.

"I got fed up with the prosthetic arms," he said. "I felt they were too heavy for me. They feel like constantly carrying a heavy bag. The doctors say it is better that I wear them more to become more independent. But I prefer to use my feet."

An extra pair of arms for purely cosmetic purposes was also supplied to Ali, and he liked to wear these to school. "They look more real and they aren't too heavy, but you can't do much with them," he said.

After a few months and endless lessons in Britain, Ali was as desperate to visit home as his surviving relatives were to see him. Yet not only was it difficult for this boy to return to the scene of the disaster that had transformed his life and robbed his family of theirs, but security arrangements had to be made to guard against the possibility that kidnappers might regard such a high-profile figure as an irresistible target. The visit was kept largely secret.

"The first time I came back, everything felt different from before," Ali said. "I used to feel safe in my country. When I returned, I was a little bit scared because I knew the violence was increasing."

He yearned to go back to his old house. "But I couldn't stay there very long, even though one of my uncles on my father's side had built a house on the same spot," he said, speaking slowly in an effort to recall his turbulent emotions calmly. "I decided I could not stay there. I couldn't stop myself from thinking that my family had died in this house. I was crying. I had to leave. I stayed with another uncle on my mother's side."

In the end, it was Ali's annual visits to the graves of his parents and younger brother that led to his becoming stuck in Iraq. He was sharing a house in London with his friend Ahmed. An uncle took care of Ali's daily needs, including washing and bathing, while Ahmed's father looked after him. The two adults and two children made the best of their situation at first. But in 2006, Ali's caregiver could no longer continue. He had to concentrate on his own family. Another uncle—Mohammed—volunteered to return to London with Ali after that summer's visit but could not obtain a visa in time. Ali returned alone and had to rely on Ahmed's father for all the personal chores that should have fallen to a member of his own family to perform. He found this intolerable.

So at the end of his visit to Iraq in 2007, Ali refused to go back to Britain unless Uncle Mohammed could come, too. In London, officials at the Home Office who had given Ali the right of residency refused to issue Uncle Mohammed with the visa he needed for even a temporary visit. The impasse meant that Ali missed the year of GCSE exams he needed to sit in order to go on to A levels and university. When I contacted him, he should have been in the final stages of his preparations for these important exams. Instead, he was twenty-five hundred miles away with nothing better to do than to kick a soccer ball around with his friends in the 35-degree-Celsius heat of Baghdad.

He liked to play in the same Manchester United shirt he wore to the Hunting Club—the number 7 shirt that had once belonged to his hero, David Beckham. It had been presented to him by Beckham during a visit to the club's Old Trafford ground. The player had even arranged for Ali's name to be inscribed on the back. Later, shirts signed by all the Manchester United players had arrived from Beckham by special delivery. The thoughtfulness of these gestures from a sporting superstar seemed in grotesque contrast to the mean spirit of the faceless Home Office official who had denied Ali the support of the uncle sitting opposite me, who was feeding Ali because he could not feed himself.

"I need to have someone with me at all times for many reasons," Ali said. "I can't understand why they refused him this visa."

Uncle Mohammed did not conceal the family's disappointment with the authorities in Britain, a country that had done so much for his nephew. He said the Home Office was demanding to be assured that he would be able to pay his way in the UK, but since he had no job he was unable to make that promise. "I am Ali's main caregiver," he said simply. "I would have thought they'd facilitate my return."

One of Ali's more mundane frustrations was that he had not even been able to watch the climax of the Champions League final because his city's electricity supply had yet to be restored to normal more than five years after the invasion of his country. Three penalties into a shoot-out against Chelsea, a power cut had blacked out the screen of the small television around which Ali's friends were gathered.

"By the time the generator was switched on, the penalties had come to an end," he said, though he made light of it by adding that the result had never been in doubt because "my team always wins."

On a more serious note, he believed that he and all the other children wounded or orphaned by misdirected American missiles should be compensated. It was exactly what Marla had believed.

"Neither the American government nor the British—nor even the Iraqi government—has ever asked us about our welfare," Ali said. "Both the American and the British governments are responsible for the killing of my parents and my family. It is only logical that they should compensate me for my losses."

Until recently, Ali had still clung to boyish dreams of emulating his other idol, the Manchester United manager Sir Alex Ferguson, by running his own club one day. His headmaster, Timothy Hobbs, had other ideas. "He's a very talented child," Hobbs said. "He picks up languages easily. He could be something amazing in public relations and politics. He has a very attractive personality and a fantastic ability to communicate."

To achieve this, however, Ali would need qualifications. His family felt that all the good work to help him overcome his epic misfortune had been halted by petty bureaucracy. I had to agree. Here was a boy who had become a symbol not only of the suffering inflicted by war, but also of the compassion shown toward its victims. Was Ali now also destined to symbolize the coalition's bungled efforts to help the Iraqi people after the fall of Saddam?

I asked Ali whether he minded having spent his teenage years being portrayed as a symbol of this, that, or the other in the media spotlight. Some would have found the attention embarrassing, especially at his age. He seemed surprised by the question.

"Of course not," he said with the utmost dignity. "This way, the world can see that wars are not a good thing and that a lot of innocent civilians get hurt as a result."

Ali spoke eloquently about the past, present, and future of his country. He said he bore no grudges against the Americans and British whose forces had spearheaded the invasion.

"I am not against the people," he said. "I know many of them were—and continue to be—against the war. I am just upset and angry with the governments that caused all this. They had smart bombs and stupid brains."

As for the state of Iraq at the time I saw him, Ali lamented the loss of friends as well as family and the inability of his step-siblings to find jobs in an economic depression that had reduced his stepmother, Leila, to dependence on his disability benefits from Britain. He summed up the conclusions of some of my own reporting of death squads driving the professional classes into exile.

"You know what the problem is?" he said. "It is that sadly all the good people have left and only the bad remain here now."

Yet despite all the opportunities open to him abroad, Ali still felt an obligation to his shattered homeland, a duty to help its people recover from the trauma of war. "Perhaps one day I can do something good for Iraq and its future," he said. "Although I haven't come to a final decision on how to help, I would like to become a doctor of sorts."

Hearing his analysis of all that had gone wrong and seeing his vision for a way ahead filled me with pride in Ali and optimism for Iraq, but the British authorities seemed deaf to the pleas from his family for Uncle Mohammed's visa and blind to the consequences of inaction for a young man eager to move on with his life. He had shown that he had the resilience, the intelligence, and the energy to be so much more than a photogenic victim of the war. How demoralizing it must have been for him to discover through personal experience that a government that had declared its intention of liberating Iraq's people from a dictator could end up failing them so badly. Ali had displayed no anger. I was enraged.

I had one last question for Ali. What had he meant about becoming "a doctor of sorts"?

He told me bluntly that without arms, it would be hard for him to practice most forms of medicine. Nevertheless, he believed he could become a psychologist capable of helping others to overcome traumatic events in their lives, as he had.

"There are probably thousands of kids like me—some with even worse injuries and disabilities—who were not as fortunate as I was, who did not receive the same chances in life that I was given," he said gravely. "It is for those people that I feel we must do something. I believe I must help in some way."

These statesmanlike words from a seventeen-year-old boy made me think of Hawra. Hawra was one of those he had spoken about. She had lost all her immediate family, just as Ali had. But unlike Ali, she had not received publicity. There had been no offers of help from well-wishers because hardly anybody knew what she had suffered. While Ali was being photographed, fêted, and educated free of charge, the opportunities for an obscure five-year-old orphan girl looked dismal and her prospects of a good education were close to nil.

Ali had inspired me.

"I believe I must help in some way," he had said.

Fifteen

FINDING HAWRA

The day of the reunion dawned bright and calm, but as I drank my second coffee of the morning and lit my fourth cigarette, I felt the adrenaline flowing faster than I would have liked. Hawra and her grandmother were due at two p.m., and I had planned it all to precision, thinking this would help me to remain composed. Instead, the thought of seeing them was already making me giddy with nerves.

I had played out the scene of our reunion over and over again in my imagination. I had thought hard about how to deliver a little speech to Grandmother, begging her forgiveness for letting Zahra die. Yet I knew that no amount of rehearsal could prepare me for my first embrace with Hawra. I did not know how I would react, let alone what I would say to a child of five who had been in my thoughts every day since she was three months old but who had no recollection of me.

By the time the early summer sun had risen high in the noonday sky, all pretense of cool detachment had evaporated as the emotions boiled up inside me. My resolve to approach this meeting rationally was melting in a hot rush of fear. What if merely setting eyes on Hawra revived visions of a home life with an adopted daughter in place of the career I had made for myself on the move from one trouble spot to the next? What if the simple act of wrapping my arms around her left me gripped not only by my old regrets at having failed to make a family, but by a renewed determination to create one?

For five years, hazardous assignments had defined the professional woman I had become. I had worked so hard, run so many risks to achieve what status I possessed. Could an hour with Hawra make the relentless, unnerving slog of month after month in Iraq seem like a grotesque mistake? Would it convince me that when I had abandoned my ambition to be a mother in favor of my aspirations for a career, I had made the worst choice of my life?

Partly to avoid raising this question with Steve and partly to distract myself from it altogether, I went to my room in the friend's house where we were staying and parceled up some clothes I had brought from London to give to Hawra. I remembered the trip I'd made to a Baby Gap in a smart part of town with my niece, Lara, and her excitement as we left with our bags bulging.

"Oh, Lollie, she's going to be the best-dressed, most up-to-date kid in Iraq," Lara had said with a giggle. And I had laughed with her, relieved that for the first time in years in a children's shop, I had not gone to pieces.

"Pull yourself together," I told myself sternly now. "What's done is done. Focus on the future."

Ordering myself around had no effect whatsoever. I could not sit. I could not settle. Disconcertingly, I found that I could barely speak. I was entering the state known to Steve as "hyper," just when I needed to be at my most levelheaded and coherent.

I rang Sean, hoping some of his calmness would be transmitted through the telephone to me.

"What if I have a total meltdown when I see them?" I gibbered. "What if everything I have worked for in the last few years suddenly dissolves?"

"What exactly is worrying you?" he asked, struggling to make sense of the lunatic on the line.

I tried to explain that I did not know if I could hold myself in check that afternoon or if my emotions were about to run away with me.

"The heart and the head never meet, Sean, they always run in parallel lines!" shrieked Crazy Woman. "I know in my head I am fine—I have taken the final decision where this issue of motherhood is concerned—but what if my heart gives way?"

What was really worrying me most was that Grandmother might suddenly turn to me and say: "I want you to take Hawra." It was conceivable that she would. Baghdad was not the brightest place in which to educate a child, and Grandmother was getting old. She would inevitably be worrying about where her orphaned granddaughter would end up when she had gone. Would she think that a journalist from London offered the best way out of this conundrum? If so, how would I respond, now that I had set my life on a different course?

Ever since Zahra's death, I had envisaged a future without children. I had built my career on that assumption. Would I be resolute enough to resist entreaties to take Hawra, or would I sacrifice my position for the child? The truth was that I was torn. Logic dictated that uprooting Hawra at a relatively late age could be unwise. But I knew in my heart that I would not be able to refuse Grandmother if she pressed the child on me.

I had no solid answers to any of these questions because I could not think straight. As two p.m. approached, my alarm was verging on panic.

I RANG GRANDMOTHER TO MAKE sure the car I had ordered for them was on its way to us.

"Oh, Hala," she said breathlessly. "The driver dropped us at the top of the road and refused to go any further and I don't know where you are. I'm lost and afraid."

That was when it hit me. All the time I had been wary of seeing Grandmother, she had been apprehensive about meeting me. When I had telephoned to make the appointment, she had rebuked me, saying: "Hawra's been asking about you since last week when you were supposed to turn up." I had thought she was setting the tone for graver reprimands when we met. But when I heard her fretting on the phone, it was clear that she was at least as anxious about the day as I was.

This poor woman had been summoned to a grand address by somebody who lived in one of the countries that had invaded her own. She had certainly believed five years earlier that I had influence and she probably did still. She would undoubtedly be feeling that her beloved grandchild might benefit in some undetermined way from an association with me if all went well this afternoon. Of course she was worried. She was bound to be. Her nervousness calmed me.

To make matters worse for Grandmother, she could not call me for directions.

"Hala, I cannot read or write, so I do not know which number is yours or how to dial it," she said candidly. "I only know how to receive an incoming call."

I assured her that I would call back every few minutes. Accompanied by one of our host's security guards, who were on constant alert for would-be kidnappers, Steve and I left the house and scanned the road for any sign of an old widow and a young girl.

We saw nobody.

Then the security guard spoke into my phone and established that our guests were close by. He told Grandmother to walk straight down the road and instructed us to go inside and wait.

"You mustn't be outside on your own," he said. "I'll find them and walk them down."

Steve and I nodded, but even when the guard left us to search for our guests, we could not bring ourselves to move from the curbside. The sun beat down fiercely on the dusty palms that lined the street, and my head throbbed with feverish anticipation. Such was the heat at this, the warmest hour of the day, that a haze obscured our view of a convoy of military vehicles rolling down the hill toward us. Then, between two vehicles, I thought I glimpsed a pair of moving shadows. No sooner had I spotted them than they flickered out of sight, but I was sure they were my adopted family.

"There!" I said to Steve, pointing. My husband peered through the lens of his camera for a clearer picture.

"Eh," he said—"yes" in Arabic. "It's her with the kid."

Then I saw them, shimmering like a mirage in the distance as they hurried toward us: the forbidding figure of Grandmother, dressed from head to toe in a black chador that flapped against her with each purposeful stride, and at her side a dainty little girl in a smart orange dress, half walking, half skipping to keep up.

It was all Steve could do to stop me from going with the security guard to fetch them. Now he could not hold me back any longer. I started walking slowly toward them, thinking this would be a more courteous way of greeting Grandmother than if I stood there like an official dignitary awaiting the arrival of a tardy visitor. I so wanted to put her at ease with a relaxed, informal welcome. But when Grandmother looked up and caught sight of me, the first tears sprang to my eyes and I could not contain myself. I felt my feet taking off. I broke into a run, oblivious to remonstrations from Steve and our guard. When I was a few yards away, Grandmother opened her arms and I flew into her embrace.

We rocked from side to side as we hugged more and more tightly. It was a relief to me to sense that Grandmother was sobbing into my chest. It meant that I had no need to stifle my own weeping on her account. We cried hard. Grandmother's tears trickled down my blouse. Mine dripped onto her abaya. I believe we were crying not for ourselves, not for each other, but for the child who had brought us together in the beginning. We reminded each other of this little girl more starkly than any photograph of her. For a few moments, we were mourning Zahra all over again.

As the wave of grief swept over me in a surge of memories, I stared into Grandmother's watery blue eyes, and we both smiled at the spectacle we were making of ourselves. She kissed my wet cheeks and I kissed hers back. I suddenly became conscious of one emotion that stood out from all the others, one that took me by surprise.

It felt as if I had been running for a long time and I had finally arrived at my destination. The journey had been long, the road hard. But as I ran into Grandmother's arms, it was as if I had been enfolded in forgiveness. This was the absolution I had been seeking ever since Zahra's death. Now that I had found it, my whole body relaxed. I was lighter somehow. The weight of the guilt I had carried over the years was lifting.

Grandmother stared back at me and said simply: "You returned, Hala."

I nodded. It was not just that I had come back to Baghdad. I had returned to the family.

It was time to turn my attention to the bewildered child at Grandmother's side. Here at last was the little girl who had been on my mind since she was a baby. As I crouched down in front of her, I knew straightaway that from this moment on, she would always be part of my life.

Hawra, the sole survivor from a family of nine wiped out in one of the most abhorrent air strikes of those early days of war, was simply beautiful. With her flawless face, the glossy hair that framed it, her graceful manner, and the affectionate way she comforted her overwrought grandmother by gently clasping her hand, Hawra was everything I would have wished for in a daughter.

She stared at me with wide brown eyes that conveyed her astonishment at the scene she had just witnessed and her wariness of the peculiar stranger before her, laughing and crying at the same time. I told myself not to overwhelm her with my feelings, but in vain. Instinct took over. I needed to pick her up and feel her in my arms. As I lifted her, I could not resist kissing her pretty cheeks and burying my face in her exquisitely perfumed hair. I was so elated, so ecstatic, that I could not put her down.

A FILM STEVE MADE of our reunion ends with the incongruous sight of me, all five feet, two and a half inches of me, walking slowly forward with Hawra, tall for her age, still clutching me. I was murmuring to her in Arabic that she should not be afraid, but the stiffness of her body in my arms suggested a certain unease, to say the least.

As we passed through the steel gates of our host's house, I apologized profusely to Grandmother for dragging her all the way out to the suburb of Mansour. I had done so on the advice of the security men, who had insisted that they must reconnoiter her street before they would take me there. Grandmother assured me that she understood, but I noticed that she looked anxiously around her as the thick oak door of our friend's house opened to reveal a lavishly furnished drawing room where the floor was carpeted by Persian rugs and the ashtrays were made of crystal glass. I thought of the modest house where I had asked to adopt her two granddaughters and hoped she would not feel uncomfortable on a sofa as opulent as the one to which I guided her. Hawra's eyes had lit up at the sight of so much splendor.

When tea had been served for our guest, it was time for my little speech. It was no less heartfelt for having been rehearsed.

"I am truly sorry," I told Grandmother. "Truly sorry that I let you down and truly sorry for not being able to save Zahra."

I expected this to be the cue for Grandmother to unburden herself of all the recriminations that must have been building up inside her over the years as she reflected on my failure to keep the big promise I had made that Zahra would live. Instead, this wise old woman responded with compassion.

"But Hala, you could not have saved her," she said calmly. "This was the will of Allah. There was nothing you could do to change Zahra's destiny."

She paused, and the anguish I had seen in the Karameh hospital returned to her face as she recalled our desperate days at Zahra's bedside.

"We do not question Allah's will," she went on. "You could not have challenged Allah's will, Hala. It was so written."

For a moment, she broke down. Then she sensed my own pain and continued to reassure me.

"Hala, my dear, I was never angry with you for that. I never held you responsible."

"But I promised you, Grandmother. I promised you I would bring her back," I protested.

"You could not have done so. It was never in your hands, Hala.

She was not meant to live. You tried for Zahra. You and Marla both tried, and for that I'll be eternally grateful."

Something in the way she looked at me told me that Grandmother was not ready to excuse my actions entirely.

"I was not angry with you about Zahra," she said. "But I was disappointed in you for abandoning Hawra—for turning your back on us and never once coming to see her. This I berate you for."

And that was it. I had been braced for a furious tirade. There was no anger in her tone, but the directness of her language signaled how far short I had fallen from Grandmother's great expectations. I had to explain to her what I barely understood myself: why I had stayed away for so long or, as she had put it, why I had abandoned Hawra. It was the vocabulary she might have used to describe a mother who had deserted a newborn infant or a cow that would not suckle her calf.

"I forced myself to stay away," I said.

"Why?"

I took a deep breath. "Because I was angry with myself," I said. "I needed to forgive myself before I could see you and sit with you like this."

She took my hand. I did not know whether she grasped what I was saying, but she knew that Zahra's death had grieved me, too, and that this bound us together. She also saw that I had not forgotten Hawra or the calamity that had befallen the family.

"My son Ali was never a soldier, Hala," she said, changing the subject abruptly, perhaps out of consideration for me. "He was just a taxi driver. All he wanted to do was to make a living for his family. They killed him and his wife and my grandchildren, and for what?"

I had no answer for her.

"These two big countries, America and Britain, they killed them all, leaving Hawra an orphan. They did not even think of compensating her," she added. "She's all alone, Hala. All she has is me, and I'm a sick old woman. As long as I'm alive, no one will dare mistreat her, but what will happen to her when I am dead and gone? Who will take care of her? They should have provided for her. They should have given her security for when I'm not here anymore. But look at me. Do you think I am capable of going to the Americans and asking them to compensate this child for all they have stripped her of? Would anyone take any notice of me?"

It was agonizing to see how much she suffered at the thought of what might happen to Hawra in a few years' time. I marveled at the strength she had found to cope with unimaginable loss and to become the substitute mother of a tiny baby at her advanced age. I also saw in her haggard face the toll this had taken; and that was before I knew the full extent of family tragedies she did not disclose to me until later.

As for Hawra, she was sitting quietly beside her grandmother, giving no sign that she understood the talk of compensation or even death but evidently moved by the anguish expressed. It was as if she sensed that the family was haunted by sorrow but was not yet old enough to know who the ghosts had been. I asked her where her mama was and she pointed to her grandmother. The pair of them lived with the old woman's two surviving sons, and Hawra called one of them Baba.

I was anxious to see Hawra happy, so I presented her with my gifts from London. There were four dresses, all sleeveless because her grandmother had told me this was her favorite style. Then there were jeans, shirts, and underwear, all in bright colors designed to bring a smile to a young girl's face. And so they did.

In return, Grandmother asked her to sing for us. Hawra was shy, but after a good deal of cajoling from Steve and me, she sighed, smiled again, and launched into a spirited rendition of some nursery rhymes.

Just when I thought we were all beginning to relax, Grandmother said something that made my heart skip a beat.

"Remember when you asked me if you could adopt the girls?" she asked. How could I have forgotten? I steeled myself, thinking that everything she had said up to that point about the child's uncertain future might have been intended to soften me up before asking me to take Hawra away with me.

"Hala, I told you I would think about it," she said, as I stroked Hawra's hair.

"The truth is that after Zahra's death I would not have been able to give you Hawra. She is all I have of my Ali and his wife. Seeing her face every day is like seeing my son. She is a constant reminder of him and the grandchildren I have lost. I can never give Hawra away now. Watching her grow before my eyes is what keeps me going. It eases the pain I still feel over my dead son."

She paused to check her emotions and collect her thoughts.

"However," she said, and I held my breath again. "I need to make sure she's all right when I'm dead. Hala, Hawra is yours in many ways. *Hawra be raqbatik*," she concluded—an expression in Arabic that commits one person to another. "She'll always be your responsibility, and you have the power to make sure she has a decent life."

Grandmother scrutinized me to see how I was reacting. She spoke slowly to emphasize the gravity of the obligation that was being placed on me. Hawra would start school the following year, she said. She was determined to see her granddaughter complete her education, graduate from college, and make something special of the only life that remained of her family.

"I want her to be free, Hala. I want her to be independent. I want her to have the ability to make choices in life. But for her to do this, she will need guidance. She will need financial support. This is the responsibility I bestow on you."

She finished bluntly. "I cannot depend on the governments that killed her family and made her an orphan. They did nothing for her then and they will not do anything for her now. So you will have to shoulder this burden. Promise me you will."

In spite of my respect for all Grandmother had done and said, I had made a solemn oath to myself that there would be no big promises that day about Hawra of the kind I had made about Zahra. The torrent of emotions raging inside me at the sight of Hawra needed to subside before I could make a sensible decision in her best interests. I knew that I would honor my obligation, but I had no idea how. I would need to talk to Steve, mull things over with my family, perhaps take some expert advice before there could be a decision. This was not one to rush.

"I am serious about helping Hawra," I told Grandmother. "But we needn't discuss this today. I have to find out the best way to help."

It was not the answer Grandmother wanted to hear.

"You won't forget, Hala? You won't just disappear again after this meeting?"

"No, I won't. I haven't come all this way after all this time just to do that." I was trying to reassure her, but I had to say this over and over again as she pressed me. I touched on some of the difficulties: Grandmother had no bank account, Iraq was not the easiest place in which to get things done, I had to come up with a practical solution if I was going to support Hawra. All the time that I was saying this, different options were flashing into my mind, each with its own complications.

It was my turn to change the subject. Steve had gone over to

Hawra to sift through the gifts with her and, given her haunted and solemn look, had resorted to making funny faces to make her smile. While the two of them were striking up a rapport, I took advantage of the opportunity to ask Grandmother how much the child knew about the deaths of her parents, brothers, and sisters. Grandmother responded with a story that sent a shiver through me.

Hawra's parents were buried in the Shi'ite holy city of Najaf, she explained. The last time she had visited, she had taken Hawra with her. Hawra saw her crying over the grave of her son. She heard her grandmother wailing for Abu Hawra, meaning the father of Hawra, and asked whose graves these were.

"I couldn't explain to her that these were her parents, so I told her they were my relatives," Grandmother said.

A little while later, when Grandmother was praying at one of the plots where the children were buried, she heard a girl weeping. She looked up to see that it was Hawra, sobbing inconsolably with her head in her hands. She was bent over her mother's grave.

"She may have wanted to imitate me, Hala, as children do," she said. "But of all the graves there, she was drawn to her mother's. I had to carry her away from it."

Picturing the scene prompted me to ask about Zahra. All afternoon, I had wanted to know more about her. I asked whether she was buried close to her parents. This answer was even more horrifying than the last.

"But Hala, didn't you know?" she said.

"Know what?"

"They never returned Zahra's body to me. I couldn't get it back." If the image of Hawra crying over her mother's corpse had chilled my blood, the vision of Zahra lying far from her family in a lonely place with nobody to visit her or tend her grave stopped my heart. For a moment, I could not draw breath. I felt the sting of tears in my eyes and an icy sweat on my palms. How was this possible? I struggled to recall what Marla had told me. I remembered her telling me that she was going to recover Zahra's body but never that she had been unable to do so. Had she spared my feelings by keeping this from me?

Grandmother was distraught. I tried to calm her by concealing the turbulence I was feeling. I asked her to explain.

Marla had tried to get Zahra back, she said. Her assistant, Faiz, had gone to the field hospital with a member of the family, but they had been turned away.

"They only sent me a death certificate, but not her body," Grandmother said, breaking down again. "I didn't see her body, Hala. I never got my Zahra back and all I know is what they told me, that she's dead. What if she isn't dead and they lied to me?"

It was hard to comprehend why fate had decreed that one simple old woman should have to endure so much pain. Was it not enough that she had lost seven members of her family in the air strike? That she had still been mourning them when Zahra died? Why did she have to go through this as well?

"If she's dead, she's buried alone," Grandmother continued. "She isn't even buried with her family in Najaf where she should be. She's all alone in the middle of nowhere and not a day goes by without me thinking about her."

I paused. I had not expected this first meeting to be easy, but neither had I anticipated that it would be this onerous. I had to fight the urge to blame myself. If I had not found Zahra, if I had never interfered, if she had simply died where she lay the first time I had seen her, she would have been spared a prolonged struggle for life, the lack of any loved ones to comfort her as she was dying, and a burial far from her family. I had to remind myself of Grandmother's conviction that these events were no fault of mine but had been determined by fate. I needed to cling to that. Grandmother's next words snapped me back to reality.

"Hala, you must try to recover Zahra's body for me," she proclaimed. "Now that you're here, you can do it." She was looking to me for a miracle, just as she had five years earlier when she had decided that I could save her granddaughter. I did not know how to respond.

"Hala, you must do this. You can do this. We need to get Zahra back and give her a decent burial with her family. We owe her this."

She gazed into my eyes.

"Promise me you will, Hala," she said.

No, I thought, this time I cannot promise. No matter how fervently I wanted to help, I did not know where to start and had no idea if I would succeed. It would have been easy to put Grandmother's mind at rest at that moment by telling her that I would find Zahra, but I knew better than to do so.

"Let's take things slowly," I said. "One step at a time," I went on, before she could protest. "Then we can decide what can and cannot be done. I'll try to help, but I'm not sure where it'll lead. We shall see."

I promised to visit her by the end of the week. I asked her to prepare copies of all the paperwork she had relating to Zahra's death. I avoided raising any hopes I might never fulfill.

It was time for Grandmother and Hawra to return home. Our security guards drove us to a main road, hailed a taxi for our guests, and made the driver promise he would deliver them to their door.

As we said good-bye, Grandmother looked me in the eye.

"Promise me one thing, at least," she said with a twinkle. "Promise you won't turn your back now that you've seen us today. Hala, promise me you're coming back."

I threw my arms around her and laughed for the first time that day. This was one promise I knew I could make.

"You'll see, Grandmother. I'm not going anywhere just yet. You'll see me at the end of the week."

I bent to give Hawra a big hug and placed her gently in the back of the car.

Sixteen

LOOKING FOR ZAHRA

The fighting I had seen in Sadr City cast a pall over the whole of Baghdad. Such was the fear caused by the Mahdi Army's threat to spread bloodshed to other areas that our security advisers warned us not to move around the city if we could help it. When we told them we needed to drive from the safety of our host's house in prosperous Mansour to Grandmother's home in the more volatile Shi'ite suburb of Hay al-Shuhada, their first reaction was that they should call in the Iraqi Army to protect us. We rejected this, saying we had no wish to see Grandmother's street cordoned off just so that we could pop in for a cup of tea. Then they said we should travel in a convoy of SUVs bristling with enough menacing weaponry to deter potential kidnappers. We argued for keeping a low profile in an ordinary sedan.

The compromise proposed by the security team was that we be accompanied by two guards at all times. Both would be armed whether we liked it or not. We did not like it but reluctantly accepted that this was the way it would have to be.

It took several days to make the arrangements, and I thought of little else but Grandmother's sorrows. I had been drained by our four-hour family reunion, dazed by the old woman's disclosures, daunted by the fresh demands she was making on me. The emotions had reached a peak, and I knew I needed to come down from my high before I could make any sensible decisions about what to do next.

Having seen Hawra, I understood some of her needs but did not know how to meet them. As for Zahra, I realized that I had very little understanding of what had happened to her. I needed to know more before I could say whether I might be able to help her, even now, five years after failing to prevent her death, by discovering where she was buried.

"Zahra and I have so much unfinished business," I told Steve as our driver wove skillfully through Baghdad's heavy traffic to hasten our journey and reduce the risk of being kidnapped. The anxiety of the guards whom our security advisers had insisted accompany us put me on edge and prompted dark thoughts. I sensed that Zahra's spirit was not at peace, that she had come to haunt me—not out of malevolence, but for the purpose of guiding me in some mysterious direction I had yet to take.

I did not like to say this to Steve, who has a very down-to-earth view when it comes to notions of ghosts and ghouls. But there was no denying that it was Zahra who had brought me together with Grandmother. It was Zahra who had made me yearn to mother Hawra. Zahra had drawn me to the inspirational figure of Marla, who in turn had urged me, until the day she died, to help this family.

Could Zahra somehow be driving me on to meet my obligations to her sister after all this time? To me, that did not seem so unreal a notion.

What I knew for certain was that it had been absurdly short-sighted of me to envisage bringing this story to a conclusion by finding Hawra. All I had done was to open a new chapter in the form of a search for Zahra. Only by discovering the details of her death could I end the family's tormented suspicion that she might yet be alive. I believed I owed it to Grandmother to establish first Zahra's fate, then Hawra's future.

Zahra's dying days were uppermost in my mind as our car stopped outside the single-story concrete house where, wreathed in smiles, Grandmother and Hawra were waiting at the gate. As our guards glared up and down the bland residential road, I was assailed by memories of my first visit here, when Zahra had still been alive. Stepping over the threshold into a small living room that doubled as a bedroom for Grandmother and Hawra, I could see damp patches on the walls. In other areas, paint was peeling. A simple curtain divided the front of the house from the back, where a dimly lit kitchen with an archaic stove and wobbly old stainless-steel basin stood. I hid my gloom by grinning at the offer of cardamom tea.

My eye was caught by two large photographs on the wall. One of them was of Ali, the father of Zahra and Hawra. The other I did not recognize. It showed a handsome young man whose pride in his military uniform was plain to see.

"Who's this?" I asked Grandmother when she brought in the tray.

"My husband," she said, with the same pride that shone from the portrait. "He died in 1980. In the war with Iran."

For a second, I was stunned. This was the first I had heard of another tragedy visited on Grandmother by a previous war. I pictured the grief that must have afflicted her and the anxiety of being left with little money to raise the family alone—the youngest of her three boys would have been six at the time. I thought of how lonely she must have felt when she was making big decisions about the children without their father and how fearful she must have been of what would become of them if anything were to happen to her.

When she had faced up to the loss of Ali and the responsibility of bringing up Hawra, she had been under no illusion about the difficulties: she had done it all before.

Grandmother directed Steve and me to a burgundy and yellow sofa so gaily patterned that it seemed to sit uncomfortably with the suffering endured within these walls. Before I could ask Grandmother more about her late husband, we were joined by her elder son, Uday. He would have been ten when his father was killed. Now, at thirty-eight, he was the head of the household. Uday was as eager as his mother to answer any questions that might help me delve into Zahra's disappearance. I asked him to start by describing the day her family had been caught in the air strike. Sitting on an adjacent sofa, dressed casually in a tracksuit and slippers, Uday recounted a sequence of events more horrifying than I could ever have imagined.

Although the family was Shi'ite, Ali, his wife, Rasmiyeh, and their children lived in the largely Sunni al-Doura district in the northwest of the city, he explained. In the early hours of April 4, 2003, the bombing of that district was fiercer and deadlier than ever. During a lull in the explosions that were shaking their street and making every family tremble, Ali consulted a friend who lived in a neighboring house. Both men agreed that they must get their wives and children as far away as they could, as fast as possible. However, they disagreed about the safest route out of the danger zone.

As each man argued the merits of his preferred route, the bombardment resumed, coming closer all the while, until their windows shattered and they saw they had no choice but to move immediately. They decided to go their separate ways.

Ali helped his wife to assemble their seven children, including Zahra and Hawra, who needed to be carried. Together, they packed their family into Ali's taxi. Ali's friend bade him good luck and Godspeed before heading off to safety. Ali took the road to hell.

Later that morning, the friend knocked on Grandmother's front door. He looked shocked, as if he had witnessed a terrible accident.

"Uday," he said urgently. "Please come with me. Your brother's been injured. He needs you to go to him in the hospital."

It was not until Uday was in his car and out of earshot of Grandmother that the friend gently broke the news that Ali had been killed and that his wife and some of the children had been injured when a missile destroyed their car as they tried to flee to the sanctuary of al-Shuhada.

"I asked him to take me to the scene of the incident straightaway," Uday said.

He would never forget what he saw there. The taxi that had provided Ali with his living had evidently turned into a death trap for the driver and his passengers. It was burned out, the metal twisted by the missile's explosive impact and charred in the ensuing inferno. Uday thought it would be a wonder if anyone had got out alive from the smoldering wreck in front of him.

Some witnesses approached with good news. They had seen a small baby dropped out of the window by the woman in the front passenger seat as the vehicle went up in flames. The infant—Hawra—had a small head wound, but it was obvious to everyone from the way she was crying and kicking and clenching her tiny fists that she was in robust health and would be fine. An elderly woman had run out from a nearby house to retrieve her from the side of the road and carry her away from the heat before it could scald her skin. She had taken Hawra home to tend to her cut and wait for her family to arrive.

Uday stared at the witnesses and saw in their faces that those who had been trapped in the car had suffered the agonies of burning, compounded by the anguish of watching those they loved most being consumed by the flames. He sensed that Ali would not be the only member of the family he would mourn that day.

"I knew Hawra was safe for now, but I had to go in search of the remaining children and my brother's wife," he said. He had raced away.

With Ali's friend, he started a systematic search of the nearest hospitals, asking in each one whether a dead man and his burned children had been brought in. Eventually, an official at one hospital asked him to inspect two bodies in the morgue. The official hoped he might be able to identify them.

The first corpse had no face, but Uday knew immediately who it was.

"Ali's entire upper body was missing. Only his lower body was there. I recognized him from his legs and the tracksuit trousers he had on," Uday said softly.

When I asked how he had known for sure, he looked at me as if he were seeing once again the pungent, blackened remains he had been forced to scrutinize that day.

"He was my brother, Madam Hala. I would always recognize his legs."

The other body was that of Ali's wife, Rasmiyeh. She had died shortly after arriving at the hospital. Her head had been wounded and a piece of shrapnel, presumably from the missile, had penetrated her heart.

This was just the beginning of the abominations that awaited Uday on a day without end.

In another hospital, Uday found the couple's spirited fifteen-year-old son, Mohammed, and their daughter Ghofran, a vivacious seven-year-old. Both were unconscious with severe burns and little chance of living through the coming night.

Close by was Muntather, the eighteen-year-old son. According to the doctor who had first alerted me to the air strike, this was the boy who had pushed open a rear door of his father's car and jumped clear of the melting upholstery with his clothes on fire. Muntather was conscious, but his blistered skin was as red as embers. He told Uday everything that had happened. His own prognosis was unclear.

The following day, April 5, Uday buried his brother and sister-in-law in temporary graves in Baghdad to await exhumation and reburial in holy Najaf ground, as the family's religious traditions dictated. There was no time to grieve their loss, reflect on their lives, or comfort Grandmother or the other relatives and friends, as would normally have been the case. Barely had the couple been lowered into the sandy soil than the news came through that Mohammed and Ghofran, the children who had failed to regain consciousness, had died.

Uday collected their bodies the following day and buried them immediately. That made four souls he had prayed for in two afternoons.

Between prayers, he made arrangements for Hawra, at three months old the great survivor, to be collected and cuddled and cared for. He also visited Muntather, who was in blinding pain as he lay in his bandages, his grip on survival weakening when his adult life had only just begun. Most urgently of all, Uday continued his search for the three other children he had been unable to locate.

It took him three days to find Zahra in the Karameh hospital. But his exhilaration at discovering another survivor was short-lived. Not only did her pitiful distress shake him to the core, but he was shattered that same day to learn that Muntather, who as the eldest son had been his father's pride and joy, was dead. The fifth burial was almost more than Uday could stand.

Grandmother was dispatched to Zahra's side and comforted her devotedly around the clock with a resilience that surprised everybody after so many shocking blows. Uday, meanwhile, kept looking for the two remaining boys. He had scoured every hospital for them, he said, blinking hard at the memory of his frustration.

Uday's account was mainly factual, devoid of any reference to the impact those dreadful days had had on him. From the raw wounds and shrieks of pain I remembered during the search of hospitals that had led me to Zahra, I knew what he must have seen and heard. But I could not imagine what he must have felt as he hunted through so much human debris for his own flesh and blood.

He never found the children—Yunis, thirteen, and Leith, eleven—but his search yielded two conflicting accounts of their fate and neither gave him any hope. According to one version, both boys had survived the first air strike, only to be caught in a second attack, this time on an ambulance taking them to the hospital and salvation. The other version was more prosaic: they had been burned to nothing but ash where they sat in the car and their remains could not be recovered.

To Uday, it mattered little which account, if either, was true. The important thing, he said, was that nobody could be sure where the children were.

"All that is known for certain is that, like Zahra, they aren't buried with their family," he said.

The room fell silent when Uday finished speaking. Even our guards were dumbfounded. Then Grandmother sniffed and sobbed, and I grasped her hand.

"I can never forget them, Hala," she cried. "To this day I am grieving. I am confused. I am angry."

Her gaze alighted on Hawra, who was sitting demurely with us, listening to every word without understanding the full story. The haunted look I had noticed at our house was back on her face.

"It is as if I'm seeing my son when I see her," Grandmother said. "She's all that's left of his smell."

I needed to know more about Zahra, but it was clear that my questions would have to wait awhile. Everyone needed a break, including Hawra. I turned to her and asked her to show me her toys. She obediently brought all of them to me, lining them up on the sofa so that I could be introduced to them one at a time. Her three teddy bears and two dolls that were still in their plastic wrapping fell a long way short of the average Western five-year-old's haul, but were perhaps all the more precious to her for being few in number.

"Do they have names?" I asked.

Hawra pointed to each one in turn. "Teddy bear, teddy bear, doll, teddy bear, doll," she explained patiently, as if speaking to a child who had never seen such things before. Obviously the Western habit of naming dolls after friends, fictional characters, and stars of the latest pop fads had yet to reach this corner of the world.

When I asked her to sing for me, Hawra showed none of the shyness that had held her back during our first encounter. She launched enthusiastically into a well-rehearsed song-and-dance act. She was beginning to feel comfortable in my company, I thought with a glow of pleasure.

"Show Auntie Hala your abaya," said Grandmother. As Hawra fetched the garment, Grandmother explained that every time they went out, the child had asked for a chador like hers. A tiny one had been made for her, and Hawra wore it on their outings together, including visits to the graves in Najaf.

For a moment, I was concerned. One of my fears during the journey to Baghdad had been that I might find Hawra in a fundamentalist Shi'ite family where she would probably receive little education as a girl and be married off in her mid-teens to a life of dim prospects with a dearth of freedom. Pressing the chador onto a girl so young might denote a degree of conservatism, I thought. But it quickly became clear that there was no need to worry on this score.

Grandmother told me how delighted the family had been with my gifts of London clothes for Hawra. If no objection had been raised to sleeveless dresses and showy tops, this was far more likely to be a family that would indulge Hawra, placing few restrictions on her.

The guards had advised us not to dally too long, in case whispers went around the neighborhood that a rich European—as Steve would have seemed to them—was ripe for plucking by any passing gangster hungry for a ransom, so I moved the conversation on as briskly as I decently could.

I prompted Grandmother to tell me everything she knew about Zahra's death. It was a subject that made the two of us apprehensive, but we both knew we had to have this conversation.

Marla had knocked on the door of her house on April 29, Grandmother recalled. She had brought Faiz, her assistant.

"Both of them were quiet as they came in," she said. Marla looked at Faiz and told him to break the news to Grandmother. Faiz could not bring himself to do so. Marla then hugged Grandmother tightly to her and began to cry. She spoke softly and Faiz translated in hushed tones. Eventually Marla's sobs reached a crescendo and Grandmother heard the words: "Zahra is dead."

"It felt as though someone had physically hit me," Grandmother said. She pushed Marla away from her and screamed: "Get out of here! Go away, both of you! Why this? Why so?"

Grandmother looked a little shamefaced as she remembered the scene. She had known this was not Marla's fault, she said. It was just that she could not bear to hear the news.

"My heart was so broken by the deaths of the rest of the family," she said solemnly. "I had so hoped that Zahra would live and that she and her little sister would keep each other company. I wanted them both to be there, not just one of them, so that they could at least have each other in the future, Hala."

Grandmother seemed transported as she remembered the bad things she had said to Marla. "Go to hell!" she had told the angel of mercy. "Never come back here. I don't want to see another American as long as I live. The Americans killed my son and his children. I never want to see you again."

Marla had stood there, weeping helplessly as her colleague stepped forward to calm Grandmother. "Hajieh," he said. "This was not in Marla's hands. She had nothing to do with it. It was Allah's will."

My tears flowed at the thought of Marla's distress.

"Hala, I said what I said in the heat of the moment. My heart was burning. I had lost my eldest son, the one who was following in his father's footsteps. After his father's death, he was our rock and now he was dead."

Grandmother broke down, too, and I did my best to console her, squeezing her rough hands. "I know, I understand," I murmured. I knew that Marla would have understood, too. She would not have taken Grandmother's outburst personally. She would have realized that the rage welling up in Grandmother was only to be expected and would eventually subside. Sure enough, Grandmother explained that Marla had stayed with her all afternoon until she was calm enough to be left.

She knew now that Zahra had died on April 28, twenty-four days after her father and mother and one day before Marla's visit, and she began to bury herself in elaborate arrangements for the family's period of mourning.

Marla, however, was still trying to arrange for Zahra's body to be recovered, but her efforts were in vain. The child had been treated at the U.S. 28th Combat Support (Field) Hospital in the town of Jurf al-Sakher. On May 11, Marla had written the following letter for Faiz to take to the field hospital:

To Whom It May Concern,

My name is Marla Ruzicka with the group CIVIC. I have been coordinating with Sgt Farishon and Watkins in Baghdad regarding the case of Zahra Ali, the little girl who was airlifted out on April 20. Thank you for doing your best to save her. Faiz, who works with me, is here to pick up her body and to arrange the burial. Please assist me as he will transport the body. Sgt Farison told me that he would give you word about the pick-up. If there are any problems you can try me at 00 88 216 6322 5770.

Thank you for your help on this hard case.

Marla Ruzicka

When Faiz had driven to the field hospital with Grandmother's third son, Firas, however, the letter proved insufficient. Instead, the two men were kept waiting at the entrance to the base for so long that they had to leave without Zahra in order to reach Baghdad by nightfall.

Firas said he had made a second attempt to collect Zahra, but this had culminated in a terrifying incident as he was approaching the field hospital. According to Firas, American soldiers guarding it had shot at him, forcing him to turn tail and flee for his life. He never returned. Faiz was apparently too busy with his work for Marla to keep driving to Jurf al-Sakher. The family was too afraid to deal with the Americans. Zahra was left where she was, perhaps in a morgue until all hope was lost that relatives would come for her, or perhaps in a grave that was never intended to be her permanent place of rest.

Grandmother, who had dreamed of reuniting the fragmented family in the holy ground of Najaf, was left to contemplate the reality that three of her son's children had vanished from the face of the earth. It tortured her soul. She sought solace with several clerics who assured her that she had committed no sin by failing to bury Zahra and her two missing brothers in the revered city. They advised her to let the innocent souls be. So she turned her back on the dead and devoted her energy to raising the infant Hawra.

As the year dragged on and the brief lull in violence that had followed the invasion gave way to the relentless bloodshed of the insurgency, the city became more and more dangerous. The first kidnappings of Westerners marked the end of Marla's visits, too. She was forced to limit her movements around the city to essential journeys only.

In the same way, I found that by the time I decided to make my peace with the family, sectarian warfare had made the drive to al-Shuhada virtually impossible. As long as the beheaders and driller killers ruled the dark streets of Baghdad, there would be no room for a compassionate gesture that might have lightened Grandmother's life. She found herself abandoned by both Marla and me, the two women who had promised support for Hawra.

Two years after the deaths of Ali and his family, Grandmother received a call from Faiz telling her that Marla was back in Iraq and was asking to see her. Since Marla could not come to her house, would Grandmother consider going to Marla's hotel?

She accepted with alacrity.

So it was that Grandmother arrived in the concrete-barricaded lobby of a once carefree hotel with the nearly three-year-old Hawra in her arms, eager to show off how fast her beautiful granddaughter had grown. Marla was ecstatic to see them, and in the photographs taken in the hotel garden that day all three are smiling happily, though

Marla was bitterly frustrated that she had still not secured any compensation for Hawra from the U.S. authorities.

"Marla cried as she said she was still trying to get Hawra compensation from the Americans," Grandmother recalled. "'I will let you know,' she told me."

But four days later, Marla was dead.

It was almost a year later when a neighbor of Grandmother's spotted one of the photographs that had been taken in the hotel garden on the front page of an old newspaper on a market stall. The newspaper was American and the neighbor did not understand the accompanying article, but she took it home to show to Grandmother, asking if that was her in the picture with the foreign woman.

Grandmother recognized the photograph but could not read the article. Only when she had it translated into Arabic did the appalling contents become clear. Like her son, Marla had been blasted and burned in her car.

When she had recovered from the shock, the consequences for the family struck her, too. It was a heavy blow to know that her last hope of security for Hawra had perished with the American angel of mercy on Baghdad's highway of death.

THERE HAD BEEN A TIME when the prospect of flying out of Baghdad would lift my mood. The nearer our departure on this occasion, however, the more downhearted I became. The lightness of spirit that followed my reunion with the family had been replaced by an oppressive sense that two new burdens were weighing heavily on me. First, I had to find out what had become of Zahra. After that, I had to decide how best to help Hawra. I felt crushed by the responsibility of two such difficult tasks. I was going through the paperwork Grandmother had given me about Zahra when I realized that the death certificate she had promised was missing. I telephoned her to ask whether she was sure she had given me all her documents.

"Yes, of course, Hala," she said.

"But where's Zahra's death certificate?" I asked.

"It's there—that paper I gave you with the English writing."

Oh, Grandmother, I thought. I had to explain that this was not a death certificate, but merely a copy of Marla's letter to the military hospital. She refused to accept what I was saying at first. Then she realized the implications.

"But it's all I have, Hala—are you telling me that I don't even have a death certificate for my grandchild?"

"Yes, I believe this is what I'm telling you if this is all you have," I replied softly. There was a long silence.

"What if she wasn't dead, Hala? What if they took her away somewhere and lied to me about her death?"

Before I could respond, she added, "Perhaps they stole her, Hala. Perhaps those people who took her to Saudi Arabia kept her there."

Saudi Arabia? Where had that come from? It was the first I had heard of it. I thought for a moment. Marla had mentioned that a Saudi doctor was interested in taking Zahra for treatment. But I had always been certain she had died before anything could be done.

I told Grandmother I would look into it.

STEVE AND I SAT TOGETHER and made a "Finding What Happened to Zahra" list of the few facts we had:

1. Marla arranged for Zahra's evacuation on April 19, 2003.
2. Just over a week later, she was told that Zahra had died.
3. Marla's assistant and Zahra's uncle went to the American base in Jurf al-Sakher to retrieve the body.

4. The body was never recovered.
5. Grandmother was under the impression that Zahra had been airlifted to Saudi Arabia for treatment.
6. There was no death certificate.

It was not much to go on.

"I need a Sherlock Holmes for this one," I told Steve sadly.

My husband manfully took on the role of Holmes. He became an Internet detective, trawling the Web for the names of American field hospitals in Iraq in 2003. Eventually, he established that the one we were looking for was the 28th Combat Support Hospital. It was the first breakthrough in our attempt to solve the mystery.

I e-mailed our details to the U.S. military in Baghdad, explaining that Zahra's grandmother was desperate to locate her body and asking for help in tracing any record of where she might have been buried. The reply was swift but left me even more despondent.

"Hi Hala," wrote a U.S. military man who gave his name only as Raoul. "Given the time frame in question, it is likely that there aren't any records available to run a coherent audit trail on this issue."

Raoul had copied his e-mail to a Captain Kay E. McKinnie, who replied that "even now in 2008 medical records are retired monthly." For good measure, she added: "It is not protocol for U.S. forces to inter local national remains."

I took the impersonal language to mean that even if Captain McKinnie could lay her hands on Zahra's American records, they would not show where my little girl had been laid to rest. It was not the captain's fault. The way she abandoned official jargon at the end of her e-mail told me that she would have come to our aid if she could. "I'm sorry I can't be of more help, but this truly is a case of a very small needle in a very large haystack," she wrote.

There were two more items to add to our list:

7. The U.S. military informed us they do not have records going as far back as 2003 to establish what happened to Zahra.
8. The U.S. military insisted they did not bury non-Americans. They handed them to their family members and/or local authorities.

No matter how many times I stared at Sherlock's list during our remaining few days in Baghdad, it did not give me a single clue as to how we should proceed. We were unable to move freely around the city, let alone drive to Jurf al-Sakher. Even if we could go there, what would we do when we arrived? We were not allowed to stay anywhere for more than fifteen minutes for fear of kidnap gangs. It would take days or weeks to scour the local cemeteries for any sign of Zahra. Besides, how did we know she had been buried in anything other than an unmarked grave?

Returning to the hotel after another visit to Grandmother, which failed to elicit any evidence of a flight to Saudi Arabia, I was as worn out, depressed, and despairing as I had ever been. When I caught sight of my reflection on my way up to our room, I barely recognized the gaunt, ghostly woman glaring back at me. The pressure was building inside me, and when I opened the door Steve felt the full force of the eruption.

He looked up from his laptop as I came in. He smiled. Big mistake.

"I don't know what you're grinning about," I snapped. And I was off. "I'm beat. I'm upset. I'm depressed. I'm a failure. I don't know what to do anymore. I go round and round in circles. Every time I meet Grandmother, I feel more weighed down with guilt for not having the answers she needs. God . . . why is this happening to me?"

Steve tried to answer, but since he was not God, I was in no mood to listen.

"All I wanted was to find them, see them, and close this dark chapter of my life, and now I'm overburdened with new worries," I yelled, slumping on the sofa and then springing up again when I realized I could not sit still for a moment.

"I mean, what is it?" I shrieked, pacing the room. "Just tell me. Is this a test of endurance for Grandmother and me? You'd think we'd both suffered enough in our different ways where families and children are concerned. What more do we have to prove to God?"

Steve's voice seemed to come from a distance.

"Hala, stop it. If you'll just be quiet for a moment, I'll tell you something great. Just calm down and listen to me for a second."

"Fine!" I shouted. "Tell me. What's so important, then?"

"I think we've found the key," he said, the smile returning to his face. "I think we can finally find out what happened to Zahra."

Seventeen

A DOCTOR'S LOVE

So it was that in September 2008, I found myself on a plane to the United States, reflecting on my good fortune in being married to such a scrupulous researcher. While I had been struggling in vain to extract any information of the slightest value from Grandmother, Steve's searches had yielded a priceless reference to a book published in hard copy and available on the Internet by one of the doctors who had served at the field hospital. It was our biggest breakthrough on the trail we hoped would lead to the truth about Zahra's death.

The doctor's name was Michael A. Hodges. On page 40 of his book, *A Doctor Looks at War: My Year in Iraq*, was a brief account of a little girl, aged about four. She had been admitted to the hospital on April 19, 2003, with burns to her head, face, arms, and feet. Her parents had died in the explosion that had caused these injuries.

Could this be Zahra? we wondered. Steve called up his pictures of Zahra in the Karameh hospital. Sure enough, the burns were precisely as described.

According to the doctor's account, the child had so charmed the hospital's military personnel that a nurse had volunteered to adopt her. The case had apparently gone all the way up to Donald Rumsfeld, the defense secretary.

I remembered one of Marla's bulletins. "Everyone from doctors to nurses has fallen in love with her," she had told me a few days after Zahra arrived. "They all seem to want to adopt your little girl, Hala. She's a star, dude!"

Not only that, but the doctor described how a Saudi plastic surgeon had paid a visit. The surgeon had said his government was willing to fund long-term treatment for the girl. Could Marla have heard about this and mentioned it to Grandmother? Was that why Grandmother thought Zahra had been flown to Saudi Arabia?

If so, it had all come to nothing. The doctor's book said the child in his care had died in the field hospital at 6:46 a.m. on April 28. I shuddered to read this. I imagined Zahra fighting through one last night to live. I tortured myself with the thought that she might have won that battle if I had been at her side to comfort and cajole her.

Was the child in the book really Zahra, though? I could not rest until we knew. An e-mail to the publisher prompted a swift response from the author: How could he help us? We sent our pictures of Zahra. Yes, he said finally. This was the girl he had cared for.

I wanted so much more information. I longed to know every detail of her time in the hospital—what had made the staff love Zahra so, how they had treated her, and whether they had spoken softly to "my" child as she lay dying. What had been done to save her in the American hospital? Why had she not been transferred to the Saudi one? What had gone wrong in the end? I craved the answers to a hundred questions.

Dr. Hodges sounded wary on the phone at first. He wanted me to know that he was proud of the U.S. mission in Iraq. He would not help any journalist discredit it, he emphasized. It was obvious that he was suspicious of me. So I told this stranger the story of my infertility, my decision to bury myself in my reporting of Iraq, the reawakening of my maternal instincts by an orphan of war, and my desire to help her sister in some as yet undefined way.

"I'm not interested in politics," I said. "This is personal."

With that, he agreed to see me.

If fate had a sense of humor, then the joke was on me, for the answers to my questions lay in Fayetteville, North Carolina, home not only to Dr. Hodges but to the 82nd Airborne Division of the U.S. Army, which had played a prominent part in Operation Iraqi Freedom five years earlier. The operation had liberated Iraq from dictatorship, but countless civilians had not survived to see their country's faltering steps to freedom. I had witnessed too many calamities in that war to respect the army that had spearheaded the invasion.

As my plane approached, I thought of Dr. Hodges and wondered what kind of doctor could see such suffering and remain proud of the mission that had inflicted it. I realized I might have to hold my tongue to avoid offending my host.

I tried to concentrate on Zahra and the reason for my long journey. At last I was going to hear answers to the questions I had been brooding over for five years. Had she woken during her last night on this earth? Had she called out for her "Mama and Baba," as she had when I was with her, or had she given up all hope of seeing her parents again and cried herself back to sleep like the orphaned Ali Abbas?

I needed to reconstruct it all in my mind if I was ever to accept what had happened. Had Zahra died quickly and painlessly? Or had her death been agonizingly drawn out? Most important of all, did Dr. Hodges know where she was buried?

Perhaps it was because of these preoccupations that my mood

plummeted as the flight touched down. Why was I flaying myself with this morbid exercise? I wished to God I had not come alone. If I had brought somebody with me, I thought, I would not have been so debilitated by exhaustion and dread. A joke, a smile, a hug, might have restored my stamina and my spirits.

More than anyone else, I longed for my sister, Rana. But she was far, far away, working in Africa, and I was so tired that I could not even figure out the time difference. Would it be too late to call her in Kenya?

"It's all going to be fine, Hala," I told myself on my sister's behalf and sighed. She would have convinced me, but I could not persuade myself.

At least I had arrived in a beautiful city, I realized, as the taxi sped toward my hotel. Fayetteville was one of the greenest places I had seen. The lushness of the countless trees linking branches along one well-tended avenue after another made a striking contrast with the hacked stumps on the road from Baghdad airport but there was something about North Carolina, a state I had never visited before, that reminded me of my home country. Everywhere I looked, I seemed to see a cedar, a national symbol in Lebanon and a native species here, too. I could only hope that I would find something in common with the people here as well.

My hopes of connecting with the inhabitants of Fayetteville were chastened by an inauspicious start. With an empty afternoon stretching ahead before my meeting with Dr. Hodges in the evening, I took the hotel receptionist's advice and strolled over to the nearest shopping mall to have a lazy lunch and watch the world go by. The first thing I saw when I looked up from my plate was a hatchet-faced young man striding purposefully past in military fatigues. My stomach knotted. I recognized the uniform from Baghdad and wondered if the wearer had served there. Then I saw another and another. I was surrounded. I have no idea why I should have been so startled when I was sitting within an hour's drive of Fort Bragg, where George W. Bush had once described the liberation of Iraq as a great turning point in the story of freedom. But something else surprised me, too.

One of these young men was walking hand in hand with his girlfriend, his head inclined toward hers, smiling as he whispered some intimacy into her ear and laughing at her response. In Baghdad, I had never thought of these hardened fighters in a foreign land as lovers longing for the joys of their homecoming. In Fayetteville, I was suddenly struck by their humanity. Some were carrying tired toddlers, others pointing out toys in shop windows to older children.

The wives who had to manage on their own when their husbands were away for six months or more looked happy to be out shopping as a family. I stared at these women and wondered how they coped with waving a man off to war, knowing that he might never return, that this could be their young children's last memory of being enfolded in the muscled arms of fathers who struggled to tear themselves away.

For a moment I mused about the hardships of army life. Then I thought of Hawra, who had never had a chance to play with her father, the father who would never take her shopping for treats because of the actions of men like those around me in the mall.

"Snap out of it, Hala," I murmured. "You don't know anything about them."

I reminded myself that I loved this country, that some of America's cities were among my favorite places on earth, that whatever I thought about the suffering in Iraq, the cruel effects of the war had been felt here, too, by thousands of families who had lost cherished fathers, sons, and sweethearts in the military. I resolved to be respectful and courteous to the military doctor I had come all this way to meet.

I DO NOT KNOW WHY I thought Michael A. Hodges would be older and sterner than he was, but my relief when he stepped forward to greet me in the hotel lobby with a broad smile and a warm handshake must have been palpable. So apprehensive was I about seeing Zahra's doctor and hearing everything he could tell me about her that I was trembling. His relaxed demeanor put me instantly at ease.

"It's so good to finally meet you," I said, and I meant it.

Dr. Hodges was a youthful forty-five, clean-shaven, clean-cut, and casually dressed in a polo shirt and slacks. If he still had any concerns about my motive in coming to talk to him, he concealed them well. He welcomed me to his hometown as generously as I hope I would have welcomed him to mine. It was important to me to know that Zahra had been in kind hands, and I was relieved to find that any doubts on that score were immediately dispelled. I tend to make up my mind about people in the first few seconds, and I decided then and there in the hotel lobby that Dr. Hodges was a considerate, compassionate man who would have been a source of great comfort for "my" child.

"Would you like to go somewhere else for a drink?" he said.

The restaurant he had chosen—Italian, run by a Greek—was a few minutes' drive away through streets bathed in bright neon light, and by the time we arrived I had already put the despondency of my dreary day behind me.

"The way things are lit here at night never ceases to amaze me," I said, anxious to make light conversation while we established some sort of rapport. "I sometimes wish I could live in the States."

"Hala," he said, momentarily concerned. "My wife, Anna, told me that maybe you didn't drink, and I forgot to ask."

"Don't worry." I laughed. "I do drink, even though I'm a Muslim. A sin, I'm sure, but one I've decided I can live with."

I was surprised to find that the restaurant catered to my other vice, too. As an honorary Londoner, I was not accustomed to seeing ashtrays on tables, and I thought the no-smoking rules had spread all the way across the United States.

"Not in Fayetteville." Dr. Hodges grinned. "You're in tobacco land, Hala. Many of the tobacco plantations are in North Carolina, so the smoking ban hasn't reached here yet."

I asked whether he minded if I lit a cigarette.

"Not at all," he teased. "Smokers are good for my business." Here was a man I could warm to, even if he defended the attack on Iraq.

We sat dipping bread in olive oil and balsamic vinegar while I answered his questions before asking my own. He wanted to know about my background, how I had become a journalist, and what I had been doing in Iraq. I tried to understand his support for the war. I asked him how he reconciled it with the Christian faith he had described in his book and heard myself confiding in him about my struggles with the uncompromising demands of Islam.

There was no doubt that we came from opposite sides of the human spectrum. I was carrying my "Arab baggage" in the form of disappointment with many years of American policy in the Middle East. He, with all his proud patriotism, was upholding his president's right to combat tyranny in a conflict I abhorred. Yet here we were, sipping wine, laughing, and talking like old friends, when the only link between us was a child we had both tried and failed to save. I sensed Zahra's presence that evening. It was as if she wanted me to know that this man had striven for her as she had struggled to keep her grip on life and finally slipped away.

I asked him to tell me everything from beginning to end; and so the story unfolded.

Zahra had arrived at the field hospital with two other female patients but no medical records. She had been admitted at 3:28 p.m. on April 19, 2003, and had been taken straight to the intensive-care unit. She was patient number 41.

Lacking firm information, the hospital staff had assumed that one of the women brought in at the same time was the child's mother, or at least related in some way. When the woman died soon afterward, there seemed to be no way of finding out anything about the girl except her name, which was marked on the registration form as "Zara." Perhaps this had been the one thing she had been able to tell them herself.

Dr. Hodges disclosed three things that astonished me. The first was that the field hospital Zahra was in had never been intended to treat civilians. It had been erected in haste to deal with U.S. military casualties. No sooner was it up and running than Iraqi doctors started begging the Americans to treat the innocent victims of weapons that had missed their military targets. The Americans responded by promptly opening the doors of their army hospital to ordinary Iraqi men, women, and children, flying them in by helicopter if necessary. These were unpublicized acts of compassion that I had been unaware of until now.

The second surprise was that not only did the hospital lack a specialist with the experience and expertise to treat a critically injured child, but everything it offered—from sophisticated ventilators to basic medicines—was for adult patients. Even putting Zahra on a drip required the nurses to improvise with tubes and catheters that were far too big for a little body. When it came to deciding what medicines to use and how large the doses should be, Dr. Hodges relied on his wife, Anna, who happens to be a pediatrician. When he could not ask her directly, he thumbed through a pediatric handbook she had tossed into his luggage on the off chance that he might come across a sick child on his travels.

"That book ended up being the bible in our hospital," he said. "We were taking children and none of us was a pediatrician. They all used it."

The third revelation from Dr. Hodges was the most shocking. When Zahra had arrived at the hospital, he said, her chances of survival had been far less than the fifty percent calculated a couple of days earlier by JB, the Merlin doctor I had taken to the Karameh hospital. This made me quiver with self-recrimination. If I had known how fast she had deteriorated in the twenty-four hours before the evacuation, I would never have been so idiotic as to promise her grandmother that she would live.

As Dr. Hodges recalled the events of five years earlier, he seemed to be transported back to Iraq, to the strains and stresses of separation from his own family and the struggles of the desperate families around him to survive the war intact. I know doctors who instinctively distance themselves from their patients—just as journalists are supposed to avoid becoming emotionally entangled with the people in their articles—and I had assumed that a military doctor, with all the machismo and discipline the job title implies, would be as clinical as any. How wrong I was. This military doctor had so missed his own three children back home that he found himself irresistibly drawn to the youngest patients in the hospital.

"The first few days when I started seeing children, I built a wall around me: I wasn't going to get involved and close to the children that were being admitted," he said. "I didn't want to see children suffering, which is the reason I didn't become a pediatrician—I couldn't deal with kids with chronic illnesses."

It had been impossible for him to remain aloof for long. "You set up the barriers but eventually you have to go behind them to see," was how he put it. "Eventually every child I saw reminded me in some way of my own kids."

Zahra was a case in point. "Her age and physical structure were about the same as my own daughter Caroline's. I kept on thinking to myself, 'What if this was my daughter, what if it was Caroline?' at the same time as having to be professional and balance my emotions." The tears in his eyes as he said this showed that it had been a losing battle to achieve any such balance.

It might have helped him to set the inhabitants of Iraq apart from his compatriots in his mind, but this struggle defeated him, too. "The reaction of the parents I saw toward their injured children was the same reaction as ours," he went on. "I don't know why I thought they'd be different."

The more the doctor confided, the faster the barriers between us crumbled away. Now that we were speaking frankly, I pressed him to tell me about Zahra. He took a deep breath.

"Zahra was hurt so badly that you have to think her injuries were quite painful," he said. I winced.

"If you have an adult that's badly burned and is awake, they make sure you know it's painful, but with Zahra I can't remember her ever communicating anything verbally. I think pretty soon after we had her, she ended up having tubes breathing for her because of problems in her airways. Most of the photos I have of her are with the tube breathing for her. She didn't do much talking but likewise she didn't do any complaining that I recall, and you would have expected that of someone as young as her."

I swallowed hard, trying to imagine the slender child who had been calling for her mother and father silenced by fat tubes down her throat.

"There was an incredible combination of beauty and ugliness,"

Dr. Hodges said tenderly, as if he had seen the picture in my mind. "Ugliness because of the burns . . . but there was a beauty and a peacefulness in her eyes. I don't know if 'acceptance' is the right word, but there wasn't the obvious struggle you would have expected to see in someone so young. There was a kind of contentment that allowed her to deal with the injuries that we were looking at, thinking how terrible they were. She was able to find a way to cope with it."

If I took comfort from knowing that Zahra had not thrashed her arms and shrieked as she had done in my worst nightmares, there was nothing heartening about the doctor's description of the medical procedures she had had to endure. I had imagined that Zahra's treatment would have been designed to soothe her. On the contrary. It turned out that her best chance had lain in the surgical removal of damaged skin. Zahra's skin had been so damaged that she had undergone this procedure—known as debridement—not once or twice but repeatedly. I asked the doctor to explain.

"With burn injuries, a lot depends on how extensive and how deep the burns are," he said, as if sketching out the fundamentals to a patient's mother. "The deeper the burns, the deeper the tissue is destroyed. The skin is the largest organ of the body. Its primary function is protection, and that includes acting as a barrier against things invading our body. It also helps to regulate temperature. So when your skin is burned away, you're susceptible to infection and problems with temperature regulation and fluids and electrolytes, which are so important for our bodies to function properly."

Zahra had suffered from all these problems, he explained. The surgeons had taken her to the operating room, sedated her, and shaved away her dead skin again and again until they reached "fresh bleeding levels." The aim had been to encourage new skin to grow in place of the burns, but it had not been easy, he said.

"The debridement process will be quite painful, even with the medicine that helps take the edge off it," Dr. Hodges told me bluntly.

When I heard this, the deep guilt I felt for having failed to find Zahra, sit with her, and reassure her turned to shame. How could I have made so little effort to discover where she had been taken and whether a relative or friend of the family could visit? I had envisaged her growing stronger each day in a remote border camp, when the reality was that she was weakening within an hour's drive of Baghdad.

Had she faded away for want of tender love and care from those closest to her? I could not restrain myself from asking Dr. Hodges whether it would have made any difference to her prospects if I—or her grandmother—had been on hand to weave a little magic, conjuring visions of a future that might have made her labor all the harder to live for it.

"It's hard to say categorically, Hala. It could have," the doctor said. "On the other hand, the chance of survival I calculated for her the day after her admission was only twenty percent to thirty percent."

It was considerate of him to emphasize that there was probably nothing I could have done. But I could no longer be in any doubt that I might have made a vital contribution to "my" daughter's care in Iraq if I had not been so eager to see my mother in Egypt.

Zahra's condition had improved for a while, just as Marla had said, despite a serious shortage of medical supplies. Dr. Hodges was candid about this, too. The field hospital had run out of some essentials, including drugs to regulate blood pressure, and was ill equipped for the range of patients who were being brought in. The doctors had made a formal complaint about this. Yet the hospital staff had been determined not to turn their backs on any patient, irrespective of age, nationality, or status.

"The thing we were able to do for her at our hospital that they weren't able to do in a hospital in Baghdad was the antibiotics for protecting her against infections—which were always going to come—and the fluids. If your skin barrier is gone, you lose fluids by simple evaporation, so you need even more than usual. If you're not drinking, the IV catheter is the ideal way to make up for the fluids that are lost. She was getting better. The longer she lived, the longer she could survive. With a burn patient, if she gets past the initial risk of infection, then she has a chance. We were making progress. Then this whole issue of transferring her to Saudi Arabia came up."

At last, the mystery of the Saudi connection was about to be cleared up for me.

"I saw her deteriorate under my eyes on that trip," Dr. Hodges said in a desolate tone.

What trip? Had Zahra indeed been flown to Saudi Arabia? The account that followed filled me with dismay.

On April 24, five days after Zahra had been admitted to the field hospital, a Saudi plastic surgeon with extensive experience in skin grafts had arrived, accompanied by a film crew. He indicated that Saudi officials were keen to help the child. Within two days, everything had been arranged. The field hospital's commander had agreed with the Saudis that Zahra, whose case was now attracting publicity in the kingdom, should be moved there for the specialist care she needed in order to reduce the inevitable scarring and increase her chances of a normal life. The job of taking her to Baghdad International Airport was given to Dr. Hodges.

Zahra and a woman who was also deemed suitable for treatment in Saudi Arabia would have been taken to the airport by helicopter but for the ill-starred onset of the *shamal*, a fierce northerly summer wind that sucks up desert sand and engulfs Iraq and Saudi Arabia in a storm that blinds, stings, and suffocates. The *shamal* strikes rarely, so it was particularly unfortunate for Zahra that the sandstorm should ground all American helicopters on the one morning she needed them to be operating.

Undeterred, Dr. Hodges ordered two ambulances, one for Zahra and one for her fellow patient. He rode with Zahra and tended her with the help of an intensive-care nurse and a respiratory therapist. But they were slowed by the storm that raged around them, hurling millions of grains of sand at their windscreen and making it impossible to see more than a few yards ahead. Then they were caught in heavy traffic crawling up the airport road through the maelstrom. Every time the ambulance started to pick up speed, it lurched to a halt after just a few yards.

The battery that powered Zahra's IV pump was the first to go, and with it her supply of fluids. Then her heart monitor flickered and faded away. The heat inside the vehicle became as stifling as the swirling sand outside. Flies filled what little air remained, and settled on eyelids and dressings. A journey of fifteen miles became a four-hour test of endurance. By the time they reached the airport, they had averaged no more than walking speed and Zahra's ventilator and oxygen monitor were the only pieces of equipment still functioning. Her blood pressure was falling. Her dressings needed to be changed. Her medication was due. But at least they had made it.

The afternoon ground slowly on and Zahra's need for intravenous fluids grew more urgent. There was no sign of the plane to take her to Saudi Arabia. At six p.m., Dr. Hodges was informed that it had never even taken off for Baghdad because of the storm. The saving grace was that the *shamal* was subsiding, as it usually does at nightfall. Realizing that his patients might not survive a further four hours in their respective ambulances, Dr. Hodges ordered an emergency airlift by Black Hawk and extracted a promise that the helicopter would be available to bring Zahra back to the airport first thing in the morning.

When morning came, however, my Zahra was no longer well enough to fly. She had survived twenty-four days of shock and agony, jarring journeys by road and air, sedation and surgery without her mother or father to whisper encouragement when she regained consciousness. Now the life force that had sustained her was draining away. The doctors fought all day to halt the deterioration in her condition. Zahra struggled all night. But at fourteen minutes to seven o'clock the following morning, the battle ended. The efforts of Merlin, Marla, Michael Hodges, and myself had all proved to be in vain.

Zahra died alone.

AS IF THIS had not been painful enough, there was another blow to come.

"Do you know what happened to Zahra after that?" I asked apprehensively. "Do you or anyone else know where she could have been buried?"

Dr. Hodges looked at me with surprise.

"No," came the flat answer. "Why do you ask?"

I recounted the efforts Zahra's family had made to recover the body. I described her grandmother's anguish that she did not know where it was to this day. I told him of my desperate wish to help.

The doctor thought hard. After Zahra's death, the physicians had mourned briefly and gone back to saving lives, he explained gently. It was up to the administrators of the hospital to decide what happened to the dead.

I explained that the army officials I had contacted said there were no records to be found.

"What about the nurse who wanted to adopt her? Surely he'd know. Wouldn't he have followed up on the girl he wanted to take home?"

Dr. Hodges looked blank. He was very sorry: he could not even remember the nurse's name.

"I'll try and check with the chaplain," he added. "Maybe he'd know something, Hala. I'll do my best to see if we can come up with anything."

It was the end of a long evening and I sensed that the doctor was almost as exhausted as I was. We agreed to call it a night.

THE FOLLOWING DAY, I invited the entire Hodges family to dinner at a local steak house. Anna, the pediatrician, had long blond hair. She had been married to Michael for seventeen years and shared his strong Christian faith.

The boys, Logan, fourteen, and Noah, ten, asked me about Lebanon and the cedar trees for which it is known. I explained that although my country made a big fuss about them, it did not have that many compared with Fayetteville.

"Yes, ma'am," one of them said. "But in Lebanon the cedars are very, very old, which is why they're special!" I smiled and nodded my agreement.

Then Caroline, the gorgeous little girl who had been Zahra's age when her father was in Iraq, piped up with the confidence of a well-loved eight-year-old used to making her voice heard above her brothers' din. She did not want to be a doctor like her parents when she grew up, she announced solemnly: "I want to be a teacher." She emphasized this with such certainty that I had no doubt she would achieve her ambition.

The family chattered away as families do, about church, soccer, and friends. It was obvious not only that they were unusually close but that Michael Hodges doted on all of them. Even when the talk turned to war and Michael spoke up for his president, saying he had acted in good faith and could not have known the claims about weapons of mass destruction were lies, I could not be angry with him. I knew this was a good man who had done his best to let Zahra live. He and his wife, who knew the details of Zahra's case, were all too familiar with the harrowing consequences of the conflict and were more sensitive to them than most.

At the end of the meal, I was invited back to the family home for coffee. The garden was brightly lit as we pulled into the drive. From the entrance hall, I was led into a study where Michael wanted to show me a painting of Anna with her mother and daughter. The beauty of the portrait lay in the serenity of the subjects and the evident bond of love between the three generations. I could not help thinking of Hawra and her grandmother, and of how much the child would miss her mother as she grew up. It reinforced my determination to fill a small part of the great gap left in Hawra's life by her mother's death.

"You have a beautiful house," I said, rather than give voice to my thoughts.

"Yes, we have been blessed, Hala."

But Michael's own thoughts were lost in Iraq, too. He seated me at the dining room table while he fetched a laptop and called up his first record of Zahra:

Zara
Registration number: 12775
Social security number: 0000
Iraqi civilian, Zara (Burn Child)
Admitted: 15.28, 19th April, 2003
ICU (intensive care unit)

I could not stifle a sharp intake of breath when his photographs flashed onto the screen. With her ventilator and her drip, Zahra looked so tiny, so fragile. I stared at her closed eyes as the doctor pointed out the burns to her brows and lashes.

"Tell me about her death," I said, searching for yet more answers to questions that had kept me awake the previous night. "What do you think caused it?"

The doctors' best guess, it seemed, was that a clot had traveled from her leg to her lungs, causing serious problems with her breathing and blood pressure. There had been complicating factors, though. Catheters made for adults had been pushed into a small child's veins. Along with an anticoagulant to prevent further clots, "very powerful chemicals" had been used to raise Zahra's blood pressure.

"That is not to say that this killed her, but it could have contributed, Hala. I went to my commander and demanded we do something. He asked me to file an incident report—something in the army that says maybe something went wrong, like the lack of pediatrics [equipment] may have hastened her death.

"I was heartbroken and angry. She was too much like Caroline. I cried for a while, but then I had to move on—other patients needed us."

We were silent for a moment, each of us remembering Zahra in our own way. I saw her trembling in my mind's eye. I could not bear the thought of her straining to breathe at the end with nobody at her bedside. I looked up at the doctor with tears welling and was about to explain how angry I was with myself when I saw that his eyes were brimming, too. He was choking from the recollection of his grief and frustration at Zahra's death. In that moment, I knew that no doctor could have cared for her more. The resentment I had felt toward the military was replaced by gratitude to this army man who had agonized over an orphan's torment, just as I had done.

"I know you did your best, Michael," I told him, "and for that I will forever be grateful."

"Hala," he responded. "Remember when you told me about your anger with yourself for making a promise that Zahra would live?"

I nodded.

"You need to know this. I've thought about what you said over and over again, and to be honest your statement to the grandmother that she was going to be fine is not unlike what physicians do on a daily basis. I liked the way you phrased it. It's not that you were saying it dishonestly—you believed it. I've said this to families before. I believe it's the right thing for me to say because the opposite gives no chance for hope whatsoever. We do it all the time, and sometimes we keep our end of the deal and the patient recovers and other times they don't. I don't think I can ever remember someone being upset at me for giving them that hope.

"Don't be angry with yourself, Hala. You did exactly what I would have done. You did not do wrong."

It was all I could do to stop myself from bursting into tears at the table. To hear this from a doctor, especially one so intimately involved with Zahra, meant more than I could have imagined. Even though Grandmother had forgiven me, it was not until now that I felt I could forgive myself. I had been absolved and the relief overwhelmed me.

Eighteen

A BOND OF RINGS

As a foreign correspondent, I have always had mixed feelings about returning from my travels. On the one hand, there are the pleasures of home comforts—the ability to cook simple dishes that suit my palate, to sit peacefully in a garden I have planted, and above all to slip between fresh cotton sheets and sleep soundly in my own bed at night. If the trip has been turbulent, familiar surroundings soothe the senses. On the other hand, there are the household chores that have piled up in my absence—overdue bills, calls to return, cupboards to clean. The professional pressures of going on the road are balanced by the escapism of an exotic assignment. Going home means confronting not only mundane responsibilities but also the burdensome realities of one's personal life. Sometimes, there are big decisions to be taken. Never more so than over Hawra.

I had set out to save two orphans of war. It had seemed important to find out as much as I could about how one had died before I resolved how the other might live. Zahra had been snatched away by a rapacious war, and even though I still sensed her with me sometimes, I knew she really belonged to the past. Hawra, the sole survivor of her family and the sunniest personality I had encountered in the whole of Baghdad, represented resilience and optimism for the future. But how could I be sure of brightening her prospects in a country whose own promise was clouded by so many uncertainties?

"I WISH YOU'D DECIDE to adopt Hawra," was Steve's answer as we mulled over it all one evening with a bottle of wine. We were sitting at opposite ends of the sofa where we do all our most important talking, facing each other with the vibrant music of my homeland playing in the background on an Arab television channel.

If the words took me by surprise, the sentiment astounded me. Steve and I had not discussed adoption since we had taken the idea to Grandmother five years earlier. When Zahra had died and I had deemed myself unworthy of Hawra, the last chance of motherhood seemed to have eluded me. Steve had never questioned that assumption.

Nor, in all the years of struggling to conceive our own child, had he once suggested that we adopt. The subject was raised only by friends in London and Beirut. They told me how to apply in Britain but warned that I might be rejected by social workers as too old, too busy, or too addicted to cigarettes. Doctor friends in Lebanon said it would be easy for them to find an unwanted newborn in one of their hospitals. Lawyer friends said it would be hard to persuade the Lebanese courts to hand over such a child to the wife of a foreigner.

Throughout these tortuous conversations, the only comment from Steve—admittedly a man of few words—would be: "Whatever you want." I was stupefied to hear him expressing a desire to adopt now. Why had he not said this ten years earlier?

"I had it in my mind to bring up the idea of adoption several times over the years," he replied. "But I knew you hadn't come to terms with facts within yourself." In other words, I was still fantasizing about getting pregnant.

"I worried that if I mentioned adoption, that would be the final blow—a blow I would have delivered. I couldn't do that. I had to be patient." So he had thought I could not take the idea that he wanted children even if they had to be someone else's.

For a while, I said nothing. I glanced around our living room, remembering the way it had been when I had believed we would have a family. There had once been a childproof green armchair and empty mantelpieces waiting to be filled with picture frames of our babies at beaches and birthday parties. Now we were surrounded by pristine Eastern furniture, and instead of family photographs above the fire, I displayed the awards I had won for my journalism and my invitations to think-tank seminars and diplomats' cocktail parties. The fine cedar dining table where I had imagined we would feed our sons or daughters was covered with laptops, newspapers, and books. Ours had become the home of an affluent, professional, singularly childless couple.

My husband was speaking again. "Things were said, but much went unsaid," he added, looking at me intensely. "I told myself our love for each other would see us through. But since I saw you and Hawra together, I've been imagining her being part of our lives. In fact, I can see myself walking her to school every morning."

"God," I thought, staring blankly at my husband. "To think of the tears these walls have witnessed. And never once in all that time did you tell me what I desperately wanted to hear—that you needed a child, too, even if it could not be our own."

I checked my emotions before saying anything out loud. I realized that during all the years I had felt Steve did not care enough about whether we had children, he had been suffering like me for the lack of them. But the opportunities that might have been open to us before had been closed off. It was too late now.

"Steve," I said quietly, topping off his glass. "Adoption would have been a beautiful event in our lives, but I am surer than ever that this is no longer an option for me or for us. Maybe five years ago I should have done this, but I wouldn't dream of it now." He sat quite still, listening impassively.

"It's not the best thing for Hawra anymore—or for me. I'm convinced in my heart of hearts that Hawra's better off with her grandmother. As for me, I no longer crave children to the point of insanity. Over the years, I've taught myself to numb the pain. I've also succeeded in mapping out a life and a career for myself that doesn't include the responsibility of children. My priority's been to protect myself by moving on with my life.

"I won't lie to you and pretend there aren't fleeting moments when I burn to have them, when seeing a child or a pregnant woman doesn't still make my heart flutter, but those moments are few and far between. I'm not obsessed anymore."

I was speaking with a conviction I had not realized I possessed. My feelings were becoming clear to me as I described them. I had resigned myself to the knowledge that there would always be moments when the desire for children would catch me unawares, but I could live with this demon now. I no longer ran home and cried myself to sleep when I caught sight of a child I wanted to mother. I had taught myself the art of equanimity.

I loved the new Hala, who was brave enough to go to the front line and tough enough to withstand all the grief that covering a war entails. Not only that, but I was coping with infertility in a way I had never thought possible before I went to Baghdad. I had new priorities. They included a child, but it did not have to be one I was raising myself. Even if I could not be the mother who got Hawra up in the morning and kissed her good night, I could be a guardian angel who would watch over her development and offer chances that other children might never have. All I had to do was decide how to go about it.

ON THE PLANE TO BEIRUT, I recalled this conversation and promptly weakened again.

Was I right to have told my husband that I did not need to hold Hawra close? That what mattered was to be a force for good in her life and the best way to help her was from a distance?

Steve had known me too well to accept this at face value. "Are you sure, Hala? Is this what you really want?"

Now that I was sipping airline coffee high above the clouds, I found myself looking at everything from a different perspective.

"I don't need to be seen as her mother in public to feel motherly toward her," I had told Steve.

"But are you certain Hawra is better off in Iraq, Hala? God knows how much you can do to make her life better if she comes here."

The truth was that I could not be certain. I knew that even if Hawra's grandmother wanted me to take her, it would be a mistake to remove the child from her home. There would be a heavy emotional price to pay for the material benefits she would enjoy in London. All the love Steve and I could give would be nothing compared with the bonds of true family that tied Hawra to Baghdad.

And yet, might there not be a middle way?

I allowed myself to contemplate another option. What if we brought her to school in London and had her stay with us during term time but took her back to Baghdad for the holidays? That way, she would remain part of her old family while allowing me to form my own. Not only that, but she would become bilingual and straddle two cultures, just as I had done. There would be many options for her later in life—in business, perhaps, if she did not wish to follow me into the media.

I knew that my niece Lara would dote on her. She had fallen in love with Hawra the moment I had e-mailed a photograph of her after our reunion. Lara had never seen anyone so beautiful yet sad.

"She's so adorable, Lollie," she had told me. "Please, please bring her over."

And yet, there were many practical problems to consider. Not the least of these would be the impact on Hawra of having two homes and all the traveling that would be required between them. I thought of my own childhood and the flights I had taken between boarding schools in England or Lebanon and my parents' house in Sierra Leone. It had been hard to be away, especially when I was as young as Hawra. Would I want her to go through the same agonies of separation that I had endured, the same perpetual longing to be thousands of miles away with my family?

I needed to talk to my parents.

THE FOLLOWING DAY, I took my mother and father to lunch at one of their favorite restaurants in Beirut. The day was sunny and the *steak frites* at Le Relais de l'Entrecôte came with a delicious sauce, but I was too preoccupied to share my parents' pleasure, as my mother was quick to notice. Gently, she asked if I was okay.

I looked first at her, then at my father.

"I have a story I need to share with you," I sighed.

They looked at me apprehensively across the table.

"Mama, remember many years ago when I told you about two girls I was thinking of adopting?"

She nodded and I smiled at her, thinking how glamorous she was looking, despite her seventy years.

"Well, it's about them," I said. My father, who had aged from surgery during the past two years and never left home without a stick, glanced at my mother, evidently hoping she would explain what his crazy daughter was talking about. I had never confided in him my hopes for adoption.

"It's about these two little girls, Baba," I began. "Two orphans I found and reported on for my newspaper when I was covering the war. They weren't just any two girls," I said slowly, sipping my wine. "Baba, in a split second they had lost everything and everyone—an entire family of seven from mother and father to brothers and sisters.

"Zahra I found in the hospital, and she was so fragile and hurt and alone that no one on earth could have looked at her and not wanted to do something. After much deliberation, I decided to try to adopt the girls. I don't know, Baba, something inside told me this would be the best thing to do, and I just followed my instincts without questioning them because I knew without a shred of doubt that it was right.

"What I hadn't told you over the years was how low I'd been about wanting children I couldn't have."

I explained to my father that there had been some personal issues my mother and I had kept from him because we knew how sensitive he could be. I said that when I had failed to conceive, I had decided on a different course in life.

"I couldn't bear the pain any longer, so I changed my life, and I know you've asked me over the years what was happening and I always told you I was fine, but I wasn't, Baba. I worked hard on myself to climb out of that hole I'd sunk into. It took me a long time to crawl out of it, inch by inch, until I felt I was fine. But then I met Zahra and Hawra."

"So what happened, Hala? Why didn't you adopt them?" I could see that tears were already forming in his eyes.

"Well, I needed to help Zahra first and get her out of there, and I did everything possible to ensure that she was transferred to a place where she could have better treatment."

"God bless you, my child," he said tenderly. "But what happened?"

I explained that I had talked to Mama when I left the country and she had said the family would approve if I adopted.

"Of course we would have, Hala. Why didn't you?"

"Because Zahra died and I felt it was all my fault at the time. Because, Baba, your daughter did something so very wrong that it took a long time for her to forgive herself."

I recounted my promises to Grandmother that Zahra would live, my devastation when she perished, and the heavy burden of guilt I had carried until it almost crushed me. At this my father suddenly burst into tears. He cried like a child. My mother scanned the neighboring tables to make sure there was nobody in the restaurant who knew us. She told Baba to get a grip.

"Oh, Hala," my father said, straining to speak. "You couldn't have done more, my child. You've tortured yourself for far too long over something that was never in your hands." He wiped his eyes, but to my mother's embarrassment, the tears kept coming.

"You didn't act out of malice," he said. "I worry about you, my daughter. I worry about the amount of guilt you seem to feel over the smallest thing, let alone the big issues. You will seriously damage yourself if you carry on like this."

My father was heartbroken, not only over Zahra's death and the loss of Hawra, but by the realization of how much pain my inability to conceive had caused me in the years before the war. My mother had witnessed my anguish, but we had concealed it from him. We wanted to spare him the distress he would undoubtedly have shared with me, so attuned was he to my feelings.

As a child, I had always felt closer to Baba than Mama. As a woman, it was to my mother that I had turned, over and over again. Her strength in dealing with events that enfeebled me was a constant source of astonishment.

"Hala," she interrupted now. "It's obvious from the way you're speaking about this and the emotions you're still struggling with that the issue of children is not over with you. Women can still have babies at a late age. You can still do it if you want to."

Dear God. She would have packed me off to the gynecologist first thing in the morning if I had let her.

"No, Mama. I'm finished with that. But just because I am does not mean I can't be emotional about babies every now and then."

I moved the subject on to Hawra. It was in the resolution of her future that I needed my parents' guidance. I told them how I had tracked down the child, how beautiful she was, and how much I loved old Grandmother, who had lost so much but still found the spirit to struggle on.

"Then why not bring Hawra to Beirut, Hala?" My mother was full of ideas that day. "Don't adopt her, just get her family to agree that you bring her here. You could place her in a good boarding school. We'll keep an eye on her when you're away."

My mother paused while she raced through the arguments in her mind. Then she enumerated them slowly, calmly, thoughtfully.

"Beirut is your home, Hala. It's more accessible to you than Baghdad. You visit often. You can always come and see her and make sure she's okay and spend time with her. And during vacations you can either send her to her family or bring her grandmother over to spend time with her here."

So wise did my mother sound and so enthusiastically did my father nod his agreement that for a moment I was almost persuaded. But as I thought about it, I began to shake my head.

"Why not?" they asked in unison. As far as my mother was concerned, she had come up with the simplest solution. It frustrated her that her difficult daughter seemed intent on complicating everything.

"To detach Hawra from her family would be hard enough, but then to dump her in a boarding school at such a young age . . . I can't bear the thought of it," I said.

I knew my mother would understand this because she had found it so painful to place her own daughters in boarding school in Beirut. To this day, she cries when she remembers waving us good-bye and flying home to her idyllic but empty villa in Africa. When she reached Freetown, she would take tranquilizers for weeks until she adjusted to life without us. She refused to cook our favorite dishes, even if my father asked for them, because they reminded her that we were not where we should have been—at her side. But she had sacrificed this invaluable time with us for the sake of our education. Forty years later, she could not understand why I failed to see that nothing mattered more than educating Hawra.

I resisted the temptation to tell my mother how difficult it had been for me as a little girl just four years old to understand why I had to board and what gain would result from the pain of my being so far away from her. Instead, I reminded her of all that Hawra had lost. I pointed out that she was more dependent on her grandmother's love than most children were on their parents.' I explained that by depriving her of her only source of security and displacing her in a foreign country where even the Arabic spoken was different from what she spoke, Hawra was certain to be lonely and isolated. Separating her from Grandmother would leave a gap that could never be filled by my parents, no matter how much attention they lavished on her.

"What good would I have done her, then?" I asked. "I wouldn't be helping her in the short term. I'd be damaging her in the long term."

TALKING TO MY PARENTS, if only to reject their ideas, had helped to clarify the limited options remaining to me. I sought further advice from my sister, Rana, in Kenya and my brother, Zu, in America. We may have been far apart, but my quandary brought us together, albeit only on Skype, for daily discussions. So complex were these meetings of minds on three continents that we mockingly referred to them as "conferences." The views from Africa, the United States, and the Middle East did not always concur, but we were unanimous in our resolve to give Hawra the best chance in life. I had e-mailed a picture of her to my siblings and both had converted it into a large print, framed it, and placed it next to Lara's photograph on their mantelpieces. As far as the three of us were concerned, Hawra was already family.

The financial options had to be considered, and both Rana and Zu were eager to contribute.

"Whatever you decide, we'll be there to help you out," Rana said. "Lara's about to graduate and make her own way in the world. Together, you and I can afford to start on Hawra and make sure she gets what she needs."

Zu came up with his own alternative.

"Listen up, Sis," he said. "Don't worry about the money. I have some good friends here who are willing to help out. Many of my

American friends were distraught about this girl, and they've told me they'll pitch in if necessary. Perhaps we should look at setting up a fund to secure her future."

Such talk made me uneasy. I was not seeking charity for Hawra. Since she was my responsibility, I did not see why others should be burdened. I was preparing to make a lifelong commitment, and I could only hope that I would be in a position to pay twenty years' worth of bills. But I was determined that whatever help she needed, I would do my utmost to provide it myself.

By the final conference call, I loved my sister and brother more than ever—not for offering money but for accepting how important Hawra was to me and for never once questioning my sense of duty to her.

My whole family knew how deeply I felt. They understood why. They respected my objectives and they encouraged me to achieve them.

"So have you decided what to do?" my father asked as I prepared to visit Grandmother in Baghdad.

"I am left with two options, Baba," I said with a deep sigh. "I'm not sure either one is great, but they're all I have."

"Allah will guide you, *habibi*," my mother said, reminding me to eat well on my travels and look after myself. "Give Hawra my love and tell her she has another *teta* [grandmother] here."

Baba hugged me and said: "I have always been proud of you, Hala. I know you will come to a wise decision. Whatever it is, know that we will be behind you."

STEVE JOINED ME FROM LONDON at a friend's house in Baghdad, just in time to see me slip into self-doubt at the decisive moment.

"Steve, do I have the right to try and change Hawra?" I asked him intently. "How much influence could I have on her life anyway?"

Despite his assurances that together we could transform her prospects, the questions preyed on me as we joined our host for dinner.

That Hawra was too young, too fragile, too vulnerable, to be separated from her family was clear in my mind when I returned to Iraq. But seeing the battered capital again reminded me of why I had wanted to get her out of there. What sort of education could she hope to receive in a poor suburb? How much freedom would she have as a young woman in a polarized society dominated by conservative men? Would an orphan girl who had become a burden to her uncles be married off in her teens to the first suitor who came along, regardless of whether he could make her happy?

Then again, it was precisely the conservatism of postwar Iraq that would make it more difficult to adapt to the liberal ways of other countries. Would she feel like an alien there after such a traditional upbringing? Would it be better to leave her alone?

Our host compounded my uncertainty.

"Tell me something, Hala," he said as we slumped on sofas after a sumptuous meal and sipped strong coffee. "Why do you want to help this child? What is it to you, anyway? There are many more like her."

"Because I want to give her a chance in life, because I owe her a chance in life, and because after everything she has gone through, she deserves a chance in life."

"But why do you believe that giving her an education abroad would be an answer to her problems? Why do you think Beirut or London is a better option for her?"

I bridled at this. Our host had led a gilded existence. His education had served him well in his flourishing business career, yet he was questioning the value of bestowing similar opportunities on a young girl.

"Look at you and the chances you got in life," I said, more heatedly than was polite. "Look at me. I was raised with options and space. Sure, I learned our traditions and was brought up conservatively in Lebanon, but I was allowed to breathe in England. I experienced both worlds and I believe that stood me in good stead."

My host was unconvinced. "Up to a degree, Hala, but you and I have been in the same boat. We sometimes felt we belonged neither here nor there. We had to work doubly hard in each environment to fit in. Hawra would find this even more difficult, given her background."

He leaned forward in his chair and punched the air to make his points hit home. "Hawra is not you," he said. "She doesn't come from the same class. What worked for you could be detrimental to her. Your intentions may be good, but think about it. Given who she is, your ideas may end up alienating her from the society you insist you don't want to sever her from."

I did not know how to answer him.

"Don't rock the boat for this one," he said finally. "Don't assume your Western ways are right for her."

IN THE END, what choice did I have but to leave the decision to Grandmother? My excitement was tinged with trepidation as I watched the car I had sent for her sweep through our host's gates. Nervously, I fingered the two rings I had bought on the day of Zahra's death and wondered how I would be able to shape her sister's life. But Hawra's reaction on seeing me banished all thoughts of dilemmas and decisions. She opened the car door herself with an ecstatic grin on her face and ran straight into my arms, where she kissed me over and over again, just as I used to kiss my mother at the end of the long term at boarding school.

Grandmother was slower to emerge, but when she saw the two of us embracing, she smiled broadly. It was the first time Hawra had shown any spontaneous emotion toward me.

"She needed time to be reassured, Hala," Grandmother explained as we hugged. "But she hasn't stopped asking about you and who you were since the day you met her. I told her you were my cousin. She's obviously accepted you in her life as a member of the family."

No words could have given me greater pleasure. I squeezed Grandmother to me.

As we sat together, I wished I could simply savor the pleasure of my visitors' company, but there was important business to attend to. The only trouble was that every time I was about to broach Hawra's future, the child leaped onto my lap to give me yet another cuddle. She kissed me so hard on the face that my cheekbones hurt. The breath was sucked out of me.

"We need to talk, Grandmother," I said solemnly, only to be reduced to a fit of giggles as I caught sight of Hawra posing in my Chanel sunglasses.

"What about Hawra? What will you do for her?" Grandmother asked, only to see me dragged off to the bathroom before I could answer because the child wanted me to undo her pants buttons.

Just when I thought we were finally getting down to a serious talk, Hawra smacked her palms against mine. This turned out to be the prelude to a long palm-smacking game in which I apparently failed to perform to the required standard.

"Harder, Auntie Hala!" Hawra squeaked. "Harder! You're not hitting me hard enough!"

There followed a tickling game, which I won on the grounds that she ended up more hysterical than I (but it was close); an exercise game inspired by stretches she had copied from daytime television, which was a tie (she was more supple, but I kept my balance); and a singing game, which she won hands down (I can't sing).

The first time I had met her, Hawra had seemed haunted by loneliness. Now she was as joyous as any five-year-old on an outing, and it was my privilege to be her playmate.

Finally, when she flopped down exhausted with a plate of rice and stew, I took a deep breath and turned to Grandmother.

"You know you always ask me this question, 'What about Hawra, what will you do for her?'" I said.

"Yes. So what about Hawra, what will you do for her?"

I thought I should run through all the possibilities, including the ones I had dismissed. I told her that although five years ago I had offered to bring up Hawra and Zahra in London, I was now convinced that adoption was not the best option. At three months, I said, it might have worked. At nearly six, it was out of the question.

"I would never give her away, Hala," she told me in typically direct fashion.

"I know, Grandmother," I said with a smile, "and I will never dream of asking you to do that."

I explained that I had wondered about arranging for Hawra to go to school in Beirut or London and for her to be returned to Baghdad at the end of each term. Grandmother looked distinctly unimpressed and said nothing.

"So, Grandmother," I said, "perhaps the best way forward is to move you and Hawra to Beirut together."

She looked at me sharply, but I could not tell what she was thinking. "I'll rent a flat for both of you. I'll ensure Hawra's enrolled in a good school. I'll provide you both with a monthly income sufficient to live on."

I described to her the mountains, the beaches, and the fun fairs where Hawra would ski, swim, and have the time of her life, and the proximity of my parents, who would keep an eye on them when I was not around. Then I looked her straight in the eye as she had so often done with me.

"Please know that I do not want to take your granddaughter away from you," I said. "Please be assured that I think she is better off with you, which is why I'm offering this option for you two together. But please understand that she means a lot to me for many reasons, which is why I would like to be involved in her upbringing, in her life."

Grandmother maintained a thoughtful silence. She seemed to want to hear more.

"I intend to help Hawra," I said, taking Grandmother's hand. "You've asked me to. In fact, you've made it my obligation. I'm trying to come up with the best solution for her. Hawra is my priority in all this and I'll do whatever it takes to make sure she gets her chance in life."

I knew of course that although Grandmother would like to be with Hawra, there was only a remote possibility that she would move from the only home she had ever known to a foreign country. Leaving behind her two sons, a daughter, and her other grandchildren would be especially grueling. Nevertheless, I believed that this frail but remarkable lady should have the power to choose.

Finally, she spoke.

"This is a big decision, Hala. I'll need time to think about it."

I HAD INTENDED to pay Grandmother the courtesy of hearing her decision in her own home, but the security arrangements proved so complicated that I asked if she would simply bring Hawra to me. Once again, I waited at the window for their car, fiddling with my jewelry and fretting over a reservation for lunch at the Hunting Club across the road. This time, however, I was ready with a fresh proposal for Grandmother and a gift to seal my bond with Hawra.

I greeted them warmly, but Hawra was burning up with a fever, and all the energy of her previous visit seemed to have evaporated. When I cuddled her, she did not hug me back. She sat floppily on my knee at the club while I ordered her a light rice dish and a cold 7Up and urged Grandmother to give her plenty of fluids until she was better. Then I remembered that Grandmother had rather more experience of children's temperatures than me. She was nodding in amusement, and it occurred to me how ridiculous I must seem as I fussed over Hawra like a mother over her first baby.

I would have laughed at myself, but my heart suddenly felt very heavy. I was weighed down by the gravity of what we were about to decide, and deflated by the thought that I would soon be returning to London, leaving Hawra behind. No matter how this meeting ended, I knew I would miss so much of Hawra's life and so many of its milestones over the years that stretched ahead.

"Grandmother," I said. "Have you thought about the offer I made you the other day?"

"Yes, Hala," she answered slowly. I felt a knot in my stomach.

"I don't think I could leave here and live in Beirut with Hawra. I would miss my two sons and my daughter, Sahar," she said, and although I was not surprised, I was saddened to think that this left only one final option.

"Also, there is Najaf and Ali and his family's graves," she explained. "I cannot be away from them." I bowed my head in sympathy.

"I wouldn't know my way round Beirut. I'm not physically strong. I can't move properly, as you can see. There's a lot that I wouldn't be able to do without my children."

"I know," I said, taking her hand. "I truly understand. But I wanted to give you the option and the chance to decide for yourself and for you to know that the offer is there if ever you want to take it. Who knows, Grandmother? Maybe in the future when she's older and you know me better we can talk about taking her to school somewhere."

"*Inshallah*, Hala," she said hesitantly. I saw from the anxiety on her face that she feared that I would leave them, now that she had turned me down.

"For now, please know that I'll try to help Hawra in whatever way I can," I said to reassure her. And then I told her about the last idea I had left.

"Grandmother, I'm left with one option and that is for me to send you a monthly income to make sure that Hawra doesn't want for anything. I'm not rich, but I'll do my best to see to her needs."

I knew this was what Grandmother wanted more than anything. She came from a background where education was important—after all, her daughter had graduated as a teacher—but people did not travel far to get it. In her world, a chance in life was a nebulous concept and ambitious talk of future prospects was virtually unknown. Cash was the commodity Grandmother valued. Cash spelled security in a city impoverished by fighting. Cash meant that Hawra would be well fed, clothed, shod, and schooled.

Grandmother looked at me with watery eyes, sensing that her family's fortunes pivoted on my pledge.

"Listen, Grandmother," I said, still hopeful of encouraging her to expand her horizons one day for Hawra's sake. "There's one thing I'd like you to do if possible. Perhaps sometime next year you and Hawra will come and visit me in Beirut for a week or two. It will give you both a break and allow Hawra to see life beyond Baghdad."

"Hala," she said delightedly. "This is the best idea I've heard so far. I promise you we will come."

Yet the smile faded and her fingers trembled. It seemed she was straining to extract some further reassurance that would give her peace of mind.

"I trust you, Hala. How can I not? After all, you did come back," she said. But I could tell she was remembering how I had broken my promise to help in 2003.

The time had come to fulfill a vow I had made to myself in my darkest hour.

"I want to tell you a story," I said. "I hope it will show you that I'm making a commitment today I'm bound to keep. Do you remember when I left Iraq five years ago after we'd arranged for Zahra to be transferred?"

"Of course," she said.

"Well, after I left you I went to see my mother in Cairo. You may not know this, but I was getting reports about Zahra at the time. Just as Marla was keeping you up to date, so she was in touch with me. My impression was that Zahra was recovering well, and one day my mother and I went out and I decided to treat myself to some jewelry. You know how we Arab girls like to look nice and how much we love these things."

"Yes, Hala. Jewelry is an investment and no girl should be without it," she replied with a knowing smile.

"The point is that the day I was buying jewelry—these two rings on my finger here—I got the call from a friend of Marla's to tell me that Zahra had died. I know one thing has nothing to do with the other, but I couldn't help feeling guilty that I was being frivolous when Zahra was dead."

Grandmother was listening earnestly. I was starting to choke up.

"But Hala, I told you before," she said. "Zahra's life was not in your hands. You could not have changed fate, whether you bought jewelry or not."

"I know, Hajieh, but I still felt bad, thinking I should have been with her instead. What I need to tell you is that I cried for Zahra a lot that night and was very angry with myself and made a pledge, one that I've been holding on to for the last five years. Now is the time to discharge it."

"What do you mean, Hala?" She was bewildered.

I removed the white-gold rings from my right hand and placed them in her palm. Their diamonds sparkled as she gazed down at them.

"They're very pretty, Hala," she said, and reached out to give them back to me.

"No, Hajieh," I said, gently pushing her hand away. "That's what I meant by my pledge. On that night, I vowed never to take them off until I found you again and asked your forgiveness. I promised that once everything was resolved between us, I would give the rings to Hawra as a legacy from her sister. It would mean a great deal to me if you'd keep them for her."

Grandmother looked from the rings to me and back again as the tears began to fall.

"Are you sure, Hala?"

"Yes, I've always felt sure about this," I said, examining the bare finger where the rings had been my constant reminder of the mission to find this family when the worst of the war was over. "I don't need them anymore. They belong to Hawra now."

The child heard her name but was too listless to show any interest in our conversation or the gold that would pass to her one day.

"Hala, I will place them with her mother's things. When she receives her mother's wedding ring, earrings, and pendant—all that was left of her—she will also have these two rings. That, I promise you."

Then she wrapped the rings in a piece of tissue and tucked them into her bosom in the old-fashioned way that Arab grandmothers still adhere to. That she no longer doubted my commitment was obvious from her serene expression. It was as if generations of money worries had suddenly been replaced by confidence in a stable future.

And so the time came to say good-bye to Hawra.

"You know what, little one?" I said, hugging her. "I'll miss you like crazy. From now on, you're my little girl. I promise to send presents for your birthday if I can't be there."

She smiled for the first time that day and a sudden realization overwhelmed me. I had known since the first time I saw her that I loved this girl. Now, after all the talk of taking Hawra with me to London or Beirut, I understood that I loved her enough to leave her in Baghdad with her family.

As for me, the events of the past few months had opened my eyes to the wondrous nature of my own family: my parents, who had sacrificed so much; my brother, Zu, and sister, Rana, whose devotion knew no bounds; and my niece, Lara, who had always been like a daughter to me. They loved me unconditionally, with all my shortcomings, yet I had failed to see how much fulfillment a childless woman could find in the family she already had. My search for Hawra had brought me closer to them and given me a new bond with a child who would remain my responsibility for as long as I lived.

I carried Hawra out to the car and kissed her good-bye again and again before placing her tenderly in her seat. Grandmother held out her arms to me and began to cry. I rested my head on her shoulder and saw my tears stream onto her abaya.

"Thank you," I whispered.

"For what, Hala?" she asked, caressing my face.

"For making me understand so many things," I said, "but most important for letting me share Hawra with you."

I stood watching and waving as the car pulled away with my child inside, and although it was painful to see her go, I smiled, marveling that after a lifetime's struggle against God's will, I was finally able to accept my fate.

Acknowledgments

For two years my agent and friend Kevin Conroy Scott encouraged me to write this book, while I dithered and hid behind every excuse about why I couldn't.

From the little details I had once revealed to him about Zahra, "Handsome K," as I've nicknamed him, was immediately captivated by my little girl's sad story in the same magical way as all of us who had come across her. Kevin instinctively knew there was something beyond what I had revealed to him, and for two years he gently pressed without pushing, nudged without pestering, and simply believed that this was a story to be told and shared.

For his friendship and encouragement, patience and guidance, through that time, I owe him a magnitude of gratitude. But more important, a huge thank you for never once wavering, even when I doubted myself.

Warmest thanks are due also to Sean Ryan, my *Sunday Times* foreign editor, collaborator, and friend. This book would not be as good or as beautiful as it is without his hard work and editorial expertise. All my words are touched by his magic, and for that I am truly grateful. Special thanks also to his children, Alastair and Charlotte Campbell Ryan, whose research and proofreading were meticulous.

Thank you to my wonderful editors and their teams at Macmillan and Riverhead, who gave me support, encouragement, and unstinting enthusiasm. They have been a joy to work with.

To my hosts in Iraq I also owe a lifetime of debt. Without them my reunion with my lost girl and her family might not have been possible. I thank them for their generous hospitality and protection in the last two years and for embracing my story and cause without questioning.

To Steve, my husband, a special thank you for always standing by me and always encouraging me to follow my dreams. I know this has not been easy for you, either. Without your arduous research we would not have been able to fill in so many of the gaps—not to mention your persistence when I was at times ready to give up.

Where do I start with my family, who put up with a roller coaster of emotions as I soul-searched for answers? My parents' unconditional love has seen me through thick and thin. Thank you for always being there for me. To my sister, Rana, no words of thanks will ever express the love I have for you. I am in awe of your selflessness; thank you for sharing your most valuable treasure in life with me. Zu, your support, encouragement, and wisdom throughout the years have meant more than you will ever know.

To all my friends in Lebanon and around the world—and the list is endless—thank you for your help, guidance, and friendship. I will never forget the times you cried with me when I ached, or the moments we laughed together and celebrated life. Your friendship has been invaluable to me.

Thanks especially to Lara, my lovely niece. Never doubt how

much I love you. You are the daughter I never had, yet everything I wished for in one. You make me proud, princess.

Finally to Grandmother and Hawra, thank you both for accepting me in your lives, for your forgiveness and love. The journey ahead of us is long, and it is one filled with difficulties, but I am hopeful that together we can overcome the obstacles and geography that separate us. I will always be there for you.